"From one distinguished federal judge of the twenty-first century, a revealing and inspiring look at one of the great judicial and public figures of the twentieth century. Our lives and decisions are guided by examples of what is possible. Through its story of William O. Douglas's achievements as an environmentalist, *Citizen Justice* will equip others to care for the planet and their communities."

—**James Fallows**, national correspondent for *The Atlantic* and coauthor of *Our Towns: A 100,000-Mile Journey into the Heart of America*

"Great women and men achieve immortality through the ideas that influence those who live after them, but William O. Douglas also achieved a more tangible and rarified immortality: protected wilderness—from the Brooks Range in Alaska, to the Red River Gorge in Kentucky, to the William O. Douglas Wilderness in Washington State. *Citizen Justice* captures Douglas's odyssey in a fascinating and poignant way."

—**Rick Ridgeway**, mountaineer, environmentalist, and author of *Life Lived Wild: Adventures at the Edge of the Map*

"A fascinating and engaging book exploring the story of iconoclastic Supreme Court Justice William O. Douglas and the dual role he played on and off the court in the world of conservation and the environment."

—**Rose Marcario**, former CEO of Patagonia

"A profound exploration of the enormous and unique contributions to conservation made by Justice Douglas even while he served on the high court, insightfully recounted by another leading American jurist."

—**David A. Churchill**, past chair of The Wilderness Society

"*Citizen Justice* is a fiercely intelligent look at how William O. Douglas, America's longest-serving Supreme Court justice, became the gold-standard conservation activist from the 1930s to the 1970s by promoting wilderness values and public lands preservation from Arctic Alaska to the Allagash of Maine. Because M. Margaret McKeown is a highly respected U.S. federal judge, she brings a stunning legal perspective to understanding Douglas's passionate secondary career championing Big Trees and Big Parks. This is environmental history at its monumental best. Highly recommended!"

—**Douglas Brinkley**, author of *Wilderness Warrior: Theodore Roosevelt and the Crusade for America*

"Like her subject, M. Margaret McKeown is a child of the West, a distinguished jurist, an incisive writer, and a lover of wild places. She brings all those assets powerfully to bear in this long-overdue account of William O. Douglas's enormously consequential contributions to the modern conservation movement. Douglas was chronically controversial, frequently cantankerous, sometimes conniving, and often cavalier about judicial ethics. But whether on the bench or on the trail, he toiled tirelessly and creatively to protect the wilderness he held so dear. This colorful and compelling book secures his rightful place in the pantheon of environmental champions."

—**David M. Kennedy**, author of the Pulitzer Prize–winning *Freedom from Fear: The American People in Depression and War, 1929–1945*

CITIZEN JUSTICE

CITIZEN JUSTICE

THE ENVIRONMENTAL LEGACY OF WILLIAM O. DOUGLAS— PUBLIC ADVOCATE AND CONSERVATION CHAMPION

M. MARGARET MCKEOWN

Potomac Books

AN IMPRINT OF THE UNIVERSITY OF NEBRASKA PRESS

An earlier version of chapter 10 was first published as
"The Trees Are Still Standing: The Backstory of *Sierra
Club v. Morton*," *Journal of Supreme Court History* 44, no. 2
(2019): 189–214. © 2018 M. Margaret McKeown.

∞

Library of Congress Cataloging-in-Publication Data
Names: McKeown, M. Margaret (Mary Margaret),
1951– author.
Title: Citizen justice: the environmental legacy of
William O. Douglas—public advocate and conservation
champion / M. Margaret McKeown.
Description: [Lincoln]: Potomac Books, an imprint
of the University of Nebraska Press, [2022] | Includes
bibliographical references and index.
Identifiers: LCCN 2022001047
ISBN 9781640123007 (hardback)
ISBN 9781640125544 (epub)
ISBN 9781640125551 (pdf)
Subjects: LCSH: Douglas, William O. (William Orville),
1898–1980—Influence. | Environmental law—United
States—History—20th century. | Nature conservation—
United States—History—20th century.
Classification: LCC KF8745.D6 M35 2022 | DDC
347.73/2634 [B]—dc23/eng/20220331
LC record available at https://lccn.loc.gov/2022001047

Set in Sabon Next LT Pro by Mikala R. Kolander.

Dedicated to Peter and Haruka for their inspiration

CONTENTS

ILLUSTRATIONS

Following page 106

PREFACE

Long before "ecology" and "environmentalist" became household words, early twentieth-century conservation pioneers—such as President Teddy Roosevelt and John Muir, founder of the Sierra Club—advocated to preserve nature. After World War II this movement took on a new urgency as the age of the automobile thrived. The nation was inundated with ubiquitous stretches of asphalt, overcrowded campgrounds, and traffic, and the last great American wildernesses were at risk.

Enter Justice William O. Douglas. Douglas, the longest-serving justice in American history, held a seat on the Supreme Court from 1939 to 1974. Hailing from the Pacific Northwest, he was a renowned legal academic, former chair of the Securities and Exchange Commission, strong-willed jurist, and dedicated advocate for the environment. During his decades on the court, he launched a crusade to galvanize activists and the public as part of his conservation army. For him, a road was like a dagger cutting through the heart of wilderness.

Douglas, an enigmatic figure, left his mark on American jurisprudence, but his influence on America's landscape was even more indelible. He became America's teacher on law, democracy, and the environment. A prolific author who wrote at breakneck speed, Douglas authored some fifty books, including *Of Men and Mountains* and *My Wilderness: The Pacific West*, homages to his beloved wilderness, and *A Wilderness Bill of Rights*, a manifesto to save American's heritage.

Douglas is often remembered for the controversies that surrounded him: four marriages, several bids for the White House, and unsuccessful impeachment proceedings led by then congressman Gerald Ford. Yet he was a legal giant and committed civil libertarian who authored landmark decisions about privacy, free speech, and criminal procedure.

By nature, Douglas was an iconoclast and a loner who was a champion dissenter on the court. One of his most famous dissents, in *Sierra Club v. Morton*, asked whether a tree, a river, or a valley should have the right to sue for its own preservation. The iconic inquiry—"Do trees have standing?"—embodied both his spiritual connection to nature and his effort to give a voice to the environment.

But perhaps Douglas's most enduring legacy is his successful conservation advocacy, particularly his passion for saving the wilderness. He grew up in the West, where he retreated every chance he had, and his heart and spirit remained there. In a manner unthinkable in this era, Douglas ran a one-man lobby shop for the environment from his chambers at the Supreme Court. He seized the tailwinds of the conservation movement and became a bandleader for wilderness preservation.

Douglas cut a striking figure in Washington DC and on the trail. With piercing blue eyes and a cowboy hat or floppy hiking hat atop his lanky figure, he exuded confidence and a western aura. For more than two decades, from the backwoods to the beltway, he was the most prominent figure in conservation circles. He brought national prominence, political connections, and boots-on-the ground credibility to his crusade.

Though he cultivated friendships with people in high places, such as Presidents Roosevelt, Kennedy, and Johnson and the secretaries of agriculture and the interior, Douglas never forgot his friends, the little guy, or the downtrodden. Nor did he forget his friends in the Sierra Club and The Wilderness Society. He railed against the federal bureaucracy and believed that the purpose of the Constitution was to get the government off the backs of the people. Though he is routinely cast as a liberal activist because of his association with the New Deal, his judicial decisions and his politics, his rugged individualism and skepticism of authority show him straddling the libertarian fence. He was provocative and unorthodox. Conservation politics became his passion.

Douglas's twenty-plus-year journey as a conservation advocate took him across America—from his first successful protest hike to save the Chesapeake and Ohio Canal near Washington DC to the Brooks Range in Alaska, the Red River Gorge in Kentucky, the big thicket in Texas, the Allagash waterway in Maine, a valley in Oregon, the last wild coastline on the Pacific Ocean, and his beloved Cougar Lakes in Washington State—now the William O. Douglas Wilderness. In between he saved scenic rivers from dams, trees from logging, and quiet places from tourist invasions. Invoking his signature strategy of marshalling the conservation army, leading public crusades, pushing his agenda in the corridors of power, inspiring the public through books and speeches, and understanding the most minute details of the political and natural landscapes, Douglas achieved stunning successes.

Serendipity brought me to the world of Douglas and the environment. As a Wyoming native, I long have been drawn to the mountains—the Tetons, the Wind Rivers, the Rockies, and later the Cascades—during my many years of hiking and climbing.

One winter while snowshoeing in Grand Teton National Park, I came across an unfamiliar homestead and discovered it was the Murie Ranch, known as "Conservation's Home." I knowingly asked, "You mean like John Muir?" No, the caretaker explained: it belonged to Olaus and Margaret "Mardy" Murie, celebrated biologists and conservationists, who helped lead The Wilderness Society in the 1950s and 1960s. Once I read their stories and journals, I was hooked, especially when I happened on a trove of correspondence between the Muries and Douglas. It was the tip of the iceberg in terms of his prodigious letters, books, articles, and campaigns to save the wild.

This book is not a biography of Douglas. Several of those have already been written, and he himself authored a three-volume autobiography plus countless other books. Nor does the book pretend to dissect his complex personality or engage in an academic critique of his legal opinions. Instead, the book traces Douglas's environmental legacy; explores the overriding ethical question of whether Douglas crossed the line in mixing his roles as a justice and an advocate; and considers whether it would be possible today to be a crusader, rabble-rouser, and high-profile advocate for the environment while serving as a Supreme Court justice.

Douglas has been called many things: Wild Bill, Mr. Justice Pangloss, the environmental justice, a public philosopher, a genius, even a Communist, and more. But most of all, he was a citizen justice. In Douglas's view, as a citizen he had a right to champion the environment, so long as it didn't interfere with the work of the court. Douglas's life work became part of the fabric of American history and its landscape. The story of his environmental legacy is one worth telling.

CITIZEN JUSTICE

1

The Man and His Mountains

When man ventures into the wilderness, climbs the ridges, and
sleeps in the forest, he comes in close communion with his
Creator. When man pits himself against the mountain,
he taps inner springs of his strength.

—WILLIAM O. DOUGLAS

The mountains are calling and I must go.

—JOHN MUIR

I t was a crisp, cloudless fall day in late 1949. On a ledge in the
Cascade Mountains, not far from Mount Rainier, Justice William O. Douglas was being crushed by his horse Kendall. After
the horse reared, Douglas had slipped off and then rolled down
the mountain, Kendall following close behind. As sixteen hundred pounds of flesh writhed atop him, Douglas lay in excruciat-
ing pain from twenty-three broken ribs.[1] He must have wondered
what was in store for his future: life or death?

This would not be Douglas's last brush with death. Nor was it
his first. More than thirty-five years earlier, as a teenager, he had
been squeezed precariously on another ledge in the Cascades,
Kloochman Rock, where he and his climbing partner had narrowly avoided a fatal fall. "Kloochman became that day," for Douglas, "a symbol of adversity and challenge—of the forces that have
drawn from man his greatest spiritual and physical achievements."[2]
Adversity and challenge became hallmarks of his life.

Despite the severity of the horse incident, Douglas recovered after months of rehabilitation and later resumed his horsepack adventures. In Washington DC Douglas cultivated the image of a rugged westerner, a five-gallon cowboy hat framing his rough-hewn face. But because he had spent the majority of his life on the East Coast, some wondered if he was "all hat and no cattle." Those skeptics were simply wrong. His writings and his life's work leave little doubt that his soul was grounded in the West, especially in the natural beauty of its mountains, valleys, rivers, lakes, and coastline.

Douglas was a man on a mission, always pushing himself and almost always succeeding. His daughter Millie once claimed that he rode his horse "like he drove his car, with his foot down on the accelerator until he got where he was going."[3] At the time of the horse fiasco, Douglas had been on the court for a decade; he was a bit bored, and his presidential hopes had been dashed. His ambition and independence found their resting place, in the years to follow, when Douglas turned his attention to his legacy to the American public: the push to preserve wilderness and save the environment.

Growing Up in the West

Born in Minnesota in 1898, William Orville Douglas was nonetheless a child of the West. After a brief stint in California, his father, a Scottish Presbyterian preacher, moved the family to Cleveland, Washington, a small town of around one hundred people, not far from the Columbia River and the Oregon border. While Douglas's father, also named William, rode his local seminary circuit among towns too small to have their own preachers, Douglas began to notice the world around him: the speed and sound of the rivers, the fleeting encounters with wildlife, the warm Western winds he would later know as "Chinooks," and the magnificent trees. By Douglas's account, Cleveland was fertile ground for a stereotypical Western upbringing, replete with "farmers and cattlemen," "God-fearing folks" of the "good, solid American stock of the kind that has made this country great."[4]

The harsh realities of life confronted Douglas at an early age, even in this picturesque setting. When he was five, his father died, leaving his mother, Julia, to cope with three children: William Orville, his older sister, Martha, and his younger brother, Arthur (Art). Though his mother called him "Treasure," the family called him "Orville" to differentiate him from his father. Douglas later settled on "Bill," reserving "William" for his formal court role.[5]

At his father's funeral, Mount Adams "stood cool and calm" in the background and "suddenly seemed to be a friend." Later Douglas often spoke of the mountain as if it were a family member, one that he would always race to see after a long absence. God, father, and nature became one in the mind of the young Douglas.[6]

Mount Adams got its name from an 1853 Pacific Railroad expedition, but Douglas preferred its more myth-laden native name, "Klickitat." The family moved to Yakima not long after the funeral, but the mountain's grand scale meant that he could still see it from his front porch. Situated in central Washington, some 145 miles east of Seattle, Yakima was a semi-arid, largely agricultural area, dotted with alfalfa, hops, orchards, and nearby foothills that offered Douglas opportunities for escape and exploration.

Even with the natural beauty around Yakima, Douglas's family struggled to eke out a living, though there are conflicting views of the family's fortune during Douglas's early years, perhaps exaggerated in part by Julia's near-constant expression of financial insecurity.[7] The array of blue-collar jobs Douglas performed shed light on his later sympathies for the "little guy." He delivered newspapers; worked in stores, creameries, packing houses, and cold-storage plants; set up bowling pins; and harvested fruit alongside migrant workers in Yakima's plentiful fields.[8] How essential these jobs were to support the family is open to some dispute, but they surely contributed to Douglas's feeling that he grew up in poverty and that he "had been born on 'the wrong side of the tracks.'"[9] Some thirty years after leaving home, Douglas dedicated one of his books to "the memory of [his] mother ... who once knew poverty in the Middle East meaning of the word."[10]

A bout with polio also sobered Douglas's childhood. Life for

Douglas was punctuated by episodes of ill health: crippling stomach attacks, psychological tensions, the horse accident, heart surgery, and, in 1974, a debilitating stroke.[11] But of these, a serious childhood illness before the age of two most profoundly shaped his personality and drove his personal narrative. Douglas became bedridden with a violent fever and lost much of the use of his legs, a condition that Douglas, his mother, and various biographers have attributed to infantile paralysis, or polio.[12] Throughout his illness, his mother and sister massaged his limbs with saltwater at all waking hours—the doctor's only prescription.[13] Whether due to this loving treatment or mere luck, Douglas improved after a matter of months. Still, his long-term recovery was not without lasting trauma—physical and emotional—for him as well as his mother.

Julia became obsessively protective and convinced herself that the infant Douglas was divinely ordained to fulfill some great, unknown purpose. This prediction of grandeur weighed on Douglas, and his relationship with his mother came to rest on her vacillation between two convictions: either Douglas would one day be president of the United States or he wouldn't "live past twelve."[14]

Discovering the Mountains

Douglas's illness left him a small, sickly child with spindly legs, making him the object of bullying. He internalized the branding that his mother, doctor, and peers offered up: "weakling." The natural world became his salvation. From his front porch view, Mount Adams and Mount Rainier became "personal friends," and these mountains "began to work a transformation." "There was a driving force," Douglas later reflected, "that took me first to the foothills and then to the mountains."[15]

Hiking at the fast clip of 4–5 miles per hour, Douglas grew stronger every summer and his hikes became harder. One day he pushed himself to finish a twenty-five-mile hike. His legs ached and common sense would have told him to quit, but because he had set a goal, he kept moving.[16] Douglas's drive at this early age offers a glimpse of the single-mindedness that played out in his personal and professional life.

Douglas quickly realized that immersion in nature brought both practical and spiritual benefits. He acquired the survival skills necessary for long mountain sojourns—woodcraft, trail finding, river fording, and salmon spearing—as well as more novel skills, such as how to use a frying pan as a toboggan.[17] Although he was never a Boy Scout, his skills would have netted him a rash of merit badges in the fields described in the *Official Handbook for Boys*: camping, conservation, forestry, horsemanship, ornithology, pathfinding, personal fitness, photography, pioneering, and scholarship.[18]

Nature was far more than a place for recuperative exercise: it was Douglas's personal religion, and he worshipped it zealously. While recuperating from the horse accident, Douglas put the finishing touches on his soliloquy, *Of Men and Mountains* (1950), which is a celebration of that spirit. It was this book that first brought him to the attention of conservationists, who would later become partners in his wilderness fight.[19] Alternating between overly dramatic and scrupulously detailed, the book affectionately chronicled his youthful adventures. With his brother Art and several close friends, the young Douglas imagined how Daniel Boone and Lewis and Clark must have felt walking in pristine wilderness.[20] Indeed, the lifelong internal clash between two opposing sides of Douglas—striving to be at the center of power while also identifying as an independent outsider—seems to be quieted only when Douglas communed with nature.

Despite his characteristic brisk pace of a man always on a mission, Douglas slowed down in the natural world to carefully observe plant life and wildlife, learning the joys of huckleberries along the trail, observing that squaw grass is a wildflower and not a grass, realizing that the kinnikinnick (bearberry) held soil in place, and waxing eloquent on the lupine as "one of the greatest of flowering plants in all the Cascades."[21] His amazing recall of details, which he routinely recorded in small black notebooks, was a talent that would later serve him well on the Supreme Court.

Douglas was a true sportsman who took pride in understanding his surroundings, and he gained a deep respect for even the most destructive events in nature. Novices may think that bears and cougars present the biggest challenge to alpine hikers, but Douglas knew that avalanches and forest fires were much greater risks. He witnessed several avalanches in his life but managed to escape harm. Recalling his drama in Oregon's Wallowa Mountains, Douglas remembered the roar of "a hundred express trains in a tunnel [that] shook the mountain itself [like] dozens of thunderstorms on an echoing hillside." Once the slide moved on, "all was silent as if death itself had passed through the ravine."[22] The sheer power of an avalanche made a strong impression and evoked in Douglas a sense of the supernatural.

Always fascinated by the seemingly paradoxical character of natural forces—destructive and creative—Douglas both respected and was in awe of nature's powers. Take fire for instance. Like avalanches, forest fires could overtake a person in an instant—"racing up trees and through forests faster than a man can run"—and devastate an entire region, "killing all life with [their] hot tongue[s], leaving behind desolation and a sterile earth that [would] not produce crops of timber for a generation or more."[23] Douglas reflected that John Muir, founder of the Sierra Club and one of his conservation heroes, also recognized the destructive nature of forest fires, whose "flames were so bright Muir could read a book at a distance of 300 yards."[24] Fire, however, was equally "a sign of life" in Douglas's mind, not to mention the spiritual warmth for those gathered around it.[25] Perhaps Douglas begin to appreciate that nature's paradox corresponded with his own internal paradox of pursuing both solitude and power.

Through his efforts to traverse and record the wild, Douglas came to an intuitive understanding of what we now call *ecology*—the study of the interconnectedness of natural systems. For Douglas this was more than a mere scientific fact; it became the basis of his personal philosophy: "It is easy to see the delicate handiwork of the Creator in any meadow. But perhaps it takes these startling views to remind us of His omnipotence. Perhaps it takes such a view to make us realize that vain, cocky, aggressive, selfish man never conquers the mountains in spite of all his boasting and bustling and exertion. He conquers only himself."[26]

The Man and His Mountains

The Star Student

When he was not working his odd jobs or wandering the hills, Douglas concentrated on his studies. For the budding lawyer and future chairman of the Securities and Exchange Commission (SEC), his schooling in Yakima "was in large measure responsible for the kind of person [he] became." To his school days Douglas traced his appreciation for "the beauty and power of words" and his sense of "the problems of costs and profits and the historic place of business in the American scheme." Perhaps more important, activities like speech and debate had transformed the "slightly crippled, nervous, frightened young man" into one with the gift of "stage presence."[27] He was quickly and consistently recognized for his agile mind, and scholastic performance became his mark of success. Douglas's mother must have been proud when her Treasure graduated from high school as valedictorian.[28] She was not alone. The yearbook inscription said it all: "Born for success he seemed, With grace to win, With heart to hold, With shining gifts that took all eyes."[29]

After taking a "last wholly carefree trip ... in the high mountains," Douglas left his Yakima cocoon for Whitman College in 1916 and began his meteoric rise.[30] Whitman, a small liberal arts college in Walla Walla, Washington (according to Al Jolson, "a valley so nice they named it twice"), gave him another opportunity to excel academically.[31] Its motto, *Per ardua surgo* (Through adversities I rise), was an apt description of how Douglas viewed himself. His air of seriousness and determination regarding academic success defined him for his peers. At one point his Beta Theta Pi fraternity brothers gave Douglas the honor of membership in the fraternity's "anti-cuss and fussing club."[32] Douglas had a good sense of humor and a joie de vivre spirit, but his reputation as a serious character stemmed in part from the fact that most often he could not *afford* to enjoy himself.

Douglas's meager funds and his mother's expectation that he send money home required him to take a host of jobs during the school year—janitor, waiter, and jewelry store assistant. On summer breaks Douglas resumed his childhood work of picking and packing fruit and also dabbled in logging and firefighting.[33] Though an academic star throughout his life, his ever-precarious financial situation would never free Douglas to dedicate himself fully to his studies.

During Douglas's early months at Whitman, patriotic fervor was high. President Woodrow Wilson engaged in a delicate effort to aid the Allies before the United States entered World War I in 1917. Douglas spent the summer of 1918 in a Reserve Officers' Training Corps camp at the Presidio in San Francisco, drilling to be sent to Europe, though he ultimately returned to Whitman as a member of the Student Army Training Corps.[34] Following that service, he received an Honorable Discharge from the U.S. Army and, years later, a resting place at Arlington National Cemetery.[35]

Douglas's college career was a consummate success: star debater, president of Whitman's student organization and of his fraternity, commencement speaker, and Phi Beta Kappa. For Douglas, however, total satisfaction was always just out of reach. In a rare setback, he didn't win a Rhodes Scholarship, a failure that, in his mind, offered proof that money, not talent, imposed a ceiling on his ability to rise from his humble beginnings.[36]

Go East, Young Man

After graduating in 1920, Douglas returned home to teach English and Latin at Yakima High School. There he met the other Latin teacher, Mildred Riddle, six years his senior, with whom he shared a love of the outdoors and a deep intelligence.[37] Although he was grateful for the steady salary, before long Douglas grew restless. After two years, he headed east to Columbia Law School, but not before getting engaged to Mildred, who stayed behind for financial reasons.

Adventurous and frugal, Douglas elected not to buy a train ticket. He made his way to Minnesota by riding in a caboose and safeguarding two thousand sheep. As to the rest of the eastward push to New York City, according to various accounts, he "rode the rods"—sneaking onto the train and riding under boxcars or passenger cars on the boards laid across the rods—or paid for a ticket in a flatcar.[38]

As he left the landscape and people he cherished, Douglas asked introspectively, "Why this compulsion to leave the valley? Why this drive, this impulse, to leave the scenes I loved?"[39] The answer, of course, was that his dreams and talents were bigger than Yakima, which to Douglas represented a place where "ideas were not congenial."[40] In the mid-1980s, Yakima sported a sign, "Welcome to Yakima, the Palm Springs of Washington."[41] Yakima was never Palm Springs and was a town of fewer than twenty thousand people at the time he left. New York and its glitz, with more than 5.5 million people and a first-rate law school, beckoned.

The urban East Coast culture at Columbia Law School was jarring as Douglas confronted "the ugliness of the city" and, again, his financial insecurity.[42] He was almost turned away at the Beta Theta Phi house in New York because of his shabby looks and had to borrow money from a fraternity brother to pay his registration fees.[43] For Douglas the contrast between his own situation and that of his blue-blooded colleagues at Columbia underscored the inequality in New York City and urban America writ large.[44]

Douglas's money woes led him to consider dropping out of school. Having packed his bags, he paid one last desperate visit to Columbia's student employment office. There he found a posting by a man running a correspondence school. Douglas was tasked with creating a course in business law, about which he knew nothing. It kept him from his own classes for six weeks as he pulled double duty, learning the material and designing the course. Soon after, Douglas began offering tutoring services for students aspiring to attend Ivy League colleges.[45] Earning enough to scrape by, Douglas decided to stay at Columbia.

The obscurity of his Western origins left Douglas more or less free to define himself for his new colleagues. He cast himself as a character out of a frontier tall tale: "The Yakima Apple Knocker." He played up the story of his early life, claiming that he had helped feed his family by knocking apples off trees.[46] While entertaining to his better-heeled colleagues, such exaggeration also gave Douglas a way to turn his outsider status, and the source of his greatest insecurity, into an asset. Despite his profession of distaste for the city and his self-identification with the West, Douglas still felt impelled to be "fashionable." His attempts to fit in resulted in taking up drinking and smoking; he would eventually kick cigarettes, but his drinking persisted and would leave its mark on his life.[47]

Even as he felt himself a stranger in a strange land full of unfriendly people, Douglas found ways to make his life in New York more livable. He lamented the absence of any semblance of the natural world. For long stretches the "only green thing" he had "was a miserable geranium plant struggling to survive" and "the only bird [he] ever saw was a pigeon." The antidote came when he was hired as an organizer of a group of low-income boys from a settlement house in New York City. He formed the "Yakima Club" and taught them about "Indians, spearing salmon, fly fishing, climbing mountains, camping out, and so on," and, to the extent there was nature to be had, they explored it together.[48]

Douglas married Mildred in 1923. Her arrival in New York was a source of cheer. She soon found a teaching job that let Douglas breathe a little easier, but because her school was outside the city, the young couple was again forced to live apart.[49]

Academic achievement and an incredible work ethic marked Douglas's law school years. After a few false starts—due in part, no doubt, to the amount of time he spent working to make ends meet—Douglas was chosen as a member of the prestigious *Columbia Law Review*.[50] This achievement meant all the more because "[it] turned not on pull, family, influence, or politics, but on grades alone."[51] Though his grades were excellent and he graduated among the top few students of his class, just as with the Rhodes Scholarship, he missed the brass ring—this time a clerkship at the Supreme Court.[52] The disappointment was one of few bumps on his path to success. At the time, Douglas was "unspeakably depressed" when the "one opportunity" he had wanted passed him by, leaving him with "little to show" for all his work.[53] Douglas spoke too soon. A mere fourteen years later, he would join the court.

In the interim, however, Douglas took a job with the famed

The Man and His Mountains

New York law firm Cravath, Henderson & de Gersdorff (now Cravath, Swaine & Moore) and taught a few classes at Columbia on the side.[54] There is, of course, some irony in that Douglas, later a critic of "the establishment," went to work for one of the most established Wall Street firms.[55] But such contradictions would continue as he straddled a life both in the center and outside of the social circle. Perhaps predictably, Douglas did not adapt easily to the long hours and constant exposure to colleagues who, it seemed to Douglas, "preferred law practice to love, compassion, family, hiking, or sunsets." After seeing his colleagues "spent before their time," Douglas knew that if he "walked their paths, [he]'d never be able to climb another mountain or wade a trout stream."[56]

Physical well-being became a priority. Before he was even thirty, Douglas again found his health deteriorating. Eventually, he accepted his doctor's diagnosis: a psychosomatic illness brought on by personal and professional stress.[57] Douglas was told that he should return west for the sake of his health—the same reason his father had moved the family from Minnesota in the first place.[58]

With mounting financial, familial, and now health imperatives to go back home, Douglas returned to Yakima. Mildred stayed behind.[59] He obtained admission to the Washington State Bar, briefly considered practicing law in Yakima, and toyed with the idea of joining a Seattle firm, Holman, Mickelwait, Marion, Price and Black (later Perkins Coie). Douglas dispensed with that notion when he realized that Seattle firms paid a fraction of what he had earned in New York—$600, compared to $5,000, per year.[60] He quickly awoke to the reality that, as unhappy as he felt in the East, he would "*never, never* be happy in Yakima."[61] After just several months, he returned to New York.

Before long, Douglas traded the onerous hours, stressful conditions, and sharp elbowing of business law for the gentler—though equally competitive—academic rivalries on the faculty of Colombia Law School. When he began teaching full time, Douglas was finally able to slow down, relatively speaking, for "the first time in [his] life." The academic world gave him a chance to "probe deeper into various problems that interested [him]" and "to reflect on [his] past and future."[62] As he grew into his role as a professor, the law seemed to come alive, representing ideas and deep sociological questions more engaging than the paper pushing he had experienced in legal practice. After only a year on the faculty, however, academic and bureaucratic rivalries within Columbia led Douglas to resign in protest.[63]

Naturally, Douglas thought again about heading west, but his growing reputation and a chance encounter with Robert Maynard Hutchins, the like-minded young dean of Yale Law School, led to a job offer. Douglas moved to New Haven, after incredulously asking Hutchins, "Where is Yale?"[64] Hutchins must have rolled his eyes. Perhaps the "aw shucks" western innocence was endearing, but it hardly rang true after six years in New York. In New Haven, Douglas finally felt "financially secure and intellectually satisfied" and settled into his personal and professional life.[65] Mildred soon gave birth to both of their children, Bill Jr. and Millie.

Though Douglas grew as a scholar, he was drawn more and more into conflict with the elitism of legal academia. Douglas saw himself as self-made and grew frustrated by the "sons of the elite . . . who in time would run the nation," treating them "as the lion tamer in the circus treats his wards."[66] This antipathy manifested itself in his teaching. Despite the fact that Hutchins had called him "the most outstanding law professor in the nation," Douglas did little to court favor with the students and was remembered as "pretty dull" and "stiff" in the classroom.[67]

Douglas's frustration extended to his colleagues. He complained that "the great names in the law were, with few exceptions, attached to men who exploited the system but brought very few spiritual or ethical values to it." Douglas's troubled relationship with some of his fellow professors spoke to a deeper discomfort with his chosen profession. He realized that academia posed questions but did not answer them. So he took a different approach, which he would later carry into his jurisprudence: "[making] the law more relevant to life."[68]

In the throes of the Great Depression, Douglas turned his scholarly attention to some of the most pressing issues of the day, including consumer credit and bankruptcy.[69] Douglas studied bankruptcy in a novel way by actually talking to those going through it.[70] His approach embraced the new trend in legal academia: law as a social science. This perspective reflected the emergence of "legal realism," which sought to use the methodology of anthropology to make "social issues and development" a priority, replacing the "strict formal interpretation of rights" that had been the academy's predominant concern.[71] Douglas's research opened his eyes to the gap between legal theory and legal reality and convinced him that there was much more to learn from direct experience than abstract ideas. This outlook mirrored the path he later preached for conservation policymakers: come and see the wilderness to understand it.

As an emerging expert in corporate and bankruptcy law, Douglas ran a study of the bankruptcy system in the federal court in New York, which foreshadowed his later work on "speculative American business practices."[72] This study attracted the attention of judges and national policymakers, allowing Douglas the time in the nation's capital that he had hoped to get as a Supreme Court clerk.[73] What began as consultations to the Hoover administration's Commerce Department would become a full-time concern under Franklin Delano Roosevelt, priming Douglas for a move to Washington DC.

Moving on to Washington

As Americans looked for hope in the midst of a worldwide depression, they elected Roosevelt as president in 1932. His famous "First Hundred Days" launched reforms that became the foundation of the New Deal, particularly the Securities Act of 1933. From his perch at Yale and through law review articles, Douglas praised the principle of the legislation but argued for the federal government to do more in protecting the public interest—a theme he championed throughout his career.[74]

Douglas developed an expertise that would give him the chance to join the new administration, writing seven major articles in the securities field in as many months.[75] These publications came as he watched legions of other bright young men and women—though mostly men—stream into Washington. As others, including another future justice, Felix Frankfurter and his "Harvard hot dogs," took up the intellectual leadership of the New Deal, Douglas yearned to join the fray and answer Roosevelt's call for "bold, persistent experimentation." That clarion call appealed to Douglas and his sense of destiny.

When new legislation created the SEC in 1934, Douglas lobbied hard to get one of the bevy of new positions for himself but to no avail. Instead, Joseph Kennedy, the commission's new chair, asked him to head up a congressionally mandated study of manipulations of bankruptcies and receiverships. Although it was less than he had hoped for, Douglas accepted Kennedy's offer, moving to the capital full time in the fall of 1934 (without officially giving up his professorship at Yale). Douglas quickly hired Abe Fortas, his former star student and future colleague on the Supreme Court, as his key staffer and began his work in earnest.[76]

Douglas and his team uncovered a staggering "trail of deceit, manipulation and outright illegal conduct" that confirmed Douglas's long-held suspicion that the law was the handmaiden of the establishment. The study's eight volumes highlighted the scourge of corporate corruption and secured Douglas's reputation as a substantive expert and public crusader for the New Deal. Douglas was keenly aware that this position brought him closer to the center of power, and he was primed to make the most of it. As James Simon, an early Douglas biographer, described it, "Douglas preferred to invest in only one stock: William O. Douglas."[77]

From the time he arrived in Washington until his appointment to the Supreme Court in 1939, Douglas dove into the web of power politics. His go-it-alone Horatio Alger story was fading further into his past. Kennedy took a liking to Douglas and sought to boost his rising star. When Kennedy stepped down as SEC chairman and was replaced by a sitting commissioner, a new seat opened. Kennedy facilitated a personal introduction to Roosevelt, who said, "You're my man," and he appointed Douglas to the commission in early 1936.[78]

The press applauded Douglas's appointment. The *New York Times* and *Newsweek* approved Roosevelt's choice, and *Time* magazine's cover story, "Walla Walla to Washington," proclaimed him "a brilliant professor."[79] His hometown newspaper, the *Yakima Daily Republic*, claimed him as Yakima's own: "He is traveling in pretty big company and takes Joseph P. Kennedy's place on the commission, though not as chairman.... Whether he reforms the world of finance and makes Wall Street a safe place for the lambs is not predictable, but he'll do it if anybody can, and Yakima will always be proud to say he lived here as a boy and started work here as a man, and above all, that he married a Yakima girl."[80]

However, as Douglas drew himself increasingly closer to the center of power in the liberal Roosevelt administration, he found himself growing distant from the West. Once he became known as a "wild" liberal, his local newspaper was not nearly as enthusiastic about its native son. A later editorial in the *Yakima Daily Republic* about his work at the SEC proclaimed, "Yakima Not At Fault."[81] The loss of hometown support would later complicate his campaign for the Supreme Court, but Douglas's commitment to the New Deal paid off almost immediately.

In September 1937 Douglas was planning to return to Yale Law School as dean after having served as an SEC commissioner for two years. But Roosevelt, at Kennedy's urging, called and said, "Unpack your bag—you are the new chairman of the Securities and Exchange Commission."[82] Only a few days later, on September 7, 1937, the New York Stock Exchange went into a tailspin.

From the stock market panic that greeted Douglas and through many attempts by industry to sideline him, he developed a working relationship with Roosevelt that gradually deepened into a more personal bond. The frequency of invitations to FDR's regular poker parties increased, alongside Douglas's bureaucratic power.[83] For Roosevelt, Douglas offered a welcome contrast to FDR's staid set of advisers, willing to correct him when he was wrong and tell him jokes "he should never hear."[84]

Though Douglas would later cast his appointment to the Supreme Court as something he "never even dreamed of," he cultivated his relationship with Roosevelt and well understood that "a Supreme Court appointment is a Presidential prerogative." On this account, his proud claim—"I had my own dreams and they were dependent solely on me, not on the whim or caprice of another"—did not exactly hold true.[85]

Douglas recognized the element of serendipity inherent in a Supreme Court appointment: "The important thing is to stay in the stream of history, be in the forefront of events—and carve out a career that will be satisfying in all other respects."[86] For Douglas the stream ran as swiftly and powerfully as the Columbia River; his rise from commission staffer to chairman spanned only three years. As Douglas's SEC term came to an end, his return to Yale—where he retained his tenured professorship—seemed inevitable.[87] Serendipity would upend these plans. Once again, Douglas would be told to unpack his bags.

When Justice Louis Brandeis informed the president of his retirement in February 1939, the justice urged Roosevelt to appoint Douglas.[88] By all accounts, Douglas was surprised by Brandeis's plans to retire.[89] Douglas was thrilled when Brandeis eventually told him, "You were my personal choice for my successor." Though Douglas frequently downplayed his aspiration, he admitted in his diary that the Supreme Court "had always been my ambition."[90]

Despite his good relationship with Roosevelt and Brandeis's recommendation, Douglas's nomination was anything but assured. Not only was he young for the appointment, but also pressure from Western senators to fix the geographic imbalance on the court made it likely that Roosevelt would look for a nominee with strong ties to the West.

As soon as he knew his name was in the mix, Douglas kicked his own private campaign into full gear. Although he considered Yakima and Washington State his "home," Douglas had spent seventeen years in the East, and his connections out West had begun to atrophy. Douglas quickly came to understand that success hinged on establishing the bona fides of his "westernness." Eventually, the tenuous ties Douglas sought to leverage became more permanent after he joined the court and acquired cabins in Oregon, in southern Washington, on the Olympic Peninsula, and finally in Goose Prairie, Washington.

Douglas orchestrated what looked like a grassroots campaign, which he combined with a personal lobbying effort targeted at well-placed officials in the administration and the press—a strategy that would later become his signature approach for getting things done. With Douglas's permission, Arthur Krock, a *New York Times* reporter and long-time Douglas booster, ran an article speculating that Douglas would be an ideal replacement for Brandeis.[91]

Douglas enlisted his brother Art, an executive of the Statler Hilton hotels, to rally the governor of Washington, members of the bar associations of Washington and Yakima, and a plethora of Washington lawyers, giving Douglas the appearance of deep Western ties as these people pressed claims of Douglas "as a son of the West."[92] Though Douglas publicly disclaimed aspirations for the nomination, he embarked on an aggressive letter-writing campaign, reaching out to key New Deal strategists: Attorney General Frank Murphy, Speaker of the House of Representatives Sam Rayburn, and Postmaster General James Farley. Each letter requested an autographed photograph to adorn his office (though perhaps he should have said "chambers"). A note to Justice Brandeis followed, along with a copy of one of Douglas's recent speeches.[93]

On Sunday, March 19, 1939, Douglas was out playing golf, most likely after his ritual weekend hike on the Chesapeake and Ohio Canal (c&o Canal). He returned home to find a summons from the White House, where Roosevelt was about to give Douglas the news of his nomination. Roosevelt first teased Douglas, telling him that he was offering him "a thankless job . . . [a] job [that] is something like being in jail." After giving Douglas enough time to panic and think he would be appointed to the Federal Communications Commission, Roosevelt announced he would nominate Douglas to be a Supreme Court justice.[94]

Even if Douglas was not quite as "overcome" and "dazed" as he later claimed, he still had reason to be surprised.[95] At age forty, Douglas would become—and remains today—the second youngest justice ever to be appointed, second only to Joseph Story (appointed in 1811 at the age of thirty-two). Of contemporary appointees, only Clarence Thomas, appointed at forty-three, rivals Douglas in his youthfulness at time of appointment.[96]

On April 17, 1939, a day that was unseasonably cold for spring in Washington, Douglas, accompanied by his wife and children, was sworn into office.[97] His quick confirmation by a vote of 62–4, just two months after Brandeis had sent his letter to the president, stands in stark contrast to the confirmation lag of some later nominees, such as Harry Blackmun (362 days after Abe Fortas's resignation) or Neil Gorsuch (419 days after the death of Antonin Scalia).[98]

Despite his strong personality and keen intellect, Douglas did not emerge as a leader on the court. His independent personality did not lend itself well to collegial decision-making. He did, however, stake out a reputation as a civil libertarian. And his judicial bent in cases involving corporations or the government foreshadowed themes that would resonate throughout his career and in his conservation battles—protecting the little guy and challenging government power.

The Supreme Court is a brass ring that few can catch; many aspirants and failed nominations dot the court's history. Once he reached that pinnacle, Douglas was adept at meeting his obligations as a justice. But he remained "a restless man," seeking his next grand challenge. "With some men, when you get to the Court, and you keep saying, 'My God, this is everything I wanted in my life. I'm the happiest man on earth.' But that wasn't Bill Douglas," his friend Clark Clifford observed. "Bill never quite knew where fate was going to lead him."[99]

Douglas spent his first decade as a justice with one foot in the court and the other in politics. There was always another frontier to conquer—overcoming his childhood illness, summiting mountains, heading east to law school, vanquishing challenges

The Man and His Mountains

in the legal academy, getting a political appointment, becoming the first this and the youngest that. He only briefly paused at each way station before starting his next quest.

In the 1940s Douglas's formula faltered. Even apart from the near-fatal horse accident, the decade was rocky for him. He soon learned that electoral politics and the Supreme Court were not a winning combination. But the political skills he had honed in Washington DC served him well when he finally found his most expansive frontier: saving the wilderness. Political Washington was a springboard for his conservation politics.

2

Political Washington—A Long Way from Yakima

Politics is perishable. The work of the
Court is long and enduring.

—WILLIAM O. DOUGLAS

When a priest enters a monastery, he must leave—or ought to
leave—all sorts of worldly desires behind him. And this Court
has no excuse for being unless it's a monastery.

—FELIX FRANKFURTER

Trading his office at the bustling sec on Pennsylvania Avenue near the White House for chambers in the more subdued and elegant atmosphere of the Supreme Court on Capitol Hill, Douglas began the job President Roosevelt had described as "like being in jail."[1] He had no intention of being cooped up and left behind neither his political ambitions nor his sense that, as a citizen, he had a mission beyond his life on the court.

Though often seen as shy and sometimes socially awkward, Douglas thrived in Washington, becoming part of the political and social fabric of the capital. He attended Washington parties four or five times a week and found himself among the president's inner circle, which included Secretary of the Interior Harold Ickes; Secretary of the Treasury Henry Morgenthau; and Tommy "the Cork" Corcoran, special counsel to the Reconstruction Finance Corporation and part of Roosevelt's brain trust.[2]

After he joined the court in 1939, Douglas continued to frequent parties with ambassadors, cabinet members, and presidential advisers. The poker parties at the White House were a social highlight, with soirees lasting from the time the president fixed the first martinis until one in the morning. Though business discussions were off limits, Douglas brought frivolity to the gatherings by taking occasional pot shots at members of the court. The president "roared" with laughter when Douglas deemed one particularly mean game "with lots of cards wild" as "Charles the Baptist," referring to Chief Justice Charles Evans Hughes.[3]

Although Douglas poked fun at the chief justice, his spirited sense of humor did not diminish his admiration for Hughes or his feeling of an almost father-son relationship.[4] When Hughes retired in 1941, Douglas wrote, "Your generosity, kindliness and forbearance meant much to me. Your professional performance . . . was a real inspiration."[5] Though he also revered some of his other colleagues, few were among the intimates at the White House parties.

Douglas also saw Roosevelt outside of group social events, dining with him, spending evenings watching movies with him, and even weighing in on speeches. Like many, Douglas felt Roosevelt was a "warm, friendly, happy man whom we all loved."[6] Though it might seem that Douglas's closest connection with Roosevelt would have come from their shared commitment to reforming corporate America, Douglas felt otherwise: "I had a deep and abiding affection for FDR. My closest bond with him was not in the work of cleaning up the capitalist system; rather it was in various expressions of his love of the earth—its grasses and trees, its manifold wildlife, its precious sanctuaries."[7]

The Beginnings of a Citizen Justice

Douglas's first term on the court forced him to confront his dual identity as a citizen and a justice. In the 1939 case of *O'Malley v. Woodrough*, the court considered whether the Internal Revenue Service's assessment of federal income tax on a federal judge's income was contrary to the constitutional provision guaranteeing that compensation of federal judges "shall not be diminished during their Continuance in Office."[8] The court quickly axed the judge's claim to a tax exemption. Justice Felix Frankfurter wrote that "to subject them to a general tax is merely to recognize that judges are also citizens, and that their particular function in government does not generate an immunity from sharing with their fellow citizens the material burden of the government whose Constitution and law they are charged with administering."[9]

Douglas joined the majority, adopting the view of two of his heroes—Justices Louis Brandeis and Oliver Wendell Holmes—who in a previous case had also rejected a judicial exemption. In a television interview more than three decades later, Douglas articulated to CBS journalist Eric Sevareid how his vote for the majority affirmed his dual identity as a citizen and a justice: "As I made this little entry into the docket sheet, I said to myself, 'Young man, you've just voted yourself first-class citizenship.' I decided that, if we were going to pay taxes like everybody else, that you should be a citizen like everyone else, except that unless the thing you are doing interferes from the work of the court."[10]

It is hard to know whether *O'Malley* actually sparked this sentiment in Douglas or whether only later it became a convenient explanation for his activities. Douglas repeated this pronouncement in the autobiography he wrote much later, but in the diary he kept for the first two years on the court, the case is referenced only in passing and without any mention of his self-proclaimed "first-class citizenship."[11]

Either way, Douglas embraced an expansive view of his role as a citizen and spent the next three decades advancing his wilderness values through protest hikes, lobbying campaigns, and advocacy—"I wrote, spoke . . . joined conservation groups. I marched, hiked, and protested against the despoilers and their tactics"—all from his mantle as a justice of the Supreme Court. Douglas tried to be "a first-class citizen to the fullest extent compatible with [his] judicial duties."[12] Apart from enabling Douglas's advocacy, *O'Malley* had a practical effect that would vex him for years: he had to pay income tax on the alimony owed to several former wives, thus making outside speaking and writing important, even necessary, sources of income.

Though Douglas often invoked *O'Malley* to justify his passion to serve as a citizen advocate for the environment, it hardly sufficed to explain how he reconciled his quest for presidential office with his role on the bench. From today's vantage point, Douglas's activities, even if discreet, were decidedly unorthodox. We perhaps myopically hew to the mantra that the Supreme Court is divorced from politics with a capital "P," and the notion of justices harboring political ambitions collides with this sensibility. But Douglas—and many of his predecessors and peers on the court—followed their own ethical star and painted a different picture of the permissive bounds of political involvement.

Politics, Ethics, and the Supreme Court

Many twentieth-century justices engaged in political activity, but William Howard Taft literally brought presidential politics to the court. After becoming a federal judge at an early age and then serving as a one-term president (1909–13), Taft was appointed chief justice. Despite his claim that "the Chief Justice goes into a monastery and confines himself to his judicial work," he continued to seek out presidential hopefuls for the Republican Party. Taft worked behind the scenes at Republican conventions and advised presidents on everything from potential judicial nominees to clemency, labor unrest, foreign debt payments, and America's role in the Permanent Court of International Justice. He also lobbied Congress until his death in 1930 on traditional judicial concerns such as court vacancies and jurisdiction. Taft's most enduring lobbying effort was his dream of a new Supreme Court headquarters. When the cornerstone of the new building, often dubbed "the Marble Palace," was laid in 1935 at the court's present location—1 First Street NE—Chief Justice Hughes gushed, "We are indebted to the late Chief Justice William Howard Taft more than anyone else. This building is the result of intellectual persistence."[13]

As chief justice, Taft is also remembered for shepherding the creation of a first formal judicial ethics code in the United States. It emerged from an American Bar Association (ABA) project Taft headed in the wake of a controversy surrounding the improbably named federal judge Kenesaw Mountain Landis. After the Chicago White Sox players were accused of "throwing" the 1919 World Series and became embroiled in what was tagged "the Black Sox scandal," the baseball leagues tried to polish their integrity by appointing Landis, known for his rectitude, as commissioner of baseball. Landis remained on the bench for another year after accepting the position, but public outrage forced him to choose: federal judge or baseball commissioner. Landis picked baseball and a job that paid almost six times as much.[14]

The Landis affair prompted a call for ethics standards, which were released under Taft's leadership as the advisory ABA Canons of Judicial Ethics (1924).[15] Over time many state courts adopted the 1924 Canons, but formal standards for federal judges were not established until 1972. Even now the Code of Conduct for Federal Judges applies only to federal *judges*, not to Supreme Court *justices*, and the lack of formal code for the justices continues to provoke controversy.[16] Nonetheless, the twenty-first-century court has taken concrete steps to follow the Code of Conduct.[17] However, in 1924 the justices did not necessarily share this commitment. Even so, they were bound by the oath in place since 1789 to "do equal right to the poor and to the rich" and "to faithfully and impartially discharge and perform" the duties of judicial office.[18] Presumably the justices also shared a collective commitment to preserve the dignity of the institution and the principle of separation of powers, and each justice had a personal moral compass as to ethical behavior. Supreme Court scholar David J. Danelski suggests that the court "collectively agreed on standards of propriety that were more specific than the 1924 canons," such as refusing even the hint of corruption, refraining from taking public positions or giving advice to other branches on matters likely to come before the Court, and abstaining from electoral campaigns.[19] Considering that the justices' conduct varied widely, it is hard to say that they adhered to the collective principles that Danelski intimates, especially the constraint on electoral politics.

Indeed, "for at least one hundred and twenty-five years, there has been no ten year period in which a Supreme Court Justice has not been seriously and soberly considered for the presidential office," Supreme Court scholar John Frank noted in 1958.[20] This figure highlights both the regard in which the justices were held and their political connections, though their colleagues often viewed these ambitions unfavorably, either because of personal rivalry and jealously, ethical concerns, or a mixture of both. So while many of the justices, including Douglas, denounced partisan political activity, their actions belied their words. While Canon 28 of the Canons of Judicial Ethics echoed Douglas's view that a judge "is not required to surrender his rights or opinions as a citizen," it went on to counsel that neither should a judge "engage generally in partisan activities."[21]

Beyond the political world, the 1924 Canons were not particularly helpful in defining the limits of extrajudicial activities. The notion of avoiding the appearance of impropriety ran broadly throughout the canons. There was some leeway given for legislative advice related to legal procedures, but the principles embraced strict prohibitions on business promotions, solicitations for charity, and the use of the office to advance "personal ambitions" or increase "popularity." The most lenient advice came in the category of social relations: "It is not necessary to the proper performance of judicial duty that a judge should live in retirement or seclusion; it is desirable that, so far as reasonable attention to the completion of his work will permit, he continue to mingle in social intercourse and that he should not discontinue his interest or appearance at meetings or members of the Bar."[22] While several justices compared the court to "living in a monastery," few actually practiced or preferred utter "retirement or seclusion," and many seized on a more permissive standard.

Extrajudicial Activities of the Justices

More than vying for political office, the justices' most prominent political roles tended to be serving as behind-the-scenes advisers to presidents and taking on special presidential appointments. Formal efforts to curb these activities, such as Senator Sam Ervin's proposal in the 1960s to prevent justices from advising the legislative and executive branches, had fallen on deaf ears.[23]

Predictably, many of the justices had close relations with the president who had nominated them and felt a continuing obligation to nurture that relationship. The appointment process is inherently political: Article II of the Constitution provides that the president "shall nominate, and by and with the Advice and Consent of the Senate, shall appoint . . . Judges of the Supreme Court."[24] The chance to appoint a Supreme Court justice is a rare presidential opportunity, and the temptation to nominate a friend or confidante plays out as part of the political dance between the president and Congress. Roosevelt was close to Douglas, Frankfurter, and Robert Jackson; Harry Truman appointed his friends Harold Burton, Fred Vinson, and Sherman Minton; John F. Kennedy selected Byron White, who had chaired Kennedy's campaign in Colorado before serving in the Kennedy Justice Department; and Lyndon Johnson looked to his lawyer and adviser, Abe Fortas. Similarly, in 1993 Bill Clinton wanted to elevate his close friend from Arkansas, Eighth Circuit Judge Richard Sheppard Arnold, whom Clinton called "the most brilliant man on the federal bench." Unfortunately, Arnold's health was uncertain. Clinton turned instead to Ruth Bader Ginsburg, whom he came to consider a brilliant choice and who had a stellar run of more than twenty-five years, though nothing approaching Douglas's almost thirty-seven-year tenure.[25]

Arguably, Taft's unique position as president before joining the court could explain his overriding urge to advise the president on a wide array of matters, but he was hardly alone. Many justices advised the executive branch after their appointment to the bench. Justice William Moody wrote memoranda to President Theodore Roosevelt on topics ranging from a reorganization of the navy to regulation on corporations involved in interstate commerce. Moody also consulted on Roosevelt's speeches, a practice justices Harlan Fiske Stone and Frank Murphy took on for their respective presidents, Herbert Hoover and FDR.[26]

Douglas's contemporary and later archenemy Frankfurter was a master insider and political adviser from the time he joined the court in 1939 until Roosevelt's death. Frankfurter was a Harvard

Law School professor who served in Washington and helped found the American Civil Liberties Union. Frankfurter and Douglas joined the court the same year and were, at least initially, friends and natural liberal compatriots who had much in common. As they began to diverge philosophically and jurisprudentially, their relationship deteriorated into bitterness.[27]

Echoing Taft's sentiment, Frankfurter famously compared the court to a monastery—a hypocritical stance in view of his political machinations. He pointedly preached that it was "inimical for good work on the Court ... for a Justice to cherish political and more particularly Presidential ambition," apparently (if unpersuasively) distinguishing between running for office and the other political extrajudicial activities that deeply absorbed him.[28] It seems fair to say that while taking direct aim at Douglas's activism, he dissembled on this subject.

Behind the scenes, Frankfurter became "an all-purpose legal adviser to the New Deal."[29] Despite his claim of living in a "marble prison" or being confined to a judicial cloister, Frankfurter was highly partisan.[30] He gave advice on the Neutrality Act and was active during Roosevelt's 1940 campaign. After Pearl Harbor, he justified his role, stating, "Everything has changed and I am going to war."[31] With that, he continued advising the president on everything from the Lend-Lease Act and weapons production to War Department appointments.[32] Frankfurter's sanctimonious denial of political activities—"I have nothing to say on matters that come within a thousand miles of what may fairly be called politics"—so collided with reality that even his friend Dean Acheson, who later served as secretary of state, claimed Frankfurter's "intimate and notorious friendship" with Roosevelt "did harm to the public reputation of both the Court and the Justice."[33]

Brandeis, Douglas's predecessor, was a prominent Zionist advocate who, while on the court, spent considerable time fund-raising, formulating American acceptance of the Balfour Declaration (the British government's support for establishing Palestine as "a national home for Jewish people"), and serving as the elected honorary president of the World Zionist Organization.[34] He resigned the honorary position when challenged but continued his advocacy less publicly—even privately supplementing Frankfurter's Harvard salary, ostensibly for the public causes Frankfurter took up, including Zionism. Bruce Allen Murphy, a judicial biographer, captured the essence of Brandeis and Frankfurter in noting that they "remained as involved in politics once on the Court as they had been before appointment. Indeed, the range and extent of their extrajudicial involvement surpassed similar endeavors by all but a handful of Supreme Court justices throughout the Court's history."[35]

Later, defending his advocacy, Frankfurter insisted that he had a right as a citizen to lobby on an issue that was "absolutely unrelated to anything that could be the concern of the Supreme Court." Like Douglas, he said, "One does not cease to be a citizen of the United States, or become unrelated to issues that make for the well-being of the world that may never come for adjudication before this Court, by becoming a member of it."[36] This expansive view envisioned a role for justices that put them in the middle of political and diplomatic disputes—a far cry from the cloistered monastic role Frankfurter preached.

The Brandeis and Frankfurter duo were not alone among the justices entangled in foreign affairs. Frank Murphy offered advice to FDR on Far Eastern policy, Chief Justice Vinson provided consult to Truman about the dismissal of General Douglas McArthur in 1951 and the legality of seizing the steel mills, and Fortas advised Johnson on both domestic and foreign affairs, including Vietnam.[37]

That they served as trusted advisers to presidents because of their personal relationships was only one measure of the justices' political influence. The symbiotic relationship was a two-way street. To fill special posts, presidents often turned to Supreme Court justices because of their national prominence and respect. Even in the face of separation-of-powers concerns, presidents seem to have regarded the justices as "floating icons" to be invoked in times of national need. Some of the more controversial political entanglements came with presidential appointments to special posts: Robert Jackson was the chief American prosecutor at Nuremberg for the first international criminal trials in history, and Chief Justice Earl Warren headed the commission to investigate the assassination of President Kennedy.

Jackson's absence for more than a year caused dissension on the court; his colleagues, including Douglas, complained that it caused them extra work. Although hailed today as a vindication of justice and the source of modern international law, the Nuremberg tribunal was not without criticism. Even years later Douglas viewed Jackson's appointment as "a gross violation of separation of powers."[38] Just before his death, Jackson said he regarded the Nuremberg trials "as infinitely more important than [his] work on the Supreme Court," though he acknowledged he should have left the court upon accepting the appointment.[39]

Two decades later, when President Johnson asked Warren to chair the investigation into Kennedy's assassination, Warren initially demurred, citing "the unhappy history of the justices' involvement in special, nonjudicial assignments." Both Douglas and Justice Hugo Black weighed in against the appointment because of the full-time demands of the court. Warren eventually agreed to accept the appointment, pulling double duty and lending his prestige to what would become known as the Warren Commission. Warren later found himself at the other end of a political gun barrel when FBI director J. Edgar Hoover dissented from the findings of the commission.[40]

More controversial still, several Supreme Court justices have sought the White House for themselves, stung by what Justice Holmes called the "presidential bee."[41] Douglas's mentor, Chief Justice Hughes, waffled about elected office. Declining to be drafted as a presidential candidate in 1912, Hughes offered this lofty justification: "If men were to step from the bench to elective office, the independence of the judiciary would be weakened along with the nation's confidence in its courts." This absolutist position withered when Hughes was drafted for an unsuccessful presidential run four years later. In the throes of World War I, Hughes accepted the nomination because of what he termed "a time of national exigency, transcending merely partisan considerations."[42] He later became secretary of state before returning to the court as chief justice from 1930 to 1941. Jackson and Owen Roberts were also bandied about as presidential timber.

It wasn't long before Vinson, Truman's political ally, adviser, and appointee as chief justice in 1946, was rumored to be Truman's choice as his successor. Vinson declined Truman's vigorous overture, insisting that "he did not think he should use the Court as a steppingstone to the presidency." He chose to remain on the court to promote unity among his then divided colleagues.[43]

Whether by stealth or begrudging acknowledgment, the relationships between justices and presidents have been intertwined over the decades. In the 1940s justices and presidents often justified their activities as special circumstances of the war and postwar period. Overt political involvement since then has apparently been more episodic. "Apparently" is the operative term since, unlike presidential papers—which the public owns under the Presidential Records Act—the justices' files are not public property and access depends on personal prerogative. Douglas's archive, like his life, is exceptional. Through access to his carefully cataloged papers maintained in hundreds of boxes at the Library of Congress, we know that Douglas stood out among political justices in his targeted lobbying of presidents, executive branch agencies, and Congress.

Douglas and His Ambition for Higher Office

Although Douglas publicly denied rumors of his political ambitions, he hoped one day to be at the top of the Democratic ticket for president. His mother is credited with instilling little Bill with big ambitions. Perhaps both mother and son took to heart the prophecy in Douglas's high school class yearbook that he would be president of the United States. Douglas gladly played the part on senior night, when he donned a silk hat and carnation in his buttonhole and took a "politician's smiling bow."[44]

By the late 1930s, Joseph Kennedy's backing of Douglas sparked speculation about Douglas's candidacy. Richard Neuberger, a journalist who later became a U.S. senator from Oregon, wrote in *Harp-*

er's that "New Dealers in Congress publicly predicted that [Douglas] would be the 1940 nominee of the Democratic Party if Mr. Roosevelt did not run again." But Roosevelt ran and was elected to a third term. When political activity heated up again in 1943, Douglas claimed, "I am more wed to the Court than ever." Washington observers took this denial with a grain of salt, believing Douglas would entertain a nomination if asked. Despite Douglas's veiled distancing from politics, Neuberger's characterization is telling: "Pussyfooting and shifting loyalties are unfortunately prevalent in American public life. The most striking characteristic of Mr. Justice Douglas is that he has never been accused of either of these."[45]

Unlike many New Dealers, Douglas came from a humble background, which finally helped rather than hindered his ambition. Roosevelt liked his backwoods, Boy Scout persona and that he "played an interesting game of poker."[46] This appeal made Douglas "presidential timber not only as a cerebral New Dealer and favorite of FDR's but as a vigorous son of the frontier."[47] Roosevelt was clearly fond of the frontier justice, and the affection was mutual—"I loved FDR," Douglas wrote.[48]

Despite claims from supporters—and Douglas's own perception—that he was Roosevelt's preferred running mate in 1944, political machinations at the Democratic convention doomed his candidacy and gave the nod instead to Truman.[49] Because of Roosevelt's failing health, selection of a vice president took on a heightened significance. Fortas and Eliot Janeway, an economist and journalist at *Fortune* and *Time* magazines, maneuvered with political operatives behind the scenes to promote Douglas. In a sealed letter to a Democratic strategist, Roosevelt signaled that he would "be very glad to run" with either Douglas or Truman, writing that "either one of them would bring real strength to the ticket." Whether Douglas's or Truman's name appeared first in the original letter, auguring a presidential preference, remains in dispute, and in any case the typed version of the letter postdated the convention by a week. Joe Kennedy allegedly offered to send one million dollars "to keep the convention going indefinitely if that would put Douglas across." Yet Douglas backer Corcoran was too toxic to be on the convention floor, and Janeway and Ickes (also a Douglas supporter) could not stop the Truman train. According to Corcoran, Douglas "wanted the Presidency worse than Don Quixote wanted Dulcinea."[50] Later, Janeway wrote to Douglas, "You were 20 minutes away from being nominated."[51]

Douglas's coyness and protective disclaimers about his ambitions also played a role in the convention's outcome. Douglas told Ickes that he would have run if Roosevelt had given him a positive signal, but Douglas sent an opposite message to others. In the days leading up to Roosevelt's decision, Douglas wrote from his cabin in Oregon to Senator Francis Maloney of Connecticut, a supporter from his Democratic political days while at Yale: "If by any chance the nomination were tendered me, I would not accept it." He incredulously proclaimed not to "know very much about the political situation" and again professed his commitment to the Supreme Court.[52] To the chief justice he wrote, "For a while, I feared that pressure might be put on me to go on the ticket. It was not. Every one of my friends knew that I had no political ambitions and that I had but one desire of staying where I am."[53] Frankfurter saw through Douglas's assurances: "It was plain as a pikestaff to me that he was not consecrated to the work of this Court but his thought and ambitions were outside it."[54] Yet at the convention's close, Douglas was where he wanted to be—at his cabin in the mountains of Oregon, with no phone, and about to leave for a pack trip into the high mountains.

Roosevelt's passing was a shock for Douglas on both a personal and political level. When he heard the radio announcement on that warm spring day, April 12, 1945, Douglas pulled his car over and "walked for hours, trying to adjust [him]self to the great void that [the president's] death had created." He remembered Roosevelt's last words to him during a luncheon at the White House, asking about his children's horses: "How are Thunder and Lightning?"[55] By this time, Corcoran lamented, Douglas, Hugo Black, and Interior Secretary Ickes were "a bunch of guys . . . that had the world in their hands last year, and now they're just a bunch of political refugees . . . a helpless bunch of sheep."[56]

While Douglas mourned with the rest of the nation, Truman and his advisers were fast at work assembling a new administration. In 1946 a coterie of Washington political operatives suggested Douglas as an ideal nominee to head the Department of the Interior. Corcoran and Ickes, who had stepped down from his post amid controversy over offshore oil leases in California, promoted Douglas's candidacy. Their effort was not selfless, as they knew their fortunes were tied to his. Douglas was cautious, worrying that a lower-level appointment would take him out of the presidential stream.

Targeting Douglas made political and practical sense. He had acquitted himself well chairing the SEC, and the Department of the Interior seemed a personal fit because of its vast jurisdiction over huge swaths of federal land, wilderness areas, the National Park Service, the Fish and Wildlife Service, Indian affairs, Alaska, and more.[57] Douglas had yet to become a public advocate for conservation, but the lands under the Department of the Interior's fold were already his personal playground and central to his communing with nature. He was the frontier justice on the court.

Truman dispatched his special counsel, Clark Clifford, to make the pitch. Douglas said he would need a few days to decide. He weighed his less-than-masked aspiration for higher office with the financial and tenure security of the court. Douglas also consulted Chief Justice Stone about the possible career switch. Stone, who had taken the helm from Hughes in 1941, was crystal clear about the impact of a vacancy on the court, especially as Jackson was still away as chief prosecutor at the Nuremburg trials. Earlier the chief justice had expressed his displeasure about Roberts's diversion to head the Commission to Investigate Pearl Harbor and his later appointment as chair of the commission to preserve cultural artifacts after World War II. Impatience with presidential poaching led Stone to demand in no uncertain terms that Truman "Please quit disturbing my court."[58] The Supreme Court was for the moment off limits as a revolving door for judicial talent.

In a lunch visit at the White House, Douglas gracefully declined the appointment, letting Truman know: "My reluctance and regret at this conclusion are not because I desire to leave the Court, but because the call to a different service, coming from you, makes a strong appeal to me." Douglas emphasized that he respected the chief justice's views and noted that his resignation in the middle of the term, "when the Court already lacks a full bench," would be unfair to his colleagues and the court. In a candid reflection about the job offered by Truman, he mildly protested, "What more will there be for me to do other than just sit there and watch the sea lion pelts and the seal fishers."[59]

In the end, Douglas repeated what would become his mantra: "I have had no desire to leave the Court. I had, indeed, resolved to make this my life work and to serve my country here to the best of my ability." Again, the proffered rationale was not wholly genuine since he hastened to tell Truman that one way to sway him to the Cabinet would be an appointment as secretary of state.[60] Despite his abiding interest in foreign affairs, that wish never came to pass. Truman chose Dean Acheson, a respected foreign policy adviser, as the next head of the State Department.

Despite these setbacks, Douglas held out hope in the electorate: "I believe that it is the privilege of Americans to seek out for high office those in whom they put great trust and confidence."[61] Discontented with Truman, liberals pushed for Douglas in 1948. At the time, Truman was taking revenge on some of Roosevelt's supporters, placing wiretaps on their phones. Transcripts of these conversations provide a pastiche of political intrigue. Truman labeled Douglas, Corcoran, and Ickes as "crackpots."[62]

Loyal to Roosevelt's legacy, Douglas never fully disavowed a draft for president. Some Democrats carried placards and covered storefronts with "Democrats for Douglas" signs, and loyalists produced "Justice Douglas for President" buttons as part of a short-lived effort by Americans for Democratic Action to promote a Douglas-Eisenhower ticket. The effort fizzled, and Dwight Eisenhower was elected president four years later—as a Republican.[63]

During the 1948 convention, Douglas's supporters, helped by the Forest Service, rigged "an ancient and rickety" nonconfidential phone line that hung from miles of trees to connect Douglas's

Oregon cabin. This was a significant undertaking for someone who disavowed an interest in presidential politics. The message came that if he would go on the ticket with Truman in 1948, Douglas would be the presidential nominee in 1952. Douglas unequivocally declined Truman's offer to become vice president. He cracked to Corcoran that he "could not be a number two man to a number two man."[64]

By the early 1950s Douglas seemed to have reluctantly settled into life on the court. The *New York Times* revealed that Douglas, while on a mountain-climbing trip to Asia in the summer of 1951, sent a handwritten note to Truman that his decision to remain on the court "was permanent in character." In letter after letter to supporters, Douglas proclaimed, "We need political rather than military management. Feeling these things as I do, I know that this is not a time for any one of us to do a purely selfish act." Despite this self-serving assessment of politics, he wrote: "After great reflection I concluded that my place in public life was on the Court. Politics are perishable. The work of the Court is long and enduring."[65]

Yet as an unofficial roving diplomat, Douglas could not resist dabbling in political affairs. Upon his return from that 1951 expedition to China, Tibet, the borderlands of Russia, Turkmenistan, and India, Douglas shocked reporters and politicians when he proposed that recognition of "Red China" was "the only logical choice."[66] Given the sensitivity of U.S.–China relations, the chair of the Senate Foreign Relations Committee immediately pounced, "We do not intend to recognize Red China. Justice Douglas is not Secretary of State." He quickly added, "Douglas is not President of the United States. He never will be."[67] Truman was no less critical: "Since you are on the highest court in the land, it seems to me that the best thing you can do is give your best effort to the Court and let the President of the United States run the political end of foreign and domestic affairs."[68]

Still the drum did not quite stop beating. Despite Douglas's continued denials, politics swirled about him. Supporters ranging from labor advocates to members of the general public still promoted him as a presidential candidate in 1952. *The Nation* ran the headline, "Justice Douglas Is Available."[69] One of his backers claimed, "There is no man in public office who understands the world situation as well as Justice Douglas."[70] Fred Rodell, a Yale law professor and Douglas confidante and hiking partner, said, "The Justice loom[ed] like a giant" compared to other party liberals, and he boldly claimed that "three times in a row" Douglas "could have made himself the Democratic heir apparent had he so much as lifted an assenting finger in his own behalf."[71] By 1956 a nasty anonymous column in the *American Mercury* portrayed Douglas as a man who had "lost the present" and whose "future appears in his dreams as the white and majestic radiance of a mansion at 1600 Pennsylvania Avenue, Washington, D.C."[72]

As late as the mid-1960s, Douglas harbored a last hope that he might be Lyndon Johnson's running mate, telling LBJ that he would resign from the court to promote Johnson for the presidency.[73] Johnson pandered to this aspiration but never acted on it. At a celebration for Douglas's twenty years on the court, Johnson showed his duplicitous finesse, claiming that many Texans had told him "that fellow Douglas ought not be on the Court." He told them in good conscience, "I have tried for fifteen years to get him off the Court." Johnson went on to explain: "I would have liked—and still would like—to see this man's talents used in the highest executive positions of the land."[74]

For Douglas, leaving the Supreme Court would have meant giving up a stable position that gave him a steady income and left him plenty of time for his other passions—dabbling in foreign policy, enjoying international travel, writing books, and spending almost half his time on conservation. As a practical matter, his divorce from Mildred in 1953—and his earlier affair with Mercedes Hester Davidson, whom he married in 1954—also helped seal his political fate.

Throughout his career Douglas's political talents provoked controversy, forcing him to defend his behavior as both justice and citizen. Yet those same talents proved invaluable in his role outside the court. A question often asked of lawyers and judges is whether in hindsight they would pick the same profession. When that question was posed to Douglas by Walter Dellinger, a law clerk for Justice Black and later solicitor general of the United States, Douglas shot back: "Absolutely not!" The reason, he explained to a group of incredulous clerks, was that "all of the action is elsewhere. All of the ability to affect action is elsewhere."[75]

As his political star dimmed and he moved on from the prospect of elected politics, Douglas saw an opportunity to begin another phase of political life and "to affect action" beyond the Supreme Court. He would find his niche as a citizen justice dedicated to the environment, combining his political instincts with his spiritual connection to nature. He later wrote to a friend: "I am doing everything within my power to help preserve the tiny bits of wilderness we have left in this country."[76]

3

Douglas and the Conservation
Movement Come of Age

In wildness is the preservation of the world.

—HENRY DAVID THOREAU

The nation behaves well if it treats the natural resources as
assets which it must turn over to the next generation.

—THEODORE ROOSEVELT

Douglas's calendar entry for March 20, 1954—"hike"—was
disarmingly understated. It turned out to be no ordinary
hike; the consequences would be dramatic and long-lasting,
for both the conservation movement and Douglas. In response
to a *Washington Post* editorial supporting a highway that would
have destroyed the c&o Canal, Douglas dared the editors to see
this special sanctuary for themselves. The hike was on. For eight
days Douglas and his entourage trekked 189 miles (the length of
the canal), from Cumberland, Maryland, to Washington DC. The
endeavor was more than a protest hike; it marked the beginning
of Douglas's public advocacy for conservation.

With the hike Douglas emerged as a leading voice of conservation, and he remained an iconic figure in the movement until his
retirement from the Supreme Court in 1975, when his health and his
national presence, though not the force of his legacy, had petered
out. Douglas joined the conservation movement as it was coming
of age but long after many of his heroes had planted the seeds.

Conservation's Founding Fathers

Although the words "environment" and "environmental" have long meant everything around us, including physical and natural forces that influence living forms, the term "environmentalist" to describe an advocate for the environment did not appear in the lexicon until the 1970s.[1] Its first use in the Supreme Court came only in 1973, when, in a partial dissent, Douglas referenced an article in the *Christian Science Monitor* in a case involving environmental groups.[2] The following year, Douglas once again employed the word.[3] After that the court was off and running, referring to "environmentalists" in a number of later opinions. Long before Douglas spoke of environmentalists, he preached the values of preservation and conservation.

In his many books, articles, and speeches, Douglas embraced men—and they were mostly men—whom he felt represented his spiritual and natural values. The ideals of Henry David Thoreau, John Muir, Theodore Roosevelt, Aldo Leopold, and Franklin Delano Roosevelt animated not only Douglas's judicial environmentalism, but also his extrajudicial activism. Alas, except for Rosalie Edge, founder of the Emergency Conservation Committee who exposed the fault lines and unmet needs in conservation protection, the movement was dominated by men until the late 1950s. The *New Yorker* proclaimed Edge as "the only honest, unselfish, indomitable hellcat in the history of conservation."[4]

Thoreau, a poet and philosopher of nature in the mid-1800s, set the stage for modern-day environmentalism. The iconic phrase from his essay on "Walking"—"In wildness is the preservation of the world"—later became a refrain for environmentalists; the title of a spectacular book of nature photographs; and an adornment on mugs, notebooks, and backpacks.[5] He recognized the interconnectedness of environmental systems—ecology—but more often led with a spiritual than a scientific viewpoint. He was especially prescient in his call for "national preserves." More than one hundred years later, Thoreau's notion of an "Oversoul," connecting every living and nonliving thing, found its way into Douglas's most well-known environmental opinion, his dissent in *Sierra Club v. Morton*.

Surprisingly, despite his iconic status today, Thoreau was ideologically lonely, and his writings were little read until the twentieth century.[6] The same cannot be said of his contemporary George Perkins Marsh, who gained more notoriety early on. Marsh also had a different focus. Rather than emphasizing the spiritual values nature provided humans, he advocated careful, science-based stewardship of natural resources in his 1864 work, *Man and Nature*, which Secretary of the Interior Stewart Udall later called "the beginning of land wisdom in this country."[7]

Though both Thoreau and Marsh presented compelling arguments for the protection of nature and natural resources, it took decades of rapacious development and the writings of a Scottish immigrant to bring these concepts to the popular imagination. That Scotsman was John Muir, who shared Thoreau's ability to convey his personal understanding of the "beauty and spirituality" of nature. But his political instincts led him toward Marsh, whose ideology and focus on tangible benefits was more accessible to a broader public.[8] Muir thus became the prototypical early conservationist, one who "acted ultimately from a love of unspoiled nature" but also took "firmly practical ground in arguing [his] cases."[9] The dialectic of these two forces would continue to fuel early discussions on conservation.

The development of a popular environmental consciousness progressed in tandem with the unprecedented expansion and development of the country. The Census Bureau's announcement in 1890 that the frontier was at its end—the official declaration that there was no more free space to be had—confirmed what many Americans already knew from experience. Rapid urbanization and industrialization made Americans yearn to escape cities and take refuge in whatever nature they could access. Americans—particularly white, upper-middle-class Americans—literally sought greener pastures, fleeing into the mountains in droves, hiking, tending gardens, and otherwise indulging in the cult of the natural. Muir approvingly wrote that "thousands of tired, nerve-shaken, over-civilized people are beginning to find out that going to the mountains is going home; that wilderness is a necessity."[10] His idea of these beneficiaries, however, was often limited to affluent whites who could afford such leisure. Partly rooted in the Progressive ideal of countering modernity's destructive effects, the early conservation movement was not immune from the era's pervasive racial bigotry. Muir's near-reverential status took a blow in 2020, when the Sierra Club acknowledged that his writings and comments "drew on deeply harmful racist stereotypes, though his views evolved later in his life," and the club pledged to increase funding in its environmental and racial justice work.[11]

One observer noted that "Muir never limited his advocacy of wilderness preservation to motives derived from nonhuman sources of value. He built the Sierra Club around the therapeutic value of wilderness recreation."[12] Today the club expressly recognizes the universal benefits of the wilderness while continuing to warn of the potential for national ruin amid environmental degradation.

Federal Protection in the Progressive Era

By the turn of the twentieth century, the groups that dominated conservation often were narrowly focused on preserving a slice of the natural world: a particular mountain range, grove, park, or hunting grounds or a species of birdlife or big game.[13] For example, when Muir founded the Sierra Club—a half-fraternal, half-lobbying organization—in 1892, it focused on saving the Yosemite Valley. Likewise, the Boone and Crockett Club, founded by Theodore Roosevelt in 1887, united the future president's sense of outdoor adventure with the conservation of game animals and their habitat. The Audubon Society, which took flight in 1886 and then was revived in 1905, was directed to the protection of birds. These organizations were not, on the whole, interested in protecting the environment writ large. Indeed the recognition of an interconnected environment would not find a place in the public debate for decades to come. Still, despite the private nature of these organizations, the solution they sought was public—that is, federal—protection.[14]

Douglas and the Conservation Movement

A good example of invoking the public domain for private gain is found in the history of Acadia National Park, which started as a private nonprofit landholding trust organized by the families who owned land around Bar Harbor, Maine. The wealthy land-owners, including Rockefellers and Vanderbilts, were spurred to conservation by the increasing presence of "numerous middle-class landowners" buying up parcels of land in the area. Federal protection, the trustees believed, was the only way to ensure that development could be curtailed.[15]

Federal protection allowed for the adoption of policies befitting the Progressive era's faith in expert management and bypassing the state bureaucracies, which were seen as beholden to local commercial interests.[16] The newly empowered federal bureaucrats would be concentrated in Washington DC and thus—for the politically connected leaders who dominated the ranks of the conservation movement at the time—highly accessible. Unsurprisingly, the early achievements of the conservation movement involved federal action and were predominantly the result of quiet personal lobbying and bureaucratic maneuvering. The most notable successes of this period followed this pattern, from the creation of Yosemite National Park in 1890, to the innovation and later designation of "forest reserves" after 1891, to the creation of the Forest Service in 1905 and the National Park Service in 1916.[17] A half century later, Douglas would launch his signature back-hall maneuvering in the capital.

No one embodied this ideal of federal conservation more resolutely than Theodore Roosevelt, who became president in 1901 after the assassination of President William McKinley. Though Roosevelt grew up in New York City, his home state was famous for the "forever wild" clause in its constitution, dictating that the forest preserves "shall be forever kept as wild forest lands."[18] Like Douglas, Roosevelt was a sickly child who pushed himself to become stronger through strenuous outdoor activity. Roosevelt developed a keen appreciation for nature and is best described as a hunter-naturalist: seeking big game and other mammals and recording what he saw in order to preserve the "memory of the natural world as it was before the onslaught of civilization."[19] He owned two ranches in the West, sponsored expeditions to Yellowstone and the Dakota Badlands, and traveled widely, including in Africa and Europe.

Though his personal interests lay more with natural history, Roosevelt made a significant mark on American conservation, perhaps inspired by his contacts with the pragmatic Muir. Tagged as "the Wilderness Warrior" and an "Audubonist," Roosevelt increasingly fell into the camp of the preservationists.[20] During his two terms, he doubled the forest land under federal protection and created fifty-three wildlife reserves, sixteen national monuments, and five new national parks.[21] For the first time, conservation and preservation were integral parts of a presidential agenda. In his lengthy "Confession of Faith" speech at the Progressive National Convention in 1912, Roosevelt exhorted, "There can be no greater issue than that of conservation in this country."[22]

Preservation versus Conservation

Roosevelt supported the creation of the U.S. Forest Service within the Agriculture Department, which was headed by famed conservationist and skilled bureaucrat Gifford Pinchot, known as "the father of modern forestry." Growing up, Douglas pondered whether one day he "could take Gifford Pinchot's place." Thinking ahead, he dreamed, "If I went to forestry school and learned all the knowledge of the woods, I too could be a ranger and from there work up to Pinchot's place." Even then, Douglas imagined, "I could carry on his fight for conservation. [Pinchot] loved the mountains; so did I."[23]

At the time, Douglas was a starry-eyed kid who knew little of wilderness politics. Douglas's view of Pinchot would change dramatically over time. Though Pinchot was fired only five years after launching the Forest Service, his political compromises stamped federal policy with a mark of utilitarian conservation rather than wilderness preservation.[24] These compromises, while arguably necessary to stave off critics in Congress and the private sector, constituted a growing source of tension with preservation activists. The

Forest Service's approach, known as its "multiple-use policy" and later codified in the Multiple Use–Sustained Yield Act of 1960, had something for everyone—recreation, wildlife, wilderness, timber, mining, and range management.[25] In later years Douglas was relentless in attacking this philosophy because he thought that in practice the Forest Service submerged environmental values.

Pinchot came to be regarded as a counterpoint to Muir, with many historians contrasting the goals of "romantic Muir [as] *preservation*" and of the "practical Pinchot [as] *conservation*."[26] Although those terms are often used interchangeably, in these early days "preservationists" were just that—advocates of protecting spaces and limiting uses such as logging, mining, and grazing. In contrast, "conservationists" embraced a broader approach that suggested a prudent, efficient use of resources, which inevitably included broader human use. Though Muir was no fan of the term, by the early 1900s "'conservation' was applied to everything that needed environmental protection."[27]

The controversy over Hetch Hetchy, a valley within Yosemite National Park, epitomized the fight over the perceived clash between conservation, marked by the multiple-use policy, and preservation. Pinchot threw the first punch by claiming in 1906 that the valley "might be dammed with no aesthetic loss" and used for everything from drinking water for San Francisco to hydroelectric power and flood control.[28] Thus began Muir's last public fight, one that he and his Sierra Club lost when Congress approved the creation of the Hetch Hetchy Dam. As a result, the valley flooded in 1913. The devastating loss solidified the Sierra Club's commitment to public advocacy. One of its leaders wrote to Pinchot: "Let me assure you that we have only begun to fight."[29]

New Friends for the Wilderness

Even if jarring to the preservationists, America was ready to open up its majestic nature to the public. Just as the forests offered opportunities for outdoor recreation, the National Park Service promoted a "See America First" campaign in the 1910s and 1920s. These efforts were aided by socioeconomic developments, such as increased leisure time and automobiles that were affordable for the middle class. Complemented by government policies like the Federal Road Aid Act of 1916, nature tourism—which some derisively called "windshield wilderness"—became a practical reality, though not one of equal opportunity because of racial segregation.[30] These trends rekindled the discussion over how to balance keeping nature pristine while keeping it accessible.

In just one decade, from 1910 to 1920, yearly visitors to the parks increased almost fivefold, to just under 920,000.[31] Skyrocketing visitation put pressure on both the Forest Service and the National Park Service and led President Calvin Coolidge to convene a National Conference on Outdoor Recreation in 1924 and 1926. In explaining his efforts to maximize the country's "national resources," he singled out the need for a "broader appreciation of nature and her works."[32]

Central to the ongoing debate of what such broad pronouncements meant in practice was Aldo Leopold, the author of *A Sand County Almanac*, a famous collection of essays about the "land ethic" and the relationship between man and his environment. Leopold wrote, "Conservation is a state of harmony between men and land."[33] Yet Leopold conceded, "We shall never achieve harmony with the land, any more than we shall achieve absolute justice or liberty for people."[34] This snippet foretold Douglas's fight for both justice and wilderness. He deemed the book his "favorite" and credited it as his "first full and complete confrontation with the ecological problems of the wilderness and of the out of doors."[35]

In the 1920s Leopold, then an employee of the Forest Service, advocated for wilderness preservation in the face of pressure to develop roads, hotels, and groomed trails.[36] He defined wilderness as "a continuous stretch of country preserved in its natural state, open to lawful hunting and fishing, big enough to absorb a two-week pack trip, and kept devoid of roads, artificial trails, cottages, and other works of man."[37] By this time, the emphasis of public debate had begun to shift subtly from the creation of parks for recreation to the preservation of wilderness for its own sake.

No organization embodied this shift more powerfully than The

Wilderness Society. Co-founder Robert Marshall had identified the need for "an organization of spirited people who will fight for the freedom and preservation of the wilderness."[38] In 1935 Marshall, remarkably an employee of the Department of the Interior at the time, helped incorporate the society to advocate for federal protection of roadless wilderness that would remain free from future development.[39] Leopold was also a founding member. (Today's conflict of interest regulations would prevent these federal employees of the key natural resources agencies from forming a conservation society to lobby their own agencies.) Later additions to the society included two luminaries who figured prominently in shaping Douglas's wilderness concepts: Howard Zahniser, credited as the drafter of the Wilderness Act of 1964, and Olaus Murie, famed naturalist and wildlife biologist. Like Leopold, Murie appreciated nature's aesthetics through a scientific lens. Roderick Nash, an environmental historian, put in context the shared style of Leopold and Murie: "This organic conception of nature, which Leopold came to share with his friend Olaus Murie, saw species functioning like organs within a body or, following one of Leopold's favorite metaphors, like parts of an engine." Their vision "was one of the hallmarks of twentieth-century ecology and a foundation of environmental ethics."[40]

Pragmatic Conservation during the New Deal

The Wilderness Society emerged during the presidency of Franklin Delano Roosevelt, who was elected in 1932 in the depths of the Great Depression. Unlike his fifth cousin, Teddy, FDR is not as closely identified with conservation in public memory, but he made environmental protection a top priority in his administration.[41] He had a "passionate response to the marvelous intricacy of nature" and emphasized the importance of "maintaining Nature's delicate balance in the organic and inorganic worlds."[42] His policies were shaped by the necessity and pragmatism of Dust Bowl politics, prioritizing putting people back to work and reshaping the economy. When he spoke of the "gospel of conservation," he was talking about the pressing need "to conserve soil, conserve water, and conserve life," not about the type of wilderness protection that became more prominent in later years.[43] His New Deal policies played a dual role, conserving the environment while also stimulating the economy. This animating principle manifested in his creation of the Civilian Conservation Corps, which put almost 3.5 million men to work in state and federal parks and on other environmental projects; the Soil Conservation Service, which targeted soil erosion; and the Tennessee Valley Authority, which provided both a soil erosion program and economic development. For FDR "conservation" meant balancing economic needs with environmental realities—that same tension that had animated the conservation debate over the past several decades.

FDR also displayed a preservationist streak by emphasizing wildlife protection and creating new protected areas.[44] By the time of his death, he had created 140 new wildlife refuges, 8 national parks, and 21 monuments (i.e., public lands similar to parks, not physical statues); added untold acreage to the national forests every year of his presidency; and vastly expanded the national park system through his 1933 reorganization of the parks.[45]

One of FDR's signature efforts, which preservationists would deride as utilitarian conservation, was the democratization of access to nature by declaring 1934 "the Year of the National Park."[46] To encourage automobile tourism, he directed millions of dollars of recovery funds toward recreational facilities, roads, and campgrounds.[47] Characteristically, this was part of the effort to get the economy moving by getting people moving. It worked. The 1930s saw a dramatic increase in visitors to national parks and monuments, from 6.3 million in 1934 to 16.2 million in 1938.[48] At the same time, Roosevelt sketched out an ambitious map of what would become the interstate highway system, which later became President Dwight Eisenhower's system of Interstate and Defense Highways.[49]

Road building and park development increased friction within the bureaucracy and deepened critical fault lines between traditional conservationists and preservationists. While FDR's allies supported greater public access, his critics bemoaned that this "industrial tourism" undercut the goal of wilderness preservation. FDR's response to critics of road building—"How [else] would I get in?"—did not placate wilderness advocates.[50] Thus groups like The Wilderness Society and the Emergency Conservation Committee, which focused on the protection of birds and animals, came to see the FDR administration as their enemy more than their ally on the issue of wilderness preservation. As one of The Wilderness Society's supporters noted in response to the encroachment on a particular wilderness area, "It was that wilderness . . . which half a decade ago we were so eagerly seeking to bring under the *protection* of the Park Service, and which now some of us are just as eagerly seeking to protect *from* the Park Service."[51]

Balancing preservation and access was no easy feat for either the government or The Wilderness Society and its allies. From the perspective of conservationists, respect for "minority rights," not elitism, drove their efforts, and a deserving minority should be able to find meaning in (relatively) untrammeled nature.[52] Though Douglas is better known for championing minority rights in his civil rights cases and his push for a fulsome First Amendment right to speech, he also preached the need for society to honor idiosyncratic lovers of wilderness. In short, he saw wilderness lovers as a minority that deserved protection: "The defenders of wilderness—no matter how unpopular they may be on a particular issue—are defending other values which so far have been important in the American saga."[53] The charge of elitism—cordoning off wilderness for a few hearty souls—would continue to plague the conservation movement.

Throughout his time in the administration and on the bench, Douglas remained a loyal New Dealer. On one key issue, however, Douglas openly broke with FDR: the building of dams. FDR was generally enthusiastic about dams as a means of conserving productive resources (even while destroying the dammed area's natural state). Following a landslide victory in 1936, FDR took a western tour that included the Grand Coulee Dam, located on the Columbia River in Washington State, where the New Deal jobs program was in full swing.[54] Douglas, who would become a lifelong opponent of dams, was outspoken about the harms the Grand Coulee Dam posed. Douglas complained about damage to the fish population and observed that the turbines were effectively "frying the fish" as they passed downstream.[55]

Recognizing a potential public relations disaster, the Department of the Interior hired folk singer Woody Guthrie to rhapsodize about the dam, and his songs, like "Roll on Columbia" and "Grand Coulee Dam," are now part of the folk-era canon.[56] Douglas was not moved and did not change his tune when he assailed big dam projects and decried the federal authorities' lack of a "conservation ethic." As to the engineers and scientists who made up the agencies in charge, Douglas noted with palpable disgust that they saw a "river [as] a thing to be exploited, not treasured" and deemed a lake "better as a repository of sewage than as a fishery or canoeway."[57] Despite Douglas's persistent protests, FDR proceeded with the construction of the Grand Coulee Dam, prioritizing citizens' immediate needs over nature's long-term well-being.

Twentieth-Century Tides

The environmental movement was beginning to come full circle. With founding figures like Thoreau and Muir, who appreciated nature not as an economic resource but as a spiritual one, the wilderness advocates of the New Deal era also began to reject the economic rationale for conservation. The "utilitarian doctrine" that had originally made conservation politically palatable was now under attack. This return to Muir meant the protection of trees "for their own sake," not for the benefit of "the puniness of man."[58] The defining conflict was again between two different ideological heirs of the wilderness tradition: those who promoted wider wilderness access and those who emphasized the need for restrictions on access.

The period during Theodore Roosevelt's presidency is often recognized as the first wave of the environmental movement. What is sometimes referred to as the second wave of the conservation movement came to an end with FDR's death in 1945. In FDR's wake, a third wave was about to begin.[59] Michael McCloskey, former

Douglas and the Conservation Movement

executive director of the Sierra Club, divides the third wave into "at least three distinct phases." The initial phase, which continued into the 1950s, "was a defensive one," with activists trying to shore up areas already protected. This period segued into an offensive phase, when conservationists realized the limits and weaknesses of a defensive posture. The third phase, aggressive advocacy, culminating in the Wilderness Act of 1964, was the hallmark during the late 1950s and into the 1960s.[60] By the late 1960s, according to McCloskey, "The movement passed into a wholly new and dramatically different phase" that expanded to encompass "the environment in its totality," not just wilderness.[61]

A 1949 report prepared by the Legislative Reference Service served as an early catalyst for the federal recognition of wilderness. The report caught the eye of Zahniser, executive secretary and later director of The Wilderness Society, who understood the importance of securing federal statutory protection. Administrative designations and bureaucratic whims simply left too much uncertainty in the scheme of protection. As the primary architect of the Wilderness Act, Zahniser slogged through some five dozen iterations of the legislation and eighteen hearings in the eight-year effort to achieve congressional approval.[62] Through a massive public relations and lobbying campaign, wilderness advocates secured permanent protection for 9.1 million acres. They laid the political and ideological groundwork for a bevy of future environmental protection legislation that led to the final phase of the progression of conservation. Sadly, Zahniser passed away shortly before President Lyndon Johnson signed the bill.

For environmental advocates, the Wilderness Act was a momentous step forward. It established the National Wilderness Preservation System and introduced to federal law the concept of "wilderness areas" as roadless plots "where the earth and its community of life are untrammeled by man, where man himself is a visitor who does not remain."[63] The secretary of agriculture and the chief of the Forest Service received the power to designate initial wilderness areas, though the law required congressional action for additional wilderness areas. Critically, the act mandated public hearings before the designation or modification of existing wilderness areas, an initiative that mirrored Douglas's advocacy for transparency in federal administrative action.

Typical of the time, Douglas's environmentalism marked a return to Muir's understanding of the spiritual value of nature to human beings. On the first page of *Of Men and Mountains*, Douglas described how, in the "thickets, ridges, cliffs, and peaks" of the Pacific Northwest, one "can find deep solitude . . . he can come to know both himself and God." Douglas echoed Muir's famous sobriquet: "I'd rather be in the mountains thinking about God than in church thinking about the mountains." Like most other things in his career, Douglas's environmental evangelism had a deliberate quality. In the three decades following FDR's death, Douglas became the "most prominent conservationist in public life."[64] At the outset, the principal object of Douglas's ire—as was the case for the early dissenters from federal conservation policy—was roads, roads, roads. But it was a specific road on the c&o Canal, one in his own backyard, that propelled him to national prominence.

4

Taking on the *Washington Post*

The C&O Canal "is a refuge, a place of retreat, a long stretch
of quiet and peace . . . a wilderness area where we
can commune with God and nature."

—WILLIAM O. DOUGLAS

The C&O Canal "is the first National Park ever
walked into existence."

—NATIONAL PARK SERVICE

Mass tourism. Roads. Loss of sanctuary. For Douglas, those
were fighting words. In the 1950s his small "wilderness
of solitude"—the towpath along the C&O Canal, starting near Georgetown in Washington DC—was in danger of being
paved over. Douglas began a campaign of "hiking and hollering" to
showcase what he called "a Gandhian protest against the highway."[1]

The Long History of the C&O Canal

The origin of the C&O Canal dates back to George Washington, who
envisioned water-borne trade connecting the Chesapeake region to
the Ohio country by way of the Potomac basin. In 1785 he became
the first president of the Patowmack Company, which sought to
improve the navigability of the Potomac River to increase trade.[2]

When it became clear that no number of skirting canals would
be sufficient to open the Potomac River to westward navigation, a
new plan emerged: build a canal that would run beside the river

from Washington DC to Cumberland, Maryland, and from there on to Ohio. Spurred on by invocations of Washington's memory, Congress chartered the Chesapeake and Ohio Canal Company (C&O Canal Company) in 1825, and on July 4, 1828, President John Quincy Adams broke ground on the project at Little Falls, Maryland.[3]

By fateful coincidence, the first stone of the Baltimore and Ohio Railroad (B&O Railroad) was laid on the same day by Charles Carroll, the last surviving signer of the Declaration of Independence. The B&O Railroad would eventually prove itself the canal's mortal rival, delaying its construction, undermining water-borne trade, and ultimately ending the waterway's commercial operation.[4]

From the beginning, the C&O Canal Company struggled to obtain both labor and land. Escalating costs were exacerbated by rapid inflation, the canal company's own "ill-advised enthusiasm," and overly ambitious construction plans. On top of these financial difficulties, the company soon found itself locked in a costly legal battle with the B&O because the path along the river could not accommodate both a canal and a railroad, and alternate routes were thought to be financially or physically impracticable. The case pitted the canal's lawyers against the likes of future secretary of state Daniel Webster and future Supreme Court chief justice Roger Taney. The canal eventually prevailed before the Maryland Court of Appeals but not before the delay had halted virtually all construction.[5]

These setbacks meant that the C&O Canal did not arrive in Cumberland until 1850, eight years after its archrival B&O and ten years later than its projected completion. Already heavily in debt, the C&O Canal Company abandoned plans for construction between Cumberland and Ohio, leaving further westward expansion to the steam engine.[6]

The company fared little better as a business than it had as a construction project. Undercut by competition from the railroad, the canal operated at a loss for all but a handful of years.[7] The Civil War, which stimulated many sectors of the Northern economy, did little for the canal. It lay right along the border of the Union

Taking on the *Washington Post*

and the Confederacy, an unfortunate location that subjected the canal to reduced trade, occupation, and (on various occasions) outright sabotage.[8]

In the end, natural disasters spelled the end to canal commerce in the Potomac basin. A series of floods, followed by the same brutal rains that caused the Johnstown Flood in 1889, decimated the canal. In an ironic twist, the resulting financial distress made it possible for the B&O Railroad to acquire most of C&O's construction and repair bonds. The B&O continued to operate the canal as a waterway for several decades until 1924, when a small flood once again stopped navigation.[9] The canal's commercial days had come to an end.

The B&O, which by the 1920s also found itself in dire financial straits, was increasingly eager to sell the canal. A potential deal with the federal government dragged on for years, even though the National Park Service was considering the possibility of a parkway running alongside the Potomac River. Presciently, one of its planners warned, "To parallel the canal with a highway would destroy much of its scenic and recreational value and filling it in would destroy its historic value." Fortunately, the canal caught the interest of President Franklin Roosevelt. He directed Harold Ickes, the secretary of the interior, to allocate the money to restore the canal, and a $2 million sale to the government was completed in 1938. Roosevelt's Civilian Conservation Corps transformed the canal into a hiking path, as it had done with the Appalachian Trail.[10] However, the war between utilitarian conservation and preservation was far from over. The canal became an important battleground. Thus Roosevelt and Ickes, two of Douglas's later allies in conservation, paved the way for his historic crusade.

In the mid-1940s the Army Corps of Engineers proposed what the Park Service saw as a far worse alternative. The corps developed a flood-control plan for the Potomac basin that envisioned fourteen reservoirs along the Potomac River and its tributaries that would submerge lengthy stretches of the canal.[11]

Opposed to the corps' proposal but unwilling to commit to the restoration of the canal for recreational use, the Park Service began considering a third alternative: a parkway along the Potomac. Residents of western Maryland, which enjoyed few decent roads, enthusiastically supported the idea. J. Glenn Beall, the region's congressman, introduced legislation authorizing a "joint reconnaissance study" by the Park Service and the Bureau of Public Roads. The bill sped through Congress without debate and the study was soon under way.[12]

Plans for a parkway proceeded virtually unopposed until Beall pushed through another bill authorizing the land acquisition necessary to build the proposed highway. At this point, conservationists began to take notice and started pushing back. They promoted restoration of the canal as a recreational area. The group included Frederick Law Olmsted Jr., the famous landscape architect and city planner, who argued that "a high-speed thoroughfare for automobiles . . . would . . . be a wasteful use of a great recreational opportunity." "The prescription for the c&o Canal is obvious," the president of the Audubon Society advocated in the *Washington Post*. "It should be restored for use by hikers, cyclists, campers, and canoers."[13] Still, conservationists were hardly in high gear, especially since the Park Service—often their powerful ally— supported the highway.

The Justice Joins the Fight against the Potomac Parkway

The future of the canal was not as "obvious" as the Audubon Society suggested. The fight highlighted the question of public access to nature. On January 3, 1954, the *Washington Post* entered the fray on the side of public access, with an editorial opposing the Olmstead position and endorsing a highway running up the Potomac River, either "on the bed of the abandoned c&o Canal or on the adjacent towpath." The newspaper dismissed the old canal as "no longer a commercial or a scenic asset." Like most parkway proponents, the *Post* justified the proposal in terms of opening up the Potomac basin for "more people to enjoy beauties now seen by very few," while still leaving "large areas of wilderness" that would be "protected permanently against further encroachment."[14]

Up to that point, opposition to the parkway had been tepid.

But the *Post*'s vision of a "great Potomac playground" provoked Douglas's ire and inspired his first conservation hike. Because Douglas—reminiscent of Thoreau—valued the spiritual benefits from communing with nature, he did not see the point of paving through it in order to deliver a warped version to more people. His involvement launched the opposition onto the front pages of newspapers across the country.

Before 1954, as an armchair critic, Douglas had written passionately about nature and the hazards of development, but the *Post* editorial unleashed in him a fervor for public advocacy that continued until his death. In his letter in response to the editorial, Douglas echoed the language of his earlier nature writings. He called the canal "a refuge," adding that it was "a place not yet marred by the roar of wheels and the sound of horns." This sanctuary would, he insisted, "be utterly destroyed by a fine two-lane highway."[15] Douglas was very familiar with the terrain; he was a frequent hiker on the towpath, and he became its neighbor when he later moved to a house near the canal on Hutchins Place NW in the District of Columbia.

Had Douglas constrained himself to poetic language, that might have been the end of it. But either because he could not help himself from throwing down a gauntlet or because he knew all too well the inefficacy of mere words in the face of a bulldozer, Douglas did not stop there. "I wish the man who wrote your editorial of January 3, 1954, approving the parkway[,] would take time off and come with me," he dared the *Post*. "We would go with packs on our backs and walk the 185 miles to Cumberland. I feel that if your editor did, he would return a new man and use the power of your great editorial page to help keep this sanctuary untouched." He concluded the invitation for a hike by assuring that "one who walked the canal its full length could plead that cause with the eloquence of a John Muir." Douglas cast himself in the role of his predecessor, Justice Louis Brandeis, who "[had] traveled the canal and river by canoe."[16] He previewed what would become one of his key strategies: calling on opponents to experience the wilderness personally and through his eyes.

The *Post*'s editors, for their part, could not resist the challenge. Two days after running Douglas's letter, the *Post* replied: "We are pleased to accept Justice Douglas's invitation to walk the towpath of the old canal—the entire 185 miles of it between Washington and Cumberland, if that meets with his pleasure. He has only to name the time and the starting point of the journey." In stepping up to the invitation, the *Post*'s editors doubled down on their endorsement of a parkway and broad public access. Their rejoinder put into play the continuing debate between public access for the masses and elitist preservation for the few. "It is only fair to warn the Justice that we are already familiar with some parts of the beautiful country that will be traversed," they wrote. "We are sufficiently enthusiastic about it to wear some blisters on our feet, but we do not believe that this backyard wilderness should be kept closed to those who cannot hike 15 or 20 miles a day."[17] So it was decided that Merlo Pusey, author of the editorial, and Robert Estabrook, chief of the *Post*'s editorial section, would accompany Douglas, along with the *Post*'s country life editor, Aubrey Graves, who sent back regular dispatches to readers in Washington.

The hikers gathered on Friday night, with the hike set to begin the next morning, March 20, perhaps because March was Douglas's favorite time to hike the canal.[18] Strategically, the hike was to end the following Saturday, March 27, capitalizing on coverage in the most widely read Sunday papers. Rather than setting out from Washington and hiking to Cumberland, as Douglas had initially proposed, the hike proceeded in the opposite direction to maximize "publicity opportunities at the finish line" in the capital.[19]

These media-savvy strategies paid off but may have been unnecessary, as the hike generated considerable publicity long before the hikers even departed for Cumberland. *Time* and *Life* both ran illustrated stories, and numerous other media outlets, including the Associated Press and all three major television networks, covered the hike. Two newsreels about the hike were screened in three thousand theaters.[20]

Public interest was high. Letters inundated the *Post* and Douglas's chambers, including many from people asking to join the

Taking on the *Washington Post*

expedition.[21] The size of the hiking party soon swelled to over two dozen, becoming, as Douglas gauged it, "a little bigger than the Lewis and Clark expedition."[22] Howard Zahniser, The Wilderness Society's executive secretary, aided Douglas in planning the hike, though he was unable to join the group. The distinguished hiking party, comprised chiefly of noted conservationists and scholars, counted among its numbers Sigurd Olson, president of the National Parks Association, and Olaus J. Murie, the prominent biologist and president of The Wilderness Society who traveled from Wyoming to join the hike.[23] Douglas's encounter with Murie began a friendship of shared values for years to come. It was Murie who would later write of his companions, "If we had deliberately sought the country over for suitable members of a formal committee to study, in the public interest, the c&o Canal question, how could we have improved on the qualifications of this haphazard collection of hikers, assembled spontaneously without formal call?"[24] (The party also picked up a pair of canine mascots along the way, including one that traveled along the canal for some fifty miles, until his family recognized him on a telecast and requested that the Park Service please send back their dog.)[25]

The *Post*'s Graves provided the services of a burro named Jose. Jose was a gift from the White House press secretary, who was tasked with disposing of the animal after President Dwight D. Eisenhower deemed it too donkey-like for a Republican White House.[26] Douglas liked to tell the story that some of the hikers tried to trick Murie, the wildlife expert, by having him identify some unknown animal tracks. He correctly noted that they came from a burro but that it was impossible since none were in the region. "They howled with laughter."[27]

The widespread publicity yielded significant creature comforts for the hikers. Rather than carrying their own supplies, the hikers enjoyed the hospitality of local conservationists and sports clubs at nearly every stop. The Potomac Appalachian Trail Club of Washington provided facilities, meals, and a truck to carry provisions.[28] To begin the hike, none other than the b&o Railroad, the canal's one-time rival and erstwhile owner, delivered the party and press representatives to Cumberland in a special rail car.[29]

Despite the seemingly cushy conditions offered by the expedition's many benefactors, the month before the hike, the *Post*'s Pusey betrayed a hint of apprehension. In a piece headlined "If Ambulant Editors Perish, So Will Justice's Argument," he pointed out that if the *Post* contingent did not survive the hike, it would only prove that a parkway was necessary to make the Potomac accessible to ordinary citizens. This charge of elitism was, of course, not the first time conservationists had faced this argument. Pusey also conceded that the editors had accepted an invitation to "commune with nature" rather than for a "foot-race or an endurance contest," presumably having been warned about Douglas's fast-paced hiking.[30]

The event kicked off in style, with a dinner of shrimp cocktails, roast beef, lobster, and chocolate cream puffs hosted at the Cumberland Country Club. Various luminaries were in attendance, including the parkway's most fervent legislative proponent, Congressman Beall.[31] Keeping with tradition, Douglas kept a little black field notebook where he listed the participants and chronicled his impressions: the congressman and the B&O lawyer "spoke for a parkway—I spoke for recreational urgency for the C&O Canal."[32]

Though the first day of fourteen miles was uneventful, the second day the party set off in snow, slogging twenty-three miles. Those who endured were rewarded with a champagne dinner at the Woodmont Club.[33] The third night was the first and only evening of camping, in Fort Frederick State Park. If some members of the party had feared that the more rustic accommodations would lower spirits—in the sense of morale or liquor—their concerns were quickly laid to rest. George Kennedy, a reporter from the *Evening Star*, came equipped with "a portable cellar."[34] The following night the hikers returned to their usual, more luxurious accommodations, enjoying the hospitality of the Potomac Fish and Game Club.[35] By the fifth day of the hike, the party was down to ten hikers.

Along the way, the brigade heard from the public on both sides of the debate. Those who favored restoration left signs nailed to trees along the path. "Justice Douglas, keep to the right. Booby traps to left are for *Post* editors," read one.[36] Even the opponents, whose goal was to convert the hikers to the parkway proposal, were cordial. They were happy to feed the hikers and met the party with coffee and doughnuts.[37]

With the end in sight and only one day to go, the hikers covered twenty-seven miles, the longest day of the trek. The long march left everyone worse for the wear—even the indefatigable Douglas ended the day suffering from a poison ivy rash.[38] On the final night of the journey, the hikers stayed in the Isaak Walton League's farmhouse, where they enjoyed a well-deserved meal of buffalo, salmon, and beef steaks prepared by the local Boy Scouts.[39]

Secretary of the Interior Douglas McKay and other government officials were waiting for the hikers when they arrived at Lock Five just before 4:00 p.m. on the final day, March 26. McKay greeted the group with a twist on a classic line: "Justice Douglas[,] I presume."[40] The *Canal Clipper*, a barge pulled by the mules Dick and Dinah, carried the hikers the final five miles into Georgetown. Douglas stood at the stern, waving to the cheering crowd of fifty thousand that welcomed the hikers home.[41]

Although thirty-seven hikers returned to Georgetown, just nine of them, none a *Post* editor, had walked the entire length of the canal of nearly 190 miles.[42] Naturally, both Douglas and Murie were among the "simon-pures," who were rewarded for their efforts with Hawaiian leis.[43] Dubbed "the Immortal Nine," they inspired the hiking party's c&o Canal Song:

Glory to the Immortal Nine
The waiting thousands roared
The conquering heroes hit on Lock 5
And hurled themselves on board.

Another verse of the song celebrated Douglas's prodigious pace throughout the hike, even while the group averaged twenty-three miles a day:

The duffers climbed aboard the truck
With many a groan and sigh,
But something faster passed them up
The Judge was whizzing by.[44]

The *Post* participants wrote, "At this point we are torn between a feeling of appreciation to Justice Douglas for luring us into this venture and irritation over the increasingly pathetic condition of our feet. But blisters heal and memories linger."[45] Appropriately, Douglas was awarded a tongue-in-cheek "Foot Health Award" from the American Foot Health Association a few months later, for having demonstrated "the usefulness 'of the lower extremities' [that] so many Americans have forgotten."[46]

More important, Douglas was proven right about the hike's effect on the *Post* editors. "After seeing it, I think the parkway ought not to go ON the canal," Pusey admitted at the trip's end.[47] A few days later, the *Post* acknowledged as much in print. Although the editors still favored opening the Potomac basin to more visitors, they noted that "in one important respect we have changed our minds." The editors no longer believed the parkway should be placed on the canal itself, urging instead that "the Park Service plan be substantially modified to avoid encroachment on the best of the natural areas" and that efforts be made to restore the canal for recreational use.[48]

Soon after the hike, Alice Longworth, Teddy Roosevelt's daughter, wrote to congratulate Douglas. She enthused that her father "would have delighted in what you did" and bemoaned that "a day in the country these days seems often to mean a six lane parkway dotted with Howard Johnsons."[49] It was Murie who summed up the link to history: "Why should we bother to preserve any historic feature? For the historic objects are not merely labeled souvenirs. History is something by which we preserve the present ... perhaps even a guide by which we might try to chart the future."[50]

Douglas's triumph with the *Post* was not the most significant consequence of the hike. The final night of the walk, a group of the hikers formed the C&O Canal Committee to continue advocating for preservation and restoration of the canal after the hike was over. Douglas, of course, was the chairman. He apparently gave no consideration whether he could take on this role as a Supreme Court justice. Other members included Murie, Olson, and Harvey Broome, the vice president of The Wilderness Society.[51] When the committee incorporated as the c&o Canal Association in 1957, Douglas signed the original Certificate of Incorporation.[52]

The c&o Canal Committee began its work almost immediately after the party arrived back in Washington. In collaboration with Murie, Broome, and Zahniser, Douglas sent McKay the committee's preliminary recommendations. Those recommendations were, it turned out, quite similar to those now favored by the *Post*. Like the *Post*, the committee supported a parkway, "perhaps at places parallel to, but not on the canal proper." It also favored developing the canal for recreational use by restoring and rewatering portions of the waterway and adding new campsites and access roads. Perhaps in a nod to gaining public support, Douglas even conceded that the area "[could] be made an attractive tourist area."[53]

McKay's encouraging response noted the government's "complete agreement on the major objectives to be achieved."[54] Douglas kept the pressure on with his letter-a-month approach to deliver the committee's evaluation of a proposed parkway and to acknowledge that he was "deeply indebted" to McKay for his "great personal efforts to save this unique wilderness strip from being destroyed or mutilated by a highway."[55]

At a Department of the Interior hearing on the proposed parkway, Douglas "put in a good word for . . . recreational development along the lines of our report." But he remained concerned about the canal's future. "We are all hoping and praying for a recreational and development program," he wrote Murie shortly after the hearing.[56]

Less than two years later, the Committee's work paid off. Douglas wrote Murie and Broome once more, this time to declare victory. "Yesterday the Secretary of the Interior announced a very interesting and imaginative program concerning the c&o Canal that was practically the same program as the one our Committee recommended." He invited his walking companions to "rejoice with me in the great victory," which made "the 180 mile hike worthwhile after all."[57]

The victory celebration over the parkway was somewhat premature. In the end, a highway was built paralleling the Maryland portion of the canal, running from the District line to the navy's facility near Bethesda, Maryland. A number of the canal's locks were destroyed to make room for construction, and today the Clara Barton Parkway can be seen and heard as one walks on long stretches of the canal. It is significant, however, that the highway was not built on the canal itself.[58] Like Douglas, the *Post* had endorsed the plan to put the parkway "well back from the canal."[59]

By the time parkway construction was under way, Douglas had his sights set on a more ambitious goal: transforming the canal into a national park. Although efforts began as early as 1956, the campaign would drag on for over a decade, repeatedly thwarted by opponents who were concerned that national park status would decrease public access and interfere with plans for dams and other river development. Douglas and the committee, now incorporated as the c&o Canal Association, were involved throughout the process. Association members relentlessly testified in favor of a park and objected to legislative amendments that would have facilitated dam construction.[60]

In what would become one of many entreaties on various subjects to his friend, Stewart Udall, then secretary of the interior, Douglas repeatedly petitioned him about the canal. "Dear Stu," he wrote in 1966, "Isn't it possible to get the c&o property that we already own made into a national park?"[61] Following his sentiment that "to see it is to feel it," Douglas next invited Udall to "come over for lunch" to discuss "getting legislative action on the c&o Canal Historical National Park."[62] And in June of the same year, Douglas, ever persistent, replied to counter, one by one, each of Udall's explanations for the delay, promising that there would be "100% support" for a "c&o Canal Bill."[63] As 1966 came to a close, Douglas approached Udall yet again, this time with the faintly threatening warning that conservationists "seemed to be pretty much up in arms about the long delay in creating the c&o Historical National Park."[64]

The delay continued another four years, but in the end the efforts by Douglas, the c&o Canal Association, and other proponents of a c&o Historical National Park paid off. Following a reunion hike in April 1970, Douglas and others signed a petition to President Richard Nixon urging his administration to support pending legislation to establish the canal as a national park.[65] Just a few weeks before the Chesapeake and Ohio Development Act became law, Senator Henry M. Jackson of Washington State, with whom Douglas collaborated on a number of environmental endeavors, gave Douglas the long-awaited good news: "I am pleased to report that at long last we were able to get your C and O Bill approved and on the way to the White House."[66]

On January 8, 1971, President Nixon signed the bill that turned 5,250 acres of the c&o Canal into the Chesapeake and Ohio Canal National Historical Park. The bill was intended "to develop the potential of the canal for public recreation, including such restoration as may be needed" and authorized funds for development and additional land acquisition.[67] It was the first national park "walked into existence."[68]

Only after this legislative success did Douglas resign as a director of the c&o Canal Association, in the belief that the association was entering a new phase as an ecological adviser to the National Park Service. In his parting letter, Douglas couldn't resist offering his advice: the association should disqualify from its board any members associated with the executive branch, such as the Army Corps of Engineers, and those holding stock in companies that polluted the Potomac.[69] There is some irony in this recommendation and sensitivity to conflicts of interest, given Douglas's sustained lobbying of the legislative and executive branches from his own perch on the Supreme Court.

Through his canal work Douglas also became associated publicly with efforts to save the Potomac River, which was a polluted mess. Because it would despoil a historic river and result in ugly mudflats, all without public benefit, Douglas joined a group of conservationists that opposed the Army Corps of Engineers proposal to flush the pollution by building the River Bend Dam. By 1979 the corps' plans for a series of dams on the Potomac were thwarted by public opposition.[70]

Douglas continued to enjoy the canal he had helped to save. The year after the historic hike, he organized a reunion hike. A party of twenty-nine hikers enjoyed a leisurely walk, then spent a nice evening under the stars. The next day, the group hiked twelve miles to a celebration typical of the c&o Canal tradition: an elegant dinner. Unfortunately, Murie suffered one of his many illnesses and could not participate. Douglas commiserated via letter, thus beginning a correspondence between the two that frequently offered mutual support during their times of illness and initiated their frequent exchanges on wilderness conservation.[71]

The following year a hike was again organized, and the group camped at Fort Frederick State Park, the site of the campout during the original hike, and then walked to the Hilltop Restaurant for dinner the following day.[72] After that, the reunions became an annual affair. A group of original participants and new additions would walk around fifteen miles at a relaxed pace before arriving at a restaurant for a celebratory meal.[73] Despite Douglas's notoriety, at the end of one of the hikes, he was refused service at the Old Angler's Inn because he was too scruffy.[74]

The reunion hikes became a highlight of the year for Douglas's law clerks. At the beginning of the clerkships, Douglas's secretary told them to expect an invitation. Some years it never came, and other times notice came the night before. On another occasion, the clerks wrote a note asking if they could take a day off for the hike. Days went by without any word. Then on evening before the hike, Douglas strode into the clerks' office with a map and pointed to the where they should camp. He warned that it was going to be cold, so he handed them something to keep them warm: a brown bag with a bottle of scotch. The day of that hike was the only Saturday they had off for the entire year.

The reunion hikes were far from the only time that Douglas would walk the c&o Canal. Sundays were his day of respite on the canal. Douglas's long-time friend Charles Reich, a Yale law professor who wrote *The Greening of America*, a best seller that celebrated the counterculture of the 1960s, recalls that Douglas would invariably call with the magic words, "Want to go for a walk, Charlie?" They walked up to twenty-four miles at Douglas's usual prodigious pace of four miles an hour, stopping only for a brief lunch or to pose for a photograph, which seemed to delight Douglas. Douglas talked and Reich listened to stories about cowboys, New Dealers, and, on occasion, the Supreme Court, but not about cases. Reich recalled those long miles were made "beautiful with our energy and our sharing of faith in a better world."[75]

On May 17, 1977, the National Park Service dedicated the C&O Canal National Historical Park—the only national park ever dedicated to a single person—to Douglas "for his immense efforts in preserving and protecting the natural and historical resources."[76] More than a hundred people, including eight Supreme Court justices and multiple senators and members of Congress, attended the ceremony. Douglas—seventy-eight, wheelchair-bound, and weak from the stroke that had forced his retirement from the court—noted that more than enough justices were present to form a quorum but that he had never been able to convince any of his colleagues to hike the length of the canal. "I promise when I'm well we'll take the hike," he said. He concluded by thanking "all those who have no portfolio but who have two strong legs and like to hike."[77]

After Douglas's death in 1980, there was a memorial for him at Great Falls on the C&O Canal. One of his admirers and fellow board members from the C&O Canal Association called his crusade one of "hiking and hollering." In that process, none more than Douglas "understood better its rich variety of flora and fauna, or wrote about the area's ecology with more sensitivity. . . . There was not a wildlife, not the most hidden bit of moss, not a migrating bird that did not attract his curiosity and become documented in his little black notebook."[78]

The canal now receives five million visitors a year, making it America's eighth most popular national park. It spans over twenty thousand acres, with more than one thousand historic structures and 113 rare or threatened species.[79] A bust of Douglas sits at the Georgetown terminus of the canal, on Thirtieth Street. The sculptor was Wendy M. Ross, a Park Service employee who became interested in sculpting Douglas after reading *Go East, Young Man* (1974).[80]

Douglas's extraordinary public effort to save the canal became a template for his future advocacy. He protested the incursion on solitude and wilderness by roads and development; organized a public protest; galvanized conservation groups and the public; headed an advocacy association (the c&o Canal Association remains active in preserving the canal); and leveraged his office and prestige to effect permanent change. It was an effective strategy that he would replicate many times—not only across town, but also on the other side of the continent.

5

Dissenting on the Road

The Arctic has a strange stillness that no other wilderness knows.

—WILLIAM O. DOUGLAS

The wildest, the most remote and, I think the most picturesque
beach area of our whole coast line lies under a pounding surf
along the Pacific Ocean in the State of Washington.... It is a
place of haunting beauty, of deep solitude.

—WILLIAM O. DOUGLAS

With one foot on the trail and the other in his Supreme
Court chambers, Douglas deftly juggled his wilderness advocacy and his judicial work. The c&o Canal
hike sparked something in Douglas that spoke to his soul and
unleashed a drive that would reach beyond his literary musings
and recreational interest in conservation. He launched himself as
a national advocate for wilderness preservation.

The canal adventure proved propitious in connecting Douglas
to conservation leaders, especially Olaus Murie. During the c&o
Canal hike, they talked about the fragility of the Alaska landscape
and an expedition Olaus and his wife, Margaret ("Mardy"), were
planning. Douglas and Olaus stayed in touch, often commiserating about their various health troubles. When Douglas learned the
Alaska trip would be postponed because of Olaus's tuberculosis,
he counseled from his own experience that "Mother Nature is a
very jealous person.... If you just take the time you will come out

a better man than you have been probably for a long time, with a lot of spring in your legs and a song in your heart."[1]

After Olaus recovered, the Muries enlisted Douglas to join the expedition. The Muries were not celebrity collectors, but they recognized the value of the imprimatur of a national figure. The way Mardy spoke of Olaus, she could easily have been talking about Douglas: "He had a kinship with untamed land wherever he found it." This explained their close association in keeping that land untrammeled.[2]

With the Alaska expedition under his belt, Douglas was receptive when conservationists corralled him in 1958 to headline a protest hike down the Olympic Beach in Washington. These early efforts in the 1950s gave Douglas both solid conservation credentials and an understanding of wilderness politics, which he coupled with his prominence to help preserve important pieces of American wilderness.

The 1956 Sheenjek Expedition in Alaska—Just Call Me "Bill"

When Douglas stepped off a pontoon plane at Last Lake in Arctic Alaska in late July 1956, he looked at home in his hiking pants and well-traveled boots. Although the expedition was already under way, Douglas and his second wife, Mercedes ("Merci")—his former researcher whom he married soon after divorcing Mildred in 1953—quickly fit in with the group. Though he had not seen Olaus since the C&O Canal hike, Douglas greeted him like an old friend. When Mardy addressed him as "Justice Douglas," he retorted, "Bill." After another round of "Justice Douglas, can I make you a cup of cocoa?" the message was clear: just call me "Bill."[3] Their friendship and Douglas's high profile proved critical to Alaska's future, but in the wilderness, "Douglas had no higher rank than a tin plate cleaner after supper."[4]

Even now Alaska is often viewed as an impenetrable, far-off frontier. In the 1940s *Time* termed it "a vast land, raw, primitive and barely scratched by civilization after 80 years of U.S. ownership."[5] Fishing and gold were the key industries, though the Soviet threat brought huge construction payrolls as military facilities were built, leading Alaskans to toast, "Here's to Joe Stalin—Alaska's best friend." The federal presence then, as now, enveloped the territory, which became a state in January 1959. Alaska was America's last frontier, filled with hearty, independent souls, many of whom loathed federal control.

The Muries were no strangers to Alaska. Olaus had studied caribou there in the 1920s as a U.S. Biological Survey scientist. He advocated habitat preservation and took the then unorthodox position that a healthy predator population was needed to maintain the equilibrium between predator and prey.[6] In 1927, three years after their honeymoon dogsledding in the remote Brooks Range, Olaus and Mardy settled in Jackson Hole, Wyoming. They were joined by Olaus's half-brother Adolph, also a prominent wildlife ecologist, who was married to Mardy's half-sister Louise. Olaus became chief field biologist with the Jackson Hole National Elk Commission of the National Fish and Wildlife Service, earning the title "the father of modern elk management" and publishing multiple books on conservation and wildlife. Mardy was his partner in exploration. Her work in Alaska and Wyoming earned her the nickname "the grandmother of conservation."[7]

The Arctic was never far from the Muries' thoughts. By 1945 Olaus was disenchanted with the federal government and transitioned to the role of director of The Wilderness Society, where he worked in tandem with executive secretary and Washington lobbyist Howard Zahniser. Together they became the scientific and intellectual leaders of the campaign to save Alaska. From his time in Alaska and Wyoming, Murie understood that "Wilderness values are subtle ones easily destroyed."[8]

Murie knew that in the early 1950s two National Park Service employees, George Collins and Lowell Sumner, had conducted fieldwork in the Brooks Range, including the Sheenjek Valley. In their assessment, the area offered "what is virtually America's last chance to preserve an adequate sample of the pioneer frontier, the stateside counterpart of which has vanished." Finding themselves at odds with government policies, the two launched a campaign to save the "Last Great Wilderness."[9]

Collins and Sumner's work built on a study by Robert Marshall (known as "Bob"), a federal forester, wilderness aficionado, and one of the founders of The Wilderness Society who was an early advocate of a wilderness frontier in Arctic Alaska. Marshall's radical proposal, contained in his 1938 report, "Alaska: Its Resources and Development," brought howls of a "federal lockup" and set the stage for a contentious debate between preservation and economic development in Alaska that continues to this day.[10]

To build support for an Alaska initiative, Murie decided to undertake a scientific expedition. Backed by the New York Zoological Society, which Theodore Roosevelt helped found in 1895, and the Conservation Foundation, with co-sponsorship from The Wilderness Society and the University of Alaska, the expedition was conceived as a "wildlife and ecological survey of the Brooks Range" in order "to lay the ground-work for the launching of a program aimed at the establishment of a wilderness in this region."[11] Costs were estimated to be just under $7,000 for the two-month expedition.

This was a serious scientific undertaking, and Murie was a fabulous talent scout. The team included George Schaller, a student in vertebrate zoology and anthropology at the University of Alaska. Schaller kept a detailed expedition journal and later became a famous biologist, conservationist, and author. As with Douglas, Schaller's adventures included travels to Tibet and Mongolia. Murie plucked Bob Krear, a doctoral student and a veteran of the 10th Mountain Infantry Division in World War II, from the Fish and Wildlife Service. Finally, there was Dr. Brina Kessell, an ornithologist at the University of Alaska who had studied with Aldo Leopold, author of the *Sand County Almanac*. They all admired Murie for his scientific accuracy and integrity and his philosophy that "collecting scientific facts is only the first step of a long process to give work meaning and value."[12] Murie counseled them to "get as much out of this as you can. Not science, hiking, fishing in themselves. Get the most you can out of it."[13] That directive captured Murie's spirit.

In this journey, a third Alaska honeymoon for Olaus and Mardy, Mardy was Olaus's indispensable partner in collecting and cataloging specimens, many of which are preserved at the Teton Science School's Murie Ranch in Moose, Wyoming. A keen observer of the mountain landscape in the Arctic, Mardy reflected that "the mountains made an unearthly beautiful frieze against the blue; numberless, snowy, streaked with dark rocks, various in shape—shoulders, domes, spires, and castles—and cliffs and screes on the slopes reaching to the darkness of the belt of forest. And then the broad valley, the winding Sheenjek, the countless lakes."[14]

Preparation for the trip was daunting; the equipment and food list ran on for pages. The group hauled in 1,243 pounds of baggage.[15] As Douglas would do later, the party flew to Fairbanks and then to Ft. Yukon—which then, as now, had a population under six hundred, mostly Gwich'in Alaska Natives—before boarding a float plane for the Sheenjek River.

Schaller and Krear left detailed logs and diaries of daily life in the outback. The weather was unforgiving, usually wind and rain mixed with clouds, interspersed with an occasional spectacular day. Days were long and hard, filled with expeditions to catalog the region. In this land there was light or near light day and night. It was striking to see the sun shining between the peaks past midnight, with one day merging "smoothly into the next with only richer colors in the northern skies at midnight to make its passing."

Camp life took on a rhythm of meals, exploration, collection, and camaraderie. Sometimes the team members camped overnight, and Schaller took a week-long expedition to explore the ridges beyond the campsite. There was plenty to fill their notebooks—more than eighty-six species of birds, herds of Caribou crossing in front of the camp, red foxes, grey and black wolves, red squirrels, porcupines, and grizzly bears. "To a bear in the Sheenjek Valley, the sight of man is probably a once-in-a-lifetimes thing," but of course "to a human the sight of a grizzly can also mean a once-in-a-lifetime experience." It was the kind of experience where a person confronts what Douglas recognized as nature's paradox of majesty and danger.

They ate well in the remote tundra: oatmeal, pancakes, freeze-dried milk, canned corned beef, skillet bread, and Jell-O. Food figured prominently in the team members' journals because meals were an opportunity to tell stories about what they had seen or caught that day. They also had caribou, fresh fish, cheese, and delicacies like peach granules and fresh oranges every week.

By the time Douglas and Mercedes arrived, the original group had moved camp upriver from Lobo Lake to an unnamed lake they dubbed "Last Lake." Douglas's insistence on first names and informality helped create an easy bond with the other members of the expedition. Although Schaller and Krear moved into the cook tent to make room for the Douglases, nothing else changed with their arrival. Douglas hiked most days with Olaus and Mardy, rafted, went fly fishing for grayling, and regaled the group with stories of his Himalaya and other foreign adventures. With long experience in the Olympic rain forest, Douglas found that the weather was no deterrent and cheerfully "sloshed around the soggy meadows."[16] But sometimes even the tundra was too wet for hiking.

As usual, Douglas recorded impressions of the trip in a small black notebook. Most of his observations were pedestrian compared to his more eloquent prose on the Sheenjek in *My Wilderness: The Pacific West* (1960). He deemed the tundra "very soft to walk on," but to hike among the tussocks, which were like "tall mushrooms with grassy heads," he reported that Mardy said one had to walk like a rag doll. Douglas's diary documented details, like the aircraft trajectory, the plants (especially the moss and flowers), and what the adventurers ate. Always obsessed with money, he noted that lunch in Fairbanks cost $2.15.[17] It surely was an unusual sight to watch a Supreme Court justice crawling around the tundra to examine the amazing details of Arctic life. Mardy marveled at "the far-ranging interest of this man of the law. What a divine thing curiosity is!"[18]

Though Douglas had visited Alaska in the early 1950s, this trip to the Arctic made a lasting impression on him. He extolled the Arctic's vast expanse and fragility. Echoing his spiritual connection with nature, Douglas wrote that "it was difficult to express my feelings as I stood beside these dark quiet pools, shaded by spruce," because "they were so beautiful, so exquisite, that they were unreal. They seemed withdrawn from this earth, though a glorious part of it."[19] In the fight to preserve this area, Douglas famously captured a sense of the region: "The Arctic has strange stillness that no other wilderness knows. It has loneliness too—a feeling of isolation and remoteness born of vast spaces, the rolling tundra, and the barren domes of limestone mountains. This is a loneliness that is joyous and exhilarating. All the noises of civilization have been left behind; now the music of the wilderness can be heard."[20]

The question of preserving the Arctic as a wilderness area was a constant theme around the campfire. Douglas's visit provided an incentive for Collins to fly in. Those discussions propelled the campaign to save Alaska. Central to the strategy was Douglas's advice that "conservation is politics." The Muries understood this message, though in their hearts they believed science and reason should be persuasive enough to prevail.

For three years after the Sheenjek expedition, the Muries crisscrossed Alaska like missionaries on a crusade. Armed with science; spectacular photos; a film made by Krear, *Letter from the Brooks Range*; and passion, Olaus perfected the soft sell/tell with sportsmen and community groups. It was a successful approach he had used in the 1940s to promote the expansion of the Grand Teton National Park boundaries. He opposed the confrontational— and in his view alienating—tactics of the Sierra Club and even Zahniser of his own Wilderness Society. Like Douglas, Olaus was a pragmatist: he wanted to preserve a vast Arctic but was not an absolutist about hunting, which helped him win over reluctant Alaskans. Realizing that a national park would not sell, Olaus and his team pitched a "refuge," which was called a "range" back then. Olaus's message blended scientific, spiritual, aesthetic, primeval, recreational, and utilitarian conservation values. He and Douglas sang from the same wilderness hymnal, warning that the Alaska question "involves the real problem of what the human species is to do with the earth."[21] And Olaus acknowledged that Douglas was "doing a great deal" in promoting the efforts to secure an Arctic wildlife range.[22]

Olaus continued his proselytizing, looking beyond the usual suspects as converts for his cause, and he was joined by a new grassroots nonprofit group, the Alaska Conservation Society, founded by former Alaska pilots Celia Hunter and Ginny Wood. The Muries' data and experience, their "easy does it" technique, and the on-the-ground army of volunteers were a winning combination.[23] Olaus's long association with Alaska lent him credibility, and Hunter and Wood were well known in a vast territory of few residents, demonstrating yet again that "all politics is local."

Despite the surge in grassroots support, the prospect of a refuge was still uncertain. Preservation efforts in the 1950s had hit a headwall with President Dwight Eisenhower's interior secretary, Douglas McKay, a former car dealer sympathetic to business interests. When McKay was replaced by Fred Seaton in 1957, the tide began to turn. Seaton navigated the complicated political divide between the purists and conservationists, competing timber and mineral interests, and general antipathy toward the federal government. Yet local chambers of commerce, mining interests, and Alaska's two Democratic senators remained roadblocks. Seaton felt that Eisenhower shouldn't go out on a limb, worrying that the Democrats might undo the refuge designation after the 1960 election. Using his relationship with the Kennedys, Douglas calmed the volatile political landscape.[24] The message transmitted through Douglas was clear: the incoming administration wouldn't embarrass Eisenhower on the Alaska front.

Seaton waited until after John F. Kennedy's election. Then, on December 6, 1960, Seaton—not Eisenhower—signed Executive Order, Public Land Order 2214. The Arctic National Wildlife Range (8.9 million acres) was created for "the purpose of preserving unique wildlife, wilderness, and recreational values."[25] With his aide, future Alaska senator Ted Stevens, Seaton was one of the heroes in the first part of the refuge saga. Olaus wept when he heard the news.

Rightfully, Douglas worried that Alaska could still fall prey to logging and oil drilling interests. Indeed, the same day the refuge was announced, Seaton declared twenty million acres of Alaska's North Slope open for leasing and mining. Controversies concerning aboriginal land claims, state ownership, and conservation punctuated debate in Alaska. Douglas would later ask, "Are we looting paradise?"[26]

In 1971 Congress passed the Alaska Native Claims Settlement Act, which endeavored to resolve these disputes. The Alaska Natives received forty-four million acres of land and payments to regional, village, and urban tribal corporations. A key provision, section d-2, directed the secretary of the interior to withdraw certain lands for conservation purposes and mandated that Congress approve these withdrawals before the lands could be reopened to development.[27]

After multiple failed proposals and with the deadline looming, in late 1978 President Jimmy Carter invoked the Antiquities Act to secure protection for fifty-six million acres as national monuments. Interior Secretary Cecil Andrus, using his management authority, withdrew forty million acres of additional lands.[28] The Antiquities Act, signed by President Theodore Roosevelt in 1906, had authorized the president to declare federal properties of scientific or historical interest as national monuments. Invoking this authority was often controversial, and Carter's proclamation was no exception. Several Alaska towns passed official proclamations deriding the federal government, and sportsmen's groups organized the "Great Denali–McKinley Trespass" to override federal regulations against guns, campfires, and snowmobiles in federal monuments.[29]

The fight was on. As a White House Fellow and special assistant to Secretary Andrus, I had the privilege to witness the denouement. Carter was burned in effigy in Fairbanks, and bumper stickers shrieked, "Lock up Andrus, not Alaska." Competing legislation, intense lobbying, and compromise followed. Adding flame to the fire, President Carter changed the name of the Arctic National Wildlife Range to the William O. Douglas Wildlife Range as a tribute after Douglas died in January 1980. In the end, the name didn't stick; it was one step too far for Alaska's Senator Stevens and others who opposed what they saw as Carter's land grab. Olaus would have agreed with the decision for a different reason: he opposed naming features of nature after humans.

In the summer of 1980, Secretary Andrus asked me to start implementing the Alaska lands legislation. "But Mr. Secretary," I protested mildly, "the bill isn't yet passed." He then told me that despite pundit wisdom, Carter would lose the election. "The sun will still come up, but it will be canted to the right," he chuckled. But he was serious. With Carter enmeshed in the Iran hostage crisis, Andrus met with him and said they needed to pressure the Alaska congressional delegation to return to the negotiating table. In an interview not long before his death in 2017, Andrus explained that "in politics, the first thing you can do is learn to count."[30] Following Carter's defeat, through deft political maneuvering, Andrus pulled a rabbit out of the hat in the lame duck congressional session—a feat that would be impossible in today's congressional environment.

Despite the timing and the resistance from key members of Congress, Andrus secured the necessary votes. Senator Henry "Scoop" Jackson of Washington provided strong support and guidance, but Senator Stevens and Utah's Senator Orin Hatch pushed back. Andrus "looked Stevens in the eye [and] convinced him the administration would rescind activities under the Antiquities Act if the bill passed." Andrus credited Stevens for bringing the deal over the line. "With Ted, a deal was a deal." Under the illusion that they would get a better deal under Ronald Reagan, the environmentalists tried to hold out for less logging and more protected areas. Andrus told them, "The problem is you are not the Secretary of the Interior and here is what we are going to do." He reflected, "In politics, once you can attest you've got the votes, there are lots of 'jumperoners.'"[31]

Compromises were brokered on logging, mining, Native subsistence hunting, and the scope of the protected lands. The resulting Alaska National Interest Lands Conservation Act (ANILCA) created more than forty-three million acres of new parkland, the addition of 9.8 million acres to the National Wildlife Refuge system, 9.1 million acres as wilderness, twenty-five wild and scenic rivers, and new national monuments and recreation areas. Douglas's name was dropped. The range was renamed the Arctic National Wildlife Refuge.[32]

A significant accommodation deferred the possible oil and gas development of 1.5 million acres in a coastal area known as the "1002 area." Andrus conceded that the "only mistake we made was giving in on the exploration aspect; we had the votes but didn't know it."[33] The shoe dropped in 2017, when Congress, as part of a wide-ranging tax bill, opened the area for resource development.[34] Just four years later, through the Department of the Interior, President Biden signaled that his administration would undertake a new environmental review of the area.[35] Whether the reserves can be economically exploited remains an open question.[36] The debate likely will continue for decades as competing legislation and studies underscore the intensity of the diverging views on oil exploration in this area.

Conservationists never abandoned hope for permanent protection for Alaska. Following the early land withdrawals, Mardy Murie continued her advocacy and was at the White House when ANILCA was signed on December 2, 1980. President Bill Clinton awarded her the Congressional Medal of Freedom for her work as "a pioneer of the wilderness movement."[37] Douglas's fourth wife, Cathy, also joined the fight and was co-president of Americans for Alaska when the legislation passed.[38]

Andrus reflected that Alaska was unique: "I believe that in Alaska we have the chance to do it right the first time."[39] Once again, Douglas played a pivotal role—this time quietly—in shaping America's landscape for future generations. At one point, Mercedes voiced concern that Douglas got too little credit for his work on Alaska.[40] Even so, it was recognized that he played a vital role as a catalyst, backroom player, and public advocate. Brochures produced by the Fish and Wildlife Service list Douglas, the Muries, Collins, and Sumner, as "among the visionaries." They also include an excerpt from the opening chapter in *My Wilderness: The Pacific West*: "This last remaining wilderness must remain sacrosanct."[41] Douglas Brinkley's *The Quiet World* also gives voice to the "prevailing opinion in conservation circles, that Douglas's participation in the Sheenjek expedition was crucial" because, as Collins from the Park Service said, he was a "goofy bird from the Supreme

Court whose name on anything in our kind of conservation was sterling and magic."[42] And that magic had special resonance in the world of Washington DC politics.

Douglas would agree with Mardy's powerful testimony in favor of a permanent refuge: "I hope the United States of America is not so rich that she can afford to let these wildernesses pass by, or so poor she cannot afford to keep them."[43] That challenge remains for the next generation.

The 1958 Olympic Beach Protest Hike—Stop the Highway

After his success with the C&O Canal, Douglas lost no time planning his next public protest. In August 1958 Douglas trained his special brand of environmental advocacy on his beloved Washington State and the Olympic National Park. The target was yet again a highway.

Douglas led a hike down the beach in the Olympic National Park, protesting a proposed extension of U.S. Highway 101 that would have interrupted the longest stretch of primitive coastline in the United States. Douglas, the wilderness lover, knew the area well—he had hiked the beach in 1953 and had a fishing cabin nearby. Douglas considered Washington's unspoiled stretch "the wildest, the most remote and, I think, the most picturesque beach area of our whole coast line. . . . It is a place of haunting beauty, of deep solitude."[44]

Douglas pleaded to the National Park Service that "a highway would destroy much of the unique values that the primitive beach now has."[45] Reflecting on the inexorable march of human progress, Douglas pondered whether any "sanctuary could be left." He asked, "Can't we have one percent of the woods and the beaches for those who love wilderness?"[46]

A fight was brewing between preservationists and residents of the Olympic Peninsula, who wanted a beach road to boost the economy and enhance tourism and transport. The choice was stark, and an article written by hiking book authors Bob and Ira Spring laid it all out: "Coastal Controversy, Highway or Trail for Ocean Strip?"[47] Highway proponents included Senator Jackson, who believed a highway would make the coastline accessible to more than a few "hardy" hikers.[48] Although, as in this instance, Douglas and Jackson butted heads over conservation issues, years later Jackson strongly supported Douglas's initiatives, especially the establishment of the Cougar Lakes Wilderness.

By 1956 Douglas was on board for this fight. He discussed a beach hike with conservation leaders like Olaus Murie and Zahniser of The Wilderness Society and David Brower, executive director of the Sierra Club, who summed up the challenge: "This is our last primitive beach, and it can be saved if somehow we do better in our effort to encourage walking to beauty that *is*, rather than motoring to beauty that *was*."[49]

Returning to his signature strategy, Douglas proposed to Murie, "We might start beating some drums about it and get a little advertising and publicity, so as to excite the conservationists in various parts of the country and mobilize them against the loss of the primitive beach areas." Unlike the c&o hike, which included only men, Douglas suggested inviting Mercedes and Mardy.[50]

To stir up political action, Douglas first wrote a note to Conrad Wirth, then director of the National Park Service: "I hope that no final decision has been made by the National Park Service to put a highway along that beach.... The highway, if close to the beach, would drive out the game and we'd end up with just another ordinary beach." He continued, "There are not many people who have hiked that beach.... As one of that small number, I would like to discuss the matter with you to see if the highway couldn't be put back a sufficiently long distance so as not to disturb the wildlife in that secluded area."[51] Douglas did not oppose a road outright, just one that ran along the beach.

The impetus for preservation of the beach was homegrown. Local leaders—like Pauline "Polly" Dyer, president of the Northwest Outdoor Club, and John Osseward, president of the Olympic Park Associates—spearheaded the grassroots effort to launch a hike. In describing the beach some years earlier, Dyer had called it "untrammeled."[52] That word resonated with Zahniser, who—crediting Dyer—later inserted the term in the Wilderness Act, which became law in 1964.[53] That description was also a favorite of Robert Marshall, a founder of The Wilderness Society.[54]

Local organizers, mainly Dyer, took care of logistics and other planning for the hike. Dyer confessed that it was "probably one of the first things [she] had really organized," but later she became a superhero of the northwest conservation movement.[55] Dyer instructed hikers to bring a Trapper Nelson packboard, sleeping bag, insect repellant, deodorant, rain hat, matches dipped in wax, and an assortment of food and drink. On the hike's organization chart, she assigned Douglas his own square, the same as she did for The Wilderness Society, the Olympic Park Associates, and the Federation of Women's Outdoor Clubs.[56]

The hike was originally planned as a perambulating debate—talking while walking—but the road proponents snubbed the walk. Even so, many reporters came along with Douglas's group. One cameraman, Louis Huber, made a movie that shows Douglas on the steps of the Supreme Court greeting conservation organizers and then walking on the beach ahead of the pack. Huber dramatically stated, "Something was at stake that affects the lives of . . . our children's children."[57] National conservation luminaries joined the group: Zahniser, Olaus Murie (who at seventy was the oldest hiker), and Harvey Broome, another founding member of The Wilderness Society. The group also recruited Dan Beard, the superintendent of Olympic National Park, and Stan McComes, its chief ranger, who radioed reports as they hiked.

The seventy-two hikers included a youth contingent. Mercedes's fourteen-year-old daughter Joan was "dragged along." Joan remembers going "through rugged territory" and said the hike "was not a cake walk." Her dog, Sandy, became the mascot, though she was peeved that Douglas claimed it was *his* dog. No one seemed to mind that dogs were not allowed in the area.[58] Apparently, Superintendent Beard joked, "How do you tell a justice that he can't bring his dog?"[59] The youngest hiker, ten-year-old Robert Serr, remembered Douglas as "a kind of introspective man, not to have to talk or be the center of attention, just another guy hiking the coast."[60]

Dissenting on the Road

Rounding out the younger hikers was Donna Osseward, current president of Olympic Park Associates, and her brother Bud. Donna recalled that Douglas gave an inspiring welcome speech at a fish fry hosted at his cabin the night before the hike.

The hike began on August 19, with a trek from Lake Ozette to Cape Alava, through a dense forest with shoulder-high ferns, and then a long march down the beach to a campsite near Sand Point. The hikers were fortunate that 1958 was unseasonably dry. Even so, hiking was treacherous and difficult with the slippery boulders, huge driftwood, and pounding surf.[61] A hearty hiker who eschewed long breaks, "Douglas moved with the tides. He rose early and moved fast."[62]

The second day began in a heavy fog with the rock islands off the beach appearing and disappearing. During this eight-mile stretch, the hikers saw deer, elk, and a bear. Along the way, Douglas greeted a group of Boy Scouts coming from the south. In his notebook Douglas recorded an impressive "Jupiter shower near the crescent moon" when he went wading in 54° water to soothe his aching feet.[63] That evening Douglas was appointed to head a watchdog committee, under the auspices of the Olympic Park Associates, to spearhead the fight against the road.[64]

Day three dawned with a heavy mist and miles of drift log piles that slowed the pace. Mercedes wrote that a "rising mist added a beauty indescribable to the beach and shoreline. The shadows of trees on wet 'smoking' sand was dramatic." The group sighted a plaque marking the shipwreck of a Chilean ship. After passing a rock base at Cape Johnson, the party continued south to an iconic rock arch known as the "eye of the needle" or the "hole in the wall," where hikers could pass through a hole in the granite cliff onto a grand stretch of sandy Rialto Beach.[65]

Unlike activities along the C&O Canal, no champagne celebration greeted the weary hikers at the end of the hike. Instead, advocates for the road stepped out to voice their opposition. On Rialto Beach, L. V. Venable, director of the Automobile Club of Washington, greeted the parties with a sign: "BIRD WATCHER GO HOME."

Douglas cordially shook his hand. Other signs carried similar messages: "We own this park too. We want a shoreline road" and "Fifty million U.S. auto owners and their families like scenery too."[66]

As was his custom, Douglas recorded the hike in a little black notebook and later chronicled the beauty of the Olympic Peninsula in *My Wilderness: The Pacific West*. He rhapsodized, "I always leave this primitive beach reluctantly. The music of the ocean front seems to establish a rhythm in man. For hours and even days afterward I can almost hear the booming of the tides on the headlands and the sound of the winds in the giant spruce."[67] Dyer praised his "leadership and impetus to focus on this precious area we cherish."[68]

When Douglas returned to the Supreme Court, with memories of the tides and winds, he knew that the crusade was not over. The National Park Service needed to be persuaded to oppose a beach road because "those in the Park Service that are against [the road] are keeping their mouths shut."[69] In 1961 Douglas got wind of "ominous news" of a potential road.[70] By 1964 a newly established federal agency, the Bureau of Outdoor Recreation, issued a report backing a highway along the ocean strip.[71]

Once it became clear that the 1958 hike was only "a temporary setback in the plans of the road builders," Douglas organized and led another protest hike in August 1964, backed by the Olympic Park Associates and The Wilderness Society. High tides and rain plagued the 160 hikers, who were buoyed by Douglas's rousing address celebrating passage of the Wilderness Act. Most members of this "Wilderness Army" were ardent supporters, but a few escaped early, with a rain-dampened sentiment: "You can have your hike, and your wilderness, too."[72]

Despite the defectors, the hikers prevailed. In 1964 John Doerr, Olympic National Park superintendent, revealed plans to keep the beach area in wilderness status, thus confirming the death of the beach road. The Park Service announced a compromise: an inland highway, which became known as the "Douglas Road," would connect Forks and Lake Ozette without impinging on the beach.[73]

Today the fight to protect Washington's coastline continues.

In August 2018 Washington attorney general Bob Ferguson led a "Save Our Coast" hike to protest the federal government's off-shore oil-drilling proposal.[74] His itinerary mirrored the twenty-two-mile coastal route Douglas hiked in 1958. This time one essential ingredient was missing: no Supreme Court justice joined the hike.

Before the 1958 hike began, Douglas made a lofty proclamation about preserving this stretch of beach: "It badly needs friends. It needs friends in order to survive." In this skirmish, Douglas and his allies prevailed. The beach road was never built, and it is still possible to hike that same stretch of beach without cars, a highway, or a hot dog stand.[75]

6

Supreme Advocate—Dissenting
in the Corridors of Power

There has never been a complete "separation" of
executive and judicial functions.

—WILLIAM O. DOUGLAS

It is not easy to pick out public enemy number one from among
our Federal agencies, for many of them are notorious despoilers
and competition is great for that position.

—WILLIAM O. DOUGLAS

I f Douglas had a business card for his activities from the 1950s
until his retirement in 1975, it might have read, "William O.
Douglas, Associate Justice of the United States Supreme Court
and Supreme Conservation Advocate."

Douglas had a knack for tapping into the corridors of power
and merging his backwoods persona with beltway advocacy. Take,
for example, a cloudy day in Washington DC in May 1962, when
Douglas found himself on the stage with Secretary of the Interior Stewart Udall to honor the hundredth anniversary of Henry
David Thoreau's death. Like Douglas, Udall had a flair for publicity and a supreme sense of timing. As the anniversary approached
and legislative efforts on the Wilderness Act began to flounder, the
commemoration became an opportunity to showcase the importance of wilderness. Udall was flanked by two conservationists and
a poet: Douglas, the high-profile justice; Howard Zahniser, the
executive secretary of The Wilderness Society; and Robert Frost.

The occasion, held on the forested grounds of Dumbarton Oaks, recalled Frost's repose in the outdoors: "Whenever I'm weary of considering, and I can stand things no longer, I always say: Give me the woods." Douglas claimed that he "traveled with Thoreau everywhere he went" and commended Thoreau's attention to "the wonders of creation . . . those wonders which are at our feet and yet which we seldom see."[1] This observance was yet another public effort, supported by Douglas, to keep the wilderness legislation on the public agenda after years of struggle.[2] Two years later, President Johnson signed the Wilderness Act of 1964.

Mixing Politics and Conservation

Douglas's advocacy represented a unique twist on judicial political involvement. By the mid-1950s and 1960s Douglas was largely a solo act in his intensive lobbying of multiple levels of the federal bureaucracy on a single subject well beyond the judicial lane: conservation. Today his approach would find little traction, but the tide was already beginning to turn during Douglas's lifetime. In his early years on the court, Douglas was not alone among the justices who offered their wisdom to Franklin Roosevelt, Harry Truman, Dwight Eisenhower, and their Cabinets. And there is episodic evidence of justices advising both the John Kennedy and Lyndon Johnson administrations, though the frequency of such contacts had begun to taper off over the years.[3] Tellingly, at his 1968 confirmation hearing to become chief justice, Abe Fortas felt compelled to stress that he had avoided advising Johnson on matters that would implicate judicial cases, though that testimony masked his advice on Vietnam and other policy matters.[4] His nomination was withdrawn and Fortas resigned in 1969 under threat of impeachment surrounding his entanglement with a private foundation. The Fortas affair prompted greater scrutiny of justices' extrajudicial activities and ethical obligations, an atmosphere that greeted Douglas during his own impeachment hearings just two years later.[5]

Despite shifting expectations on justices' behavior, Douglas never accepted that his advocacy was exceptional. Citing historical examples of justices consulting with presidents and serving on commissions, Douglas contended, "There never has been a complete 'separation' of executive and judicial functions."[6] For a justice to declare such a blurred line is bold, especially given the Constitution's clear provision for an independent judiciary. Presumably Douglas meant the statement as a one-way ratchet: judges should be free from the president's and his advisers' thumbs on the scale of judicial decisions but also free to advise on executive branch policies. Notably, Douglas did not name other justices who pursued his signature style of advocacy: sustained lobbying before Congress and the federal agencies on a singular cause that implicated cases before the judiciary. Of course, interaction between the judiciary and the political branches is inevitable and appropriate on matters related to judicial business, such as the budget and judicial reform. Douglas's cause—conservation and the environment—did not fall into that category.

Douglas defended his colleagues for "leaning over backwards to observe the appearance of propriety as well as proprieties themselves," but his was a more flexible vision.[7] He vocally objected to Supreme Court proposals to impose internal rules that would chip away at the justices' freedom, such as the public reporting of outside income. And the notion of approval for travel, lecturing, and writing truly galled him as judicial censorship, driving judges "into a cloistered life."[8] He balked at the ABA ethics committee or his colleagues telling him what to do. Though recognizing that partisanship might raise a conflict of interest, Douglas was adamant that "prior advocacy or promotion of one side or another of a cause, long identification with a particular program for legal or constitutional reform do not disqualify a Justice."[9] Both of his hobbies, international travel and the environment, turned out to be "controversial" according to his wife Cathy. In later years, he was aware that he needed "to adjust his activities" and not be as vocal because of "conflicts regarding cases that might come before the court."[10] In practice, however, he felt largely unrestrained from lobbying federal officials on conservation issues that he believed to be in the public interest. His approach surely glossed over the ethical importance of the *appearance* of propriety, which bolsters public perception of the judiciary's integrity and independence. Still, Douglas's conception was consistent with his self-image as a citizen justice. His commitment to the First Amendment right to petition the government did not falter, even if the petitioner was a Supreme Court justice. He pushed the envelope in extending judicial independence to his passion for the wild.

While Douglas's early protest hikes gained publicity and notoriety—indeed, that was the point—his behind-the-scenes advocacy for environmental causes is less well known. But it was a crucial element of his effective strategy. Through his academic studies and stint at the SEC, Douglas became a master of the intricacies of the administrative state, developing a subtle understanding of the soft spots of the bureaucracy and learning which levers to pull. Douglas applied this knowledge broadly; after consultation with a White House aide, he once suggested to his hiking buddy and intellectual muse, Charlie Reich of Yale Law School, that they initiate a comprehensive overhaul of Forest Service regulations to provide "for a public hearing in cases where there was about to be a dangerous or substantial invasion of the public domain."[11] He had started the initiative earlier with the Sierra Club, urging, "We should move fast and mobilize all the troops—or we are lost."[12] Rewriting Forest Service rules was definitely outside the judicial lane, but his wish was granted when the Wilderness Act incorporated public hearing requirements.

Douglas did not acknowledge the irony that his work to expand transparency and democracy through public hearings and citizen participation took place in the cozy world of back-channel politics. Of course Douglas operated in an atmosphere very different from today—before the Freedom of Information Act, which gave the public access to documents of federal agencies, took effect in 1967; before C-SPAN shed light on the congressional world; and before the internet opened up the world of "private" communications. In describing "a Washington that worked" in the 1960s, *Washington Post* editor Robert Kaiser would likely agree that Douglas operated "in a political context that looks now like something from another planet in a parallel universe."[13]

Supreme Advocate

Douglas's calling card was prestige, not the money of paid lobbyists. His advocacy took many forms: a word to the president; a quick call, note, or visit to a member of Congress; a quiet entreaty to a Cabinet member; or a memorandum cursing a bureaucrat. Given his gift for nurturing political friendships, Douglas was at ease going to the highest levels—Presidents Kennedy and Johnson; Interior Secretary Udall; Agriculture Secretary Orville Freeman—to support his environmental causes. And we know, from his careful record keeping and extensive correspondence preserved at the Library of Congress and other archives, that his was not an occasional letter, visit, or call to the halls of power. His efforts were frequent and persistent until he succeeded. And successful he was—mostly at stopping or delaying approval of federal projects, but also in protecting parks and his beloved wilderness.

Targeting Federal Agencies—Public Enemy Numbers One and Two and Three and . . .

To appreciate Douglas's high-level advocacy, it helps to understand the federal agencies that were the targets of his opprobrium. Just as he demonized corporations and big business, Douglas targeted federal agencies for their lack of environmental sensitivity. "It is not easy to pick out public enemy number one from among our Federal agencies," he explained in a *Playboy* article, "for many of them are notorious despoilers and the competition is great for that position."[14] Douglas's federal foes included the Tennessee Valley Authority, the Bureau of Mines, the Public Roads Administration, the Soil Conservation Service, the Forest Service, and even, at times, the supposedly conservation-friendly National Park Service. These agencies were at the core of Douglas's efforts because he saw them as responsible for encroaching on the solitude of the wild and diminishing the prospects for an environmentally sensitive future.

Douglas did manage to pick an ultimate enemy: the Army Corps of Engineers, a little-understood agency with an outsized presence, especially in the West, and an obsession for building dams. From 1935 to 1965 the "big dam" era swept the country. The corps and the Bureau of Reclamation spearheaded engineering feats, like the Hoover Dam and the Grand Coulee Dam, which aimed to spur an economic transformation through reduced flooding; improved navigation; irrigation; and development of hydroelectric power.[15] In his *Playboy* article, "The Public Be Dammed," Douglas pulled no punches. He claimed, "The Corps has no conservation, no ecological standards. It operates as an engineer—digging, filling, damming, the waterways. And when it finishes, America the beautiful is doomed."[16] He cataloged these "pork barrel" travesties: dams despoiling the Everglades in Florida; the Middle Fork of the Salmon River in Idaho; and the Bosque River in Waco, Texas. Publicly assailing agencies that often came before the Supreme Court was unorthodox; doing it in *Playboy* was extraordinary. But, as usual, Douglas was willing to risk scandal to save the wilderness, and he strategically selected the magazine "to reach the young people . . . on conservation."[17]

Even before Douglas became politically engaged in the dam wars, environmentalists had scored a big victory at Echo Park, situated on a tributary of the Colorado River. They stopped a dam that would have flooded the Dinosaur National Monument, which spans the boundary between Colorado and Utah. Congress's 1954 decision to delete budget authorization for the dam was a watershed event for wilderness preservation and for the nascent environmental movement.[18]

Douglas's far-flung personal interventions included a canoe trip to protest the red-brown scum on the Buffalo River in Arkansas (which in 1972 became the first national river) and a high-profile hike and rally to save the Sangamon River in Allerton Park in Illinois.[19] Closer to his home, Douglas headlined a rally against building the Ben Franklin Dam on the last free-flowing stretch of the Columbia River. He understood the importance of the river and its tributaries to salmon spawning, steelhead trout, and breeding grounds for the Canada goose, but he lamented that "the river has few knowledgeable friends."[20] In highlighting potential ecological disasters, Douglas often used the "few friends" language. Joining a rally and issuing a statement opposing the dam made Douglas a valuable friend of the Columbia River.[21]

In his crusade against the Army Corps of Engineers, Douglas's Supreme Court seat proved a powerful pulpit. For instance, in 1963 and 1971, the court considered dam disputes involving the corps. Douglas dissented both times, critiquing the corps' procedures and defending waterways.[22] At least by the time of the 1971 case, Douglas had vilified the agency publicly in his *Playboy* article and in correspondence, thus raising the ethical question of whether he could decide the case fairly or, at the very least, whether his sitting on the case raised an appearance of impropriety. Apart from dissenting, politicking, and floating the rivers, Douglas urged that the corps condition project approval on conservation standards. Douglas proposed a novel solution to save the rivers: "We pay farmers not to plant crops. Let's pay the Corps not to build dams, dredge estuaries, convert rivers into sluiceways, or build inland canals."[23] An unlikely crew of environmentalists, tribal leaders, and fishing enthusiasts eventually came to the aid of the Columbia River. Together they prompted the corps to postpone the Franklin Dam in 1970 and abandon the project in 1981.[24]

Today environmentalists are still fighting to stop new dams and remove existing ones. Douglas would have endorsed these environmental remediation efforts. The arguments to restore river ecosystems and protect fish populations echo Douglas's cry of the 1960s, and several large dams have been demolished in recent years in the Pacific Northwest and elsewhere. All together, 241 dams were removed across the country between 2006 and 2010. Yet the battle continues: as the *New York Times* noted in 2012, "It's Fish vs. Dams, and the Dams are Winning."[25]

Leveraging Presidential Politics

Douglas's protest at the Red River Gorge in Kentucky illustrates the intersection of his remarkable political friendships, his prominent role with the Sierra Club, his antipathy toward the Army Corps of Engineers, and his talent for publicity. Though the protest began as a grassroots campaign, Douglas took it all the way to the White House and the Cabinet.

Boasting natural stone arches and dramatic cliffs, the gorge is part of a canyon system on the Red River, part of what Douglas called "the spiritual inheritance of America."[26] In the early 1960s, the Army Corps of Engineers proposed building a flood-control dam on the river, a project that soon became controversial. Taking a page from earlier organizers, the newly formed Cumberland Chapter of the Sierra Club invited Douglas and his wife Cathy to join a protest hike in the fall of 1967.

In 1966 Douglas was newly married to Cathy Heffernan, a twenty-three-year-old college student from Oregon whose school-of-hard-knocks upbringing fit with Douglas's sense of himself. Little time had elapsed since the end of his not-quite-three-year marriage to his third wife, Joan Martin, whom he had also met while she was in college. Cathy's appearance fed the Washington gossip mill, though it was hardly a scandal among the hikers. (She later became an accomplished environmental lawyer and philanthropist.) With Cathy enlisted in his conservation army, Douglas rallied round the Sierra Club: "We live by the great spiritual values. That's why I think your fight for the little Red River Gorge is symbolic of the great fight that's going on round the United States."[27]

It is a miracle Douglas found time to headline the protest, given the Supreme Court's heavy docket that November and December. Just a few weeks after the hike, Douglas announced his dissent to the court's decision not to review a case in which he had warned of the environmental harms of unregulated garbage and sewage disposal.[28] He had to squeeze the weekend hike between his ongoing court duties, in a year in which he cataloged four other major protest hikes. Douglas understood that his name and presence guaranteed publicity. So did the Sierra Club. One organizer bluntly explained the motive behind inviting Douglas: "We wanted national attention and I thought that was one way of getting it . . . [and] I'm not sure we could have stopped the dam if he hadn't come."[29]

The march in the rugged country of the Red River Gorge attracted several hundred demonstrators. As with the Olympic

Beach hike, Douglas was "very friendly to both those who opposed and those who favored the dam." He faced counter-protestors with signs that read "Dam the Gorge" and "Sierra Club Go Home," reminiscent of the "Bird Watcher Go Home" placard that had greeted him on the Olympic Beach. Though intimidated by the celebrity factor, opponents arranged for a rebuttal speech for the dam. Douglas's intuition that spending time in nature produces conservationist converts again prevailed. Reflecting on the power of place, one counter-protester years later changed his view and supported preservation of this "magical place."[30]

The press described Douglas as "a showboat," but that was precisely the point: the Sierra Club hoped to use him to capture public support to save the gorge. With Douglas out ahead of the spirited entourage, Diane Sawyer, then a *New York Times* local correspondent and Louisville reporter, worked hard to keep up and keep her camera aimed at the justice and his young wife.[31] Anxious to see how the hike was received, Douglas checked the Sunday morning headlines the next day and chuckled that "every paper I saw had a wire-service story saying that we had been driven out of Kentucky by 200 armed men who did not want a 'senile judge' telling them how to run their affairs."[32] He was sixty-nine years old.

The conclusion of the hike was not the end of Douglas's advocacy, and he wasted no time intervening on behalf of the gorge with his Washington connections. He went straight to the top, writing to President Johnson the day that he returned to chambers. Douglas knew LBJ well—they had formed an "instant friendship" after Johnson's victory in a special election to the U.S. House in 1937 and were often at the same parties and dinners. After Douglas's horse accident in 1949, LBJ wrote that he was "afraid [to have Douglas's] health and vigor snatched from us," and he continued to keep tabs on Douglas's health in later years, even visiting him in the intensive care unit at Walter Reed Hospital.[33]

Now, to flatter the president and appeal to his conservation legacy, in a note to LBJ Douglas analogized the gorge to the "interesting and unique bits of Americana that you and Lady Bird have worked hard to preserve." He even painted the limestone cliffs of

Kentucky as being "reminiscent of your part of Texas." Douglas then raised the proposed dam project: "I, myself, do not know what the answer is; but when I saw it and when we were flying back on the plane, I decided to send you this note." He advised Johnson, "You might want to hold everything say for 30, 60, or 90 days and ask your Water Resources Council of which Udall, I think, is Chairman, to look at it and give you a report before it is all too late."[34] Douglas had one of the president's special assistants attach a note, explaining that Douglas wanted the president to receive his message "right away."[35]

Johnson replied promptly and favorably, pledging that the "conservation values [would] be carefully weighed by all concerned," and he promised to pass the matter on to Secretary Udall. Douglas surely appreciated the sentiment but was perhaps frustrated that the president skirted direct intervention.[36] Douglas understood, however, that in the hierarchy of Washington, a note passed from the president to a Cabinet member was significant. It was part of the game that reinforced Douglas's role as a political player in the capital.

Douglas did not wait for President Johnson to involve Udall. He sent Udall a copy of his original note and soon after asked him "to look at some of the strip mining operations which I believe are the worst in the country, and . . . to take a quick look at the Red River Gorge."[37] Udall later responded, "We almost lost the gorge fight (due to the Corps machinations. I'll tell you about [it] sometime). I'm getting some action initiated however that may get a re-study underway."[38] Delay, study, and reconsideration were music to Douglas's ears; he knew delay often sounded the death knell for a project.

A dam had seemed inevitable until Udall and others, likely nudged and influenced by President Johnson, slowed the process. By the early 1990s the project was dead, and 19.4 miles of the Red River were added to the National Wild and Scenic River System.[39] The Douglas magic had worked again.

Despite the success of his entreaty, Douglas did not consider Johnson a fellow traveler on environmental causes. Ultimately, they broke over Johnson's views on environmentalism and his handling of the Vietnam War. Douglas was skeptical of LBJ's sincerity and considered him a promoter of "consensus conservation," a tactic that promised something for everyone. Whereas Douglas encouraged the Sierra Club to celebrate Lady Bird, he took "with a grain of salt the so-called conservation achievements of LBJ" and pronounced him "a complete phony as a conservationist."[40] Douglas was even dismissive of Johnson's role on the Red River Gorge and later complained, "I don't think any credit is coming to him for the Red River Gorge or Allerton Park in Illinois, both of which I had something to do with. Everything that was done was in spite of LBJ's attitudes."[41]

This criticism was somewhat harsh in light of Johnson's signature on the Wilderness Act and support of more than three hundred progressive environmental laws during the expansion of government oversight of the environment.[42] True, Lady Bird had stronger conservationist credentials than her husband, and she championed numerous initiatives on behalf of wilderness legislation and protective legislation. She and Douglas bonded over their fondness for hiking, and, partly to curry Johnson's favor, Douglas invited her along on at least one of the C&O Canal walks.[43] Lady Bird championed highway beautification and saving the California redwoods. Supporting the passage of the National Trails System Act and the National Wild and Scenic Rivers Act were among her other initiatives. While Johnson did cast a critical eye on some projects and worked political angles when necessary, he deserves credit for promoting a clean environment. Even if Johnson's conservationist commitment did not meet Douglas's exacting standards, Douglas's bold entreaties evidently pushed the president in the right direction. The presidential contact was golden but didn't always produce gold.

Engaging with the "Most Environmentally Conscious" Secretary of the Interior

While Douglas realized the value of high-level contacts with the president and his inner circle, he knew that key decision-making on conservation took place within the federal agencies. In the same way that dams sparked his ire, Douglas decried the foibles of federal land management. Most of America's public lands fall under the Department of the Interior, which includes the National Park Service, and the Department of Agriculture, which includes the Forest Service. Then, as now, the vast majority of these lands were concentrated in the western United States.[44] Because Douglas focused on preserving wilderness and saving public lands, these two departments consumed much of his energy. As Douglas blossomed into a full-blown conservationist, these agencies and their leaders became both allies and opponents, and he learned to juggle the complexity of their conflicting and intersecting interests.

The Department of the Interior, nicknamed "the Department of Everything Else," was created in 1849 to take up the slack on domestic issues not covered by the Departments of Foreign Affairs and War. Its early responsibilities ranged from exploration of western wilderness and management of public lands to oversight of the District of Columbia jail.[45] Today the department oversees more than five hundred million acres of public land, one-fifth of all land in the United States.[46]

Two of the department's agencies, the National Park Service and the Bureau of Land Management (BLM), figured prominently in Douglas's world. The work of the National Park Service posed a dilemma for Douglas. He supported the creation of new parks, like the North Cascades National Park in Washington, but parks also meant roads, tourism, and a loss of solitude. The BLM induced less ambivalence. Tasked with managing vast public lands for livestock grazing, energy development, and recreation, the agency collided more directly with Douglas's conservation principles.

Douglas had a special relationship with Udall, a four-term progressive congressman from Arizona who was appointed secretary of the interior by President Kennedy in 1960. Udall was a longtime conservationist who championed protection of the forests, promoted outdoor recreation, and tackled pollution. Key environmental legislation of the 1960s—the Clean Air Act, the Clean Water Act, the Endangered Species Preservation Act, and the Wilderness Act—all bore his mark.[47] Udall was a keen collaborator and a friendlier ally than his cross-town counterpart, Orville Freeman, the secretary of agriculture under Kennedy and Johnson.

Soon after Udall's appointment, he and Douglas began a stream of correspondence that attests to their warm relationship and details Douglas's full-on lobbying efforts. The letters spanned a wide range of projects, from a reservoir at Bumping Lake (near Douglas's Goose Prairie cabin) to wetlands in Toppenish, Washington, and a BLM fencing program in Wyoming.[48] No project was too small to escape Douglas's attention. Udall once responded to Douglas's support for a study in the North Cascades that if Douglas was for the study, "I am for it too."[49] It is hardly a surprise that Douglas's efforts carried such weight; during their years of friendship and collaboration, Douglas participated in multiple Supreme Court decisions in which Udall, in his official capacity, was a named party.[50] Douglas's true allegiance was to the environment, not to Udall, but from an outsider's perspective, the relationship certainly raised an appearance of conflict.

Douglas and Udall were aligned in friendship as well as politics. At one point, perhaps after one of their hikes together, Udall suggested that Douglas was miscast in life. After Udall's close friend Attorney General Robert ("Bobby") Kennedy repeatedly told him that "Bill Douglas says you should do so and so," Udall imagined, "I bet he'd trade jobs with me straight across if I'd offer it, and I am not sure that it wouldn't be a good idea for the Department."[51] Both men remained where they were; together they made a formidable team.

Udall and Douglas both pushed for passage of the Wilderness Act at the Sierra Club's 1961 biennial Wilderness Conference. Club organizers asked Douglas, "the key man in our hopes," to secure President Kennedy's attendance and even drafted remarks for Kennedy titled "Wilderness and the New Frontier." Douglas tried, but with the press of business for the new administration, the president reluctantly turned him down.[52] Along with paying tribute to Douglas during the conference, Udall celebrated JFK as "a final supreme court," declaring, "There is only one President and he is President of the parks and the forests too."[53]

President Kennedy was an imperfect ally. He sympathized with the conservationists' values during his short tenure in office, but he and Douglas, who kept in touch about international affairs and politics, never shared a true wilderness connection.[54] Douglas lamented, "The trouble is, Jack, you've never slept on the ground."[55] Nevertheless, he acknowledged Kennedy's charms: "I think if you were up here more often, it would help dispel the gloom that always seems to fill the courtroom."[56] Ironically, Douglas deemed Kennedy "a playboy in public office."[57] And though they saw each other often, there is scant correspondence between them because there was no need—Douglas's close friendship with Bobby Kennedy, with whom he fished and hiked and even traveled to Russia—was perfect backdoor access. Whatever the president's personal views, the most significant thing Kennedy did for the environment was to appoint Udall—no small contribution.[58]

At the wilderness conference, Douglas counseled conservationists to get out in the limelight: "We should be like the Salvation Army, out on the street with a band!" He also let Udall know that being battle-ready did not mean the conservationists were not in concert with him. Douglas assured, "And so, Mr. Secretary, when we sound the alarm, we are with you, we are not against you. We stand ready to serve as amicus curiae to use an ancient and honorable phrase."[59] Invoking the Latin phrase *amicus curiae*, briefs filed by lawyers as "friends of the court," Douglas melded his metaphors and his role as a jurist. Again, he saw himself as a spokesman for conservation and an adviser to top administration officials like Udall, roles that, in his mind, posed no conflict with his role as a justice.

Throughout his sometimes contentious dealings with the Department of the Interior, Douglas maintained respect for its leaders. Time and again, Douglas reminded Udall, "Mr. Secretary, consider it our constitutional right to lay siege to the Secretary of the Interior, the Chief Forester, and all the other people in the government." That, he emphasized, is "part of the greatness of America."[60]

The National Park Service was at the receiving end of many Douglas invectives, but he also had a soft spot for many who worked there, including Conrad Wirth, its longest-serving director (1951–64). Douglas cast his relationship with the Park Service in a positive light: "I may not be the best friend of the Park Service in the country but it would be difficult to prepare a list of the top ten best friends and exclude me."[61] Douglas amicably sparred with Wirth about the Park Service's devotion to roads and hotels rather than to wilderness.[62] Wirth curtly replied: "Everybody, especially our friends, seem to jump to conclusions without knowledge of the facts."[63] As was typical, Douglas had the last word: "One of the prerogatives of friends is criticism—not malicious criticism, not destructive criticism, but criticism in the sense of helping improve conditions and policies."[64]

The Douglas-Udall partnership (1961–69) overlapped in part with the 1954–64 period that the Sierra Club's David Brower called the "decade of the last chance to decide in favor of wilderness."[65] It was a critical time in America's awakening to environmental issues, and it spanned the years of Douglas's most active advocacy. Udall has been hailed as one of the "most successful" secretaries of the interior "in terms of conservation of natural resources and environmental protection."[66] The Sierra Club remembered him as the most "environmentally conscious" interior secretary, praise that could be equally heaped on Douglas as the most "environmentally conscious" justice.[67]

Getting through to the Forest Service

Though the Army Corps of Engineers was first on his hit list, Douglas reserved some of his harshest words for the Forest Service, an agency of the Department of Agriculture. The agency ranked among his top ten public enemies because it "listened attentively to the lumbermen's talk and cut, cut, cut for commercial purposes."[68] The vendetta against this agency was somewhat surprising as Gifford Pinchot, America's first chief forester, had been Douglas's childhood hero. Yet in the same way that Douglas chastised the Park Service for its "roads, roads, roads" approach, he believed the "cut, cut, cut" mantra of the Forest Service would be the downfall of the wilderness.

In 1905 forest lands were transferred from the purview of the Department of the Interior to the Department of Agriculture and placed under the auspices of the newly created U.S. Forest Service, which now manages 193 million acres across the country.[69] From the outset, forest management was squeezed between agency mandates to support farmers and to ensure food safety. Until 1941 the Forest Service concentrated on a custodial role of range and timber management. According to Charles Wilkinson, a noted University of Colorado environmental law professor emeritus, "Setting aside lands for wilderness or other recreational purposes was relatively uncontroversial because the pressure for reconciling other national forest uses was not yet acute."[70]

All that changed with the high demand for timber during World War II, followed by a national housing boom. From 1946 to 1949 timber sale receipts tripled and then tripled again between 1950 and 1956.[71] Increased logging also meant expansion of access roads. During "the production years" (1942–66), Congress enacted the Multiple-Use Sustained-Yield Act of 1960, which, for the first time, treated the development of key forest resources—timber, range, water, recreation, and wildlife—equally.[72] The years 1967–76 were a prelude to national environmental policy planning, which led to the National Forest Management Act of 1976. Over time, tensions flared between the competing imperatives of preserving land for wilderness, allocating land for recreation, and exploiting federal land for minerals and timber.

This pivotal period for the Forest Service coincided with Douglas's awakening as a conservationist and advocate, and he learned to seize on these conflicts within the bureaucracy's mission. In the late 1940s Douglas was friendly with the Forest Service, consulting with foresters about map details in the Wallowa and Cascade Mountains and sharing plant specimens from his foreign travels.[73] Even in the mid-1950s, Douglas held out hope that the Forest Service might share his dismay over the vanishing wilderness.[74] Over time Douglas and the Sierra Club accused the agency of tilting toward resource development rather than resource protection and stripping out the notion of "multiple" in "multiple use" when it came to conservation.[75]

With this critique in mind, Douglas leveraged his access to Agriculture Secretary Freeman. A three-term governor from Minnesota with no experience in federal land management, Freeman found himself overseeing the only agency with designated wilderness under its purview. Freeman gave no signs of being a wilderness aficionado. Despite Douglas's efforts, Freeman clung to the notion that the agency's broad statutory mandate was to manage forest resources, not to advantage wilderness areas. As a consequence, Douglas complained bitterly about local forest leadership, calling Forest Supervisor L. G. Barrett—who would become something of a Douglas antagonist—"intellectually dishonest" and decrying "mutilation" of the forests.[76] Douglas made only limited headway with Freeman and his team, despite efforts to stop logging, delay development with hearings, and expand wilderness.[77]

Yet Freeman was not totally unsupportive of wilderness options. Pressure from Douglas and conservationists in the early 1960s resulted in the "the high mountain policy," which kept logging to a minimum in certain parts of the Pacific Northwest.[78] In January 1963 Freeman and Udall wrote a historic letter to President Kennedy, known as the "Treaty of the Potomac," which outlined a "new era of cooperation in the management of Federal lands for outdoor recreation," including a study of the North Cascades, an area dear to Douglas. Among other endeavors, the study group proposed four new wilderness areas, including the expansion of Glacier Peak Wilderness (created in 1960) and the establishment of a North Cascades National Park.[79] Freeman also headlined one of the Sierra Club's biennial Wilderness Conferences, where he opposed Kennecott Corporation's effort to put a copper mine in the Cascades.

To maintain Freeman's favor, Douglas invoked his signature "come with me and see" strategy, asking decision makers to join him on the trail. It had worked on the C&O Canal and the Olympic Beach campaigns, and in later years he asked leaders from the Forest Service and Park Service to see for themselves the joy of solitude and the impact of encroaching roads, noise, logging, and development. He even went with Barrett on a trip to see "the problem areas" in Cascade country.[80]

At least once, the tables were turned. In 1962 the chief of the Forest Service took Freeman and Douglas on a horsepack trip in the Bob Marshall Wilderness to see up close the challenges faced by wilderness managers. This spectacular area in western Montana, near Glacier National Park, is named after one of the founders of The Wilderness Society. Douglas was in his element, riding remote trails and trading tales with companions who knew exactly where he stood on wilderness politics. One day Freeman was complaining about being miserable after being on a horse for three days when a family with two children emerged from the woods. After talking with that family, Freeman realized the value in having "an ordinary family of modest income means" tell its outdoor story. The result was a pamphlet, "Backpacking in the National Forest Wilderness."[81] This was wilderness music for Douglas, a strong proponent of families getting out of their cars and into the backwoods. Later the Forest Service sent Douglas a set of striking photographs from the trip.[82] Whether Douglas was host or guest, these trips to experience wilderness first-hand were a Douglas hallmark and a potent weapon in his advocacy arsenal. Through such subtle politicking, Douglas kept his enemies close and made some inroads with the Forest Service.

Tapping into Congressional Contacts

The intricate dance between Congress and the agencies administering federal environmental policies meant Capitol Hill was prime territory for Douglas to exert his influence. That the Capitol was just a few blocks from the Supreme Court allowed Douglas to develop important relationships with members of Congress, especially those from the West.

The adage that "all politics are local" held true in the conservation world. Douglas knew that while agency policy is made at the Washington headquarters, implementation takes place on the ground. He also understood that although members of Congress may cite the national or public interest, their allegiances rested with their local constituents.

Douglas's early foray into congressional advocacy targeted the delegations from Oregon and Washington, where he had personal connections with the land and its politicians. Douglas and Wayne L. Morse, Oregon's senior senator, were ideological compatriots on the environment and later on the Vietnam war. Morse was one of two senators to oppose the Gulf of Tonkin resolution authorizing the war, and Douglas was the lone dissenter when the court declined to hear cases challenging the constitutionality of the draft in the absence of a declaration of war.[83] Douglas also relied on Washington's senators, Henry M. "Scoop" Jackson and Warren G. "Maggie" Magnuson, who were nicknamed the "Gold Dust Twins" because they were so successful in bringing home federal money and legislative successes for their constituents. Their heyday in the 1960s and 1970s coincided with the prime of Douglas's advocacy.[84] Douglas was in touch with them about protection for the Minam River and the North Cascades and a host of other projects, such as keeping a timber mill in southern Washington in operation.[85] He was particularly close to Jackson, chair of the Senate Committee on Interior and Insular Affairs, who championed major environmental legislation, including the National Environmental Policy Act, and was instrumental in the ultimate success of the Cougar Lakes wilderness designation, which became the William O. Douglas Wilderness.[86]

These were big-picture projects for the public good, but Douglas also worried about his own solitude. When sonic booms from military aircraft began interrupting his seclusion at Goose Prairie and panicking the horses, Douglas triangulated by pleading to Jackson, President Johnson, and Secretary of Defense Robert McNamara for relief. His caustic reply to Secretary McNamara highlights Douglas's frustration with the "disastrous effects of your sonic boom in the wilderness": "I assure you, Mr. Secretary that your 'villagers' here are not as voiceless and unimportant as your 'villagers' in Viet Nam."[87]

Douglas's Washington State roots gave him particular sway

with senators from the Pacific Coast, but from his desk in DC, he cultivated contacts with members of Congress from across the country. When an issue sparked his ire or interest, he sent letters highlighting environmental problems and asking for support, whether explaining a mounting problem of overcrowding in the High Sierra in California for Maryland Senator Charles Mathias or reaching out to California's Senator Clair Engle about the Forest Service's multiple-use policy in the Sierra Nevada Mountains.[88]

To complement his dissenting on the road and in court, Douglas was also dissenting in the corridors of power. He ran a one-man lobby shop from his chambers, cajoling presidents, secretaries of the interior and agriculture, leaders of the National Park Service and Forest Service, and members of Congress to intervene in pending administrative decisions and to stop logging, dams, and road construction. Douglas developed friendships with powerful players in the executive and legislative branches but still disapproved when they grew complacent or too compromising. As he had reminded the Park Service, Douglas considered constructive criticism "one of the prerogatives of friends."[89] Vocal, persuasive, and untroubled by the appearance of conflict, Douglas was impossible to ignore.

Supreme Advocate

1. Douglas in his teenage years, outfitted for a hike in the Cascades near his home. Douglas grew up in modest circumstances in Yakima, Washington, with his mother, sister, and brother. His father passed away when he was five years old. Courtesy of the Yakima Valley Museum.

2. (*opposite top*) Beta Theta Pi Fraternity, Whitman College, 1917–18. Douglas was an enthusiastic member of his fraternity, calling initiation a rare spiritual experience. Courtesy of Whitman College and Northwest Archives.

3. (*opposite bottom*) Douglas in a tuxedo at a dinner in Washington DC. After moving from Yale Law School to Washington DC, Douglas led an active social life, from poker parties with President Roosevelt to embassy galas. Courtesy of the Estate of Charles Reich.

4. (*above*) Supreme Court, 1939. President Franklin Roosevelt appointed Douglas to the Supreme Court when Douglas was forty. He was (and remains) the longest-serving justice—36 years and 211 days—when he retired in 1975. He died in 1980. Courtesy of the Archives of the Supreme Court.

5. The Immortal Nine: just nine hikers finished the entire historic 189-mile hike on the c&o Canal in 1954, a hike that launched Douglas's conservation advocacy career. The Chesapeake and Ohio Canal National Historic Park became the only national park walked into existence. On that trip Douglas met Olaus Murie, head of The Wilderness Society, with whom he formed a close friendship and advocacy partnership. National Park Service photo.

6. Douglas leading a commemorative hike on the c&o Canal. Until his illness in the 1970s, Douglas hiked on the canal almost every week during the court term. In *My Wilderness: East to Katahdin*, he decried the pollution in the Potomac River but celebrated the "glorious days along the old canal." National Park Service photo.

7. Douglas with Mardy Murie at Last Lake, Alaska, 1956. Douglas joined with conservationists Olaus and Mardy Murie of Wyoming for part of their exploratory Sheenjek Expedition in Alaska. Together they successfully advocated for preservation of the Arctic wilderness, which later was included in the Alaska National Interest Lands Conservation Act. Courtesy of the Wildlife Conservation Society. Reproduced by permission of the WCS Archives. Photography by George Schaller.

8. Douglas leading seventy-two hikers down the Olympic Beach in Washington State in 1958 to protest a proposed highway down the beach. He lamented that the area "badly needs friends." Douglas's lobbying efforts resulted in the relocation of the proposed byway by the National Park Service. Courtesy of the Yakima Valley Museum.

9. Douglas hiking on the Olympic Beach, the longest stretch of wild coastline in the continental United States. The beach, with its iconic Point of the Arches, is now part of Olympic National Park. At the conclusion of the protest hike, Douglas was met with counter-protesters who counseled, "Bird Watchers Go Home."
Courtesy of the Yakima Valley Museum.

10. Mineral King Hike-In: The clash between environmentalists and the U.S. Forest Service and Disney Corporation over the proposal for a ski resort in Mineral King Valley in California culminated in a Hike-In at Mineral King. Douglas's iconic dissent in *Sierra Club v. Morton* in 1972 highlighted the controversy and queried whether the lawsuit could be brought in the name of the valley itself.

Courtesy of usc Special Collections.

11. Douglas's chambers at the Supreme Court. Douglas was a fast and prolific writer with a love of books. Legend has it that when he learned a clerk had written in one of the law books, he threw it out the window. Courtesy of Judge William Aslup.

12. Cabin at Goose Prairie, Washington. Douglas had cabins in Oregon, southern Washington, and on the Washington coast before he built a cabin in the Cascade Mountains, not far from where he grew up in Yakima, Washington. Courtesy of the Yakima Valley Museum.

13. Douglas with his wife, Cathy Heffernan Douglas, near their Goose Prairie cabin. Goose Prairie became his summer refuge from the Supreme Court, and he even entertained petitions from lawyers on his front porch. This was one of Cathy's favorite photos. Courtesy of Cathy Douglas.

14. Douglas and the Double K girls, 1969. Kay Kershaw and Isabelle Lynn owned the Double K Ranch, adjacent to Douglas's cabin at Goose Prairie. They collaborated with Douglas on achieving wilderness status for what would become the William O. Douglas Wilderness. Courtesy of Ed Kershaw.

15. Douglas contemplating nature. Courtesy of the Yakima Valley Museum.

16. Douglas at the campfire on a hiking trip. Douglas was a born storyteller, both in his books and in gatherings with friends and fellow hikers. He paid tribute to his love of wilderness and the mountains in *My Wilderness: The Pacific West* and *My Wilderness: East to Katahdin*. Courtesy of the Yakima Valley Museum.

17. Douglas leading a party up Mount Gilbert. In addition to being an avid hiker, Douglas was a skilled climber. This trip in the Sierra Nevada Range took him to the crest at 13,104 feet. Courtesy of the Yakima Valley Museum.

To Bill Bayard
Over the years – always a true friend
Lyndon B. Johnson

18. (*opposite top*) Douglas at a White House meeting with President John F. Kennedy. Though he admired Kennedy, unlike his brother Bobby—Douglas's hiking and travel companion—Jack was not a traditional outdoorsman. As Douglas wrote, the trouble with Jack was that he "never slept on the ground." Courtesy of the Yakima Valley Museum.

19. (*opposite bottom*) Douglas and President Lyndon Johnson. Although Johnson championed significant environmental causes, he had an uneasy relationship with Douglas, who dismissed him as a phony when it came to the environment. This was a harsh view in light of Johnson's considerable contributions to the environment. Courtesy of the LBJ Library.

20. (*above*) Douglas was a chronicler of events and an inveterate record keeper. He kept a small black notebook for each significant hike, with entries detailing his observations of the flora and fauna, as well as impressions of the people. This photo was taken on one of his hikes in Texas, which he featured in *Farewell to Texas: A Vanishing Wilderness*. Courtesy of the Yakima Valley Museum.

21. Douglas fishing on the Salmon River in Idaho. Although he disdained hunting, Douglas was an enthusiastic fisherman. Courtesy of the Yakima Valley Museum.

22. Douglas with his movie camera. Although his friend Charles Reich joked that Douglas would always stop to have his photograph taken, Douglas also loved to document his trips through numerous photos, many of which are housed at the Library of Congress and the Yakima Valley Museum. Courtesy of the Yakima Valley Museum.

23. Douglas in Maroon Bells, Colorado. He loved pack trips but suffered a near fatal fall in the Cascades in 1949. He celebrated his love of mountains and the spirituality of wilderness in the first book of his autobiographical trio, *Of Men and Mountains*. On the court, he became a one-man lobby shop for the environment. Courtesy of the Yakima Valley Museum.

24. William O. Douglas Wilderness sign in the Wenatchee National Forest. After years of lobbying and congressional fits and starts, the William O. Douglas Wilderness was designated in 1984 and now encompasses more than 169,000 acres. Courtesy of Tom R. Hulst.

25. Mount Rainier from the William O. Douglas Wilderness, 2006. Douglas could see Mount Rainier from his porch in Yakima, Washington, and the wilderness area is near his Goose Prairie cabin. "The William O. Douglas Wilderness is designated in remembrance of Justice Douglas's lifelong efforts to preserve Cougar Lakes for the recreational benefits of future generations." U.S. Congress. Courtesy of Jo Miles.

7

America's Teacher—Writing a New Script for Conservation Action

Books must serve as powerful agencies of social,
economic, or political reform.

—WILLIAM O. DOUGLAS

We inherited the loveliest of all continents. We should bequeath
it to our grandchildren as a land where the majority is
disciplined to respect the values even of a minority.

—WILLIAM O. DOUGLAS

From his perch at the Supreme Court, Douglas became a bandleader for the conservation movement. He brought the prominence of a national figure, coupled with passion and true boots-on-the ground conservation credentials. Just as he considered the role of dissenting opinions to prick "the conscience of our people," Douglas saw a broader opportunity to raise the environmental conscience of the country.[1] The man who once wrote a concurring opinion describing the power of books and pamphlets to "reach the minds and hearts of the American people" was now determined to do just that.[2] Douglas became America's teacher for the conservation movement.

Building Coalitions

Though Douglas initially conceived of saving the C&O Canal as a singular mission, the relationships he developed in that effort led him to embrace coalition building for a much broader conservation advocacy. Douglas could get only so far on his own, serving as the point person in the nation's capital and showing up at select hot spots across the country. For the conservationists to become a truly formidable force, Douglas realized that their national organizations had to combine with grassroots efforts. Two of those organizations, The Wilderness Society and the Sierra Club, were at the heart of Douglas's efforts to build conservation coalitions. Both groups—The Wilderness Society as its tag line and the Sierra Club in its publications—invoked Thoreau's famous sentiment, "In wildness is the preservation of the world."[3]

Douglas's association with The Wilderness Society began around the time of the C&O Canal hike. The society's executive director, Howard Zahniser, thanked Douglas for his "signal service to the cause of conservation in the Nation's Capital as well as in the United States" and helped Douglas plan the protest hike.[4] Olaus Murie, then president of the society, became one of the nine intrepid souls to finish the hike. In addition to consulting Murie about other protest hikes, Douglas also consulted him on scientific questions and wilderness particulars.[5] But with Murie located in Wyoming, save for a short stint in Washington DC, the society recognized the need for a political presence in the capital. Zahniser became the national spokesman, the political go-between, and key drafter of the Wilderness Act. For Douglas, The Wilderness Society represented a spiritual link, plus an accessible ally.

Throughout the 1950s and early 1960s, as he emerged on the national conservation scene, Douglas publicly supported The Wilderness Society, writing to members of Congress on its behalf and publishing frequently in *Living Wilderness*, the group's newsletter. Zahniser enthused to Douglas, "You have been genius, Bill, in so many ways and we are heartened by your support."[6] The feeling was mutual. Douglas returned a twenty-five dollar check sent to him for a short piece in the newsletter with a note: "I would prefer you add it to the assets of the Society. What I have done for you I consider in the realm of public service."[7] After Murie's death in 1963 and Zahniser's in 1964, Douglas's focus shifted to other conservation groups. Yet Douglas and The Wilderness Society had come of age together, and the partnership would continue to influence him.

The Sierra Club, which evolved from John Muir's hiking club into a political powerhouse, became an important strand in Douglas's coalition tapestry. Douglas likely first interacted with its charismatic leader, David Brower, when Brower stepped up his political and personal appearances in Washington DC in the late 1950s. Their association took on a new and personal dimension in 1959, however, when Douglas appealed to Brower to help stop logging in the Minam Valley, near Douglas's cabin in Oregon.[8]

By the early 1960s Brower found himself at a tense crossroads with the organization over his leadership. Although the board already included luminaries like renowned photographer Ansel Adams, to solidify his position, Brower decided to add more famous names. He invited Douglas to join, along with other national figures, including author Wallace Stegner and John Oakes from the *New York Times*.[9]

Douglas was not long for the board, resigning after only a year. He explained, "The reason that I am resigning is that I understand from some of our mutual friends that the Sierra Club, like other conservation agencies, may be engaging in litigation in the state [or] federal courts on conservation matters which at least in their potential might reach this court."[10] In an earlier letter to Charles Reich, Douglas had offered the same logic, saying that he had resigned "because the Club may, I hear, get into litigation."[11] This rationale was dubious: nothing had changed during Douglas's year on the board, and surely any perceived conflict existed even when he decided to join the board. Years later Douglas offered another explanation: it was impossible to get to the club's meetings in San Francisco.[12] The reality was that he was bored with the business of the board; as he confessed to Brower, the meetings depressed him.[13] Despite the resignation, the club hoped it could continue to benefit from Douglas's "broad experience on behalf of conserving some of the not-completely-spoiled as well as wilderness parts of the earth."[14]

Leaving the board did not mean leaving the Sierra Club. Douglas continued as a life member until 1971 and worked closely with the local and national offices to promote the club's agenda. The relationship was not always smooth, especially as the club made an acrimonious transition from Brower to Michael McCloskey as the new executive director. Douglas's ability to both praise and polarize, whether in his chambers or in conservation circles, was on display soon after the transition, when he was the keynote speaker at a Sierra Club event in New York. Despite praising the club's work, Douglas warned against the club's "going soft" without Brower. McCloskey, sitting in the front row, understandably "felt let down, even insulted," in light of his earlier work with Douglas in Oregon and beyond.[15]

Whatever the hiccups in the relationship, Douglas was closely associated with the club, even referring to "We of the Sierra Club."[16] Whether being asked to contact Chief Justice Warren and Governor Pat Brown of California about a crisis in Sequoia National Park—which he declined to do—or collaborating with the club on protests in Washington, Oregon, Arkansas, Maine, and beyond, Douglas became the high-level go-to contact for difficult problems. His trademark response was, "I will fight all I can."[17]

Over the years, as the Sierra Club's influence continued to grow, it expanded operations, became more politically active, and worked closely with other conservation organizations. Like his relationship with The Wilderness Society, Douglas admired and augmented the Sierra Club's coalition power, and the club lauded him as "the highest-placed advocate of Wilderness in the United States."[18]

Committees of Correspondence

Even as Douglas remained a collaborator with national and local organizations, he forged his own brand of a conservation organization. His did not have a board or an office beyond his chambers at the Supreme Court. Douglas chose to speak to the American public directly in personal letters, best-selling books, and even television appearances. Through words, he formed his own "conservation army"—one made up of ordinary citizens.

Long before the internet, Douglas took social networking to

America's Teacher

a high art form in the analog world. Letter writing became his hallmark tool, with his 1954 missive to the *Washington Post* about saving the c&o Canal serving as a catalyst for enlisting citizens as foot soldiers in his conservation army.

Douglas championed a vehicle he called "Committees of Correspondence," a concept he borrowed from the Revolutionary War era.[19] In the 1770s such committees comprised a loosely organized communications network intended to keep revolutionaries abreast of British activity and to work for a common cause.[20] Douglas enlisted his own Committees of Correspondence to protect not America itself but its wilderness—though he certainly considered the two inextricably intertwined.[21] To supplement his personal entreaties to top agency leadership, Douglas envisioned legions of citizens pelting agencies with petitions, letters, testimonies, and data.

Douglas debuted this strategy in an article for *Ladies' Home Journal* in 1964, "America's Vanishing Wilderness," which made such an impression on Alaska senator Ernest Gruening that he inserted it into the *Congressional Record*.[22] Energizing the public to take charge of public lands, Douglas urged, "Committees of Correspondence to coordinate the efforts of diverse groups to keep America beautiful and to preserve the few wilderness alcoves we have left." "Local groups," he wrote, "need national assistance; and that means joining hands in an overall effort to keep our land bright and shining."[23] Douglas was hardly the first advocate to draw connections between national and local organizers, but he lent the tactic a moniker and national prominence.

In letter after letter Douglas transformed into something of an inspirational reference librarian. He offered personal encouragement to citizens he had never met, suggesting how they could access information, where they could send petitions and inquiries, and how they could become conservation activists. For citizens seeking referrals to conservation organizations, he recommended the Sierra Club, The Wilderness Society, the National Parks Association, and the Appalachian Mountain Club, touting his association with each. He explained to Marian G. Laurie, a stranger from Brookfield, Illinois, "All I can do is urge that every group get thoroughly organized and extremely vocal to make sure that the basic values are not sacrificed as our population expands and as our highways multiply."[24]

Receiving a letter on Supreme Court letterhead from a justice of the nation's highest court was no small matter. Douglas received hundreds and hundreds of letters. On top of that, every new Douglas book prompted a raft of fan mail and requests. Yet he did not treat letters from citizens like cold calls and unsolicited inquiries that others might quickly toss in the trash. From Douglas came personally crafted messages. One of his earliest forays into citizen-justice correspondence came in 1955, when the United Conservation Fund in Milwaukee, Wisconsin, asked for a statement to further its public education program. Douglas promptly sent a telegram. Harkening back to the desolate land in the Middle East, he chastised those who were "cutting too much timber, grazing too many cattle or sheep," and he warned that "the river that runs red is taking precious topsoil to the ocean."[25] In a letter to a Florida resident who had listened to one of Douglas's television interviews, Douglas expounded on sewage treatment and the problem "[that detergents with] a carbon molecule do not break down."[26] From detergents to DDT, Douglas engaged the American public. Whether encouraging citizens to form informal committees to support environmental causes or responding to far-flung inquiries, like complimenting leaders in Ruanda-Urundi, Africa, on efforts to preserve the mountain gorilla, Douglas's message was the same: individual citizens can make a difference.[27]

Ever a savvy strategist, Douglas also cultivated a national television presence to reach the public. Always in the vanguard, he appeared on programs with Mike Wallace (1958) and Eric Sevareid (1972), both renowned journalists, and even on *Good Morning America* in 1975.[28] Douglas did not limit himself to news shows. In 1956 he appeared as a "mystery guest" on the popular television game show *What's My Line*. Trying to guess Douglas's profession, a blindfolded panelist asked, "Do you get your orders directly from Washington?" Douglas paused long enough to flash a look of mischievous incredulity before answering, "No." After figuring out that the mystery guest was a justice, another panelist posed, "Are you the author of several best sellers?" "Yes." The identity of the mystery guest became immediately obvious: "Bill Douglas!"[29]

Douglas's television appearances were remarkable for a justice in that era. In 1958 his colleague and friend, Justice Hugo Black, gave an interview on CBS News, but he and Douglas were the only justices to do so in the first three decades after television became part of the mass media. By the 1980s that had begun to change; Justice Antonin Scalia, for example, became a recognized figure on CNN, C-SPAN, and Fox News. Today the justices are a familiar presence on YouTube and on programs ranging from *The Late Show with Stephen Colbert* to CBS *Sunday Morning* and PBS documentaries.[30]

The Advocate as Author

At heart Douglas was a storyteller. Whether around the campfire, at poker parties, during Washington dinners, in chambers after hours, on the trail, or on a long overseas trip, Douglas loved to regale his audience with tales of the wilderness, backroom politics, and foreign adventures. Those stories became the backbone of his myriad writings. His books ranged from a personal and patriotic reflection on democracy—*Being an American* (1948)—to the purely legal—*Stare Decisis* (1949), *We the Judges* (1956), and *The Living Bill of Rights* (1961)—to travelogues and to a celebration of his beloved wilderness. Over the course of his life, Douglas wrote more than fifty books and several hundred articles, which became yet another platform for his national advocacy.

Unique among the justices of his time, Douglas did not shy away from writing an autobiography. He authored an autobiographical trilogy: *Of Men and Mountains* (1950), a national best seller that was a paean to his spiritual connection with mountains; *Go East, Young Man: The Early Years* (1974), the story of his childhood up to the time of his appointment to the Supreme Court; and *The Court Years: 1939–1975* (1980), a chronicle of his time on the court until his retirement. While judicial autobiographies are more common today—such as those by Justice Sandra Day O'Connor (*Lazy B: Growing Up on a Cattle Ranch in the American South-west*, 2003); Justice Clarence Thomas (*My Grandfather's Son*, 2007); Justice Sonia Sotomayor (*My Beloved World*, 2013); Justice Ruth Bader Ginsburg (*My Own Words*, 2016); and Justice Paul Stevens (*The Making of a Justice: Reflections on My First 94 Years*, 2019)—in Douglas's time they were rare.[31] Douglas's autobiographical works have been called "a remarkable achievement: the first attempt by a Justice to transform the raw material of his life into a resonant American myth of personal and professional transcendence."[32]

As he neared his first decade on the court, Douglas was churning out at least a book a year. His view, alone among the justices, that the court work took only four days a week did not endear him to his brethren. At one point, not totally tongue in cheek, Douglas suggested abolishing law clerks for a year: "Why don't we experiment with doing our own work? You all might like it for a change."[33] In one of his last opinions, Douglas jangled the justices again: "In all frankness, no Justice of this Court need work more than four days a week to carry his burden. I have found it a comfortable burden carried even in my months of hospitalization."[34] So for years Douglas addressed "what to do with the other days" with his conservation, political, and other activities, which included writing for the public.[35]

Douglas wrote his book drafts longhand on yellow legal pads (though sometimes he dictated drafts), surrounded by his iconic little black notebooks that detailed hikes and protest campaigns; correspondence with Olaus Murie, David Brower, and other conservation leaders; news clippings; letters from political leaders; stories from *National Geographic*; naturalist guides; and his own photographs and pressings of flora from the woods. At times he sketched out drafts while he sat on the bench hearing cases. Douglas had a brilliant mind and saw no problem in multitasking when oral arguments droned on. The drafts resembled jigsaw puzzle pieces, with Douglas's extensive inserts (which he called "riders"), addenda, and edits.

Writing became not only a vehicle for his conservation advocacy, but also a source of income when his several divorces stretched

America's Teacher

him financially. An article might bring $1,000. His first national bestseller, *Of Men and Mountains*, brought almost $33,000 (around $350,000 in today's dollars), at a time when the annual salary for Supreme Court justices was $25,000.[36] While writing helped him achieve personal financial stability, Douglas, first and foremost, wrote for the public. Douglas believed that "books must serve as powerful agencies of social, economic, or political reform."[37]

Douglas approached articles with the same imperative and penned an impressive array for popular periodicals. To reach the broadest audience, he published in outlets as wide-ranging as *Playboy*, *Reader's Digest*, *American Forests*, *Look*, *Life*, *National Geographic*, *Home and Highway*, *Outdoor Life Magazine*, and the *Bulletin of Atomic Scientists*.[38] His publishing in *Playboy*—albeit on civil liberties and conservation topics—was grist for his critics, but he was pragmatic about his choice: he wanted to reach the "18 million youngsters" that read the provocative periodical.[39] Douglas also deliberately reached out to women's magazines—*Mademoiselle*, *McCall's*, *Family Circle*, and *Ladies' Home Journal*—not only because they sought content and paid well, but also because he realized that women, particularly those at home, were on the front line of conservation challenges. That sentiment was echoed by his friend Mardy Murie in a letter to *Ladies' Home Journal*: "It was encouraging to see that at long last the editors of the most important woman's magazine have realized that the American woman could be[,] or should be, interested in conservation."[40] The articles, which often recycled Douglas's speeches and his standby themes of conservation, wilderness protection, and citizen action, brought nature to America's living rooms.

Indeed, during a time when it was unusual for an ordinary citizen to travel around the world for recreation, Douglas brought the places to the people and cultivated a collective appreciation of nature as a place of beauty and restful solitude. So he chronicled foreign adventures to the Middle East in *Strange Lands and Friendly People* (1951) and the Far East in *Russian Journey* (1956), and he provided a blueprint for a free Asia in *North from Malay: Adventure on Five Fronts* (1953). *Strange Lands* was an eclectic cross between a travelogue, adventure narrative, and political commentary. With an abiding interest in people and their cultures, Douglas took readers on foot and horseback to villages, tribal settlements, places of worship, and farmlands, exploring subjects as diverse as communism, nationalism, and India's welfare state.

Douglas painted vivid pictures of his exciting expeditions. In *Beyond the High Himalayas* (1952), he celebrated Central Asia, with descriptions of blizzards, mules, rancid yak butter tea, and the hazards of the high peaks. Exploring the areas now familiar to famous climbing expeditions, K2 and Nanga Parbat, he found himself in a tight spot at high altitude, but "it seemed that unseen hands reached out and helped me over the last stretch."[41] Like his life, the book reflected adversity, hope, and redemption. In 1954 this chronicle took on a special cache with its cameo in the Alfred Hitchcock thriller *Rear Window*, which featured Grace Kelly reading the book before she put it down to read a fashion magazine.

Douglas also helped his readers to appreciate America's backyard; his writings on America's wilderness and nature are some of his best. These works from the heart reflected Douglas's passion for conservation, his distaste for politicians who undermined the environment, and his remarkable knowledge of ecology and the grammar of nature.

Douglas's nature writings evince his gift for expressing his love of nature through poetic descriptions. For example, his debut outdoor book, *Of Men and Mountains*, was part memoir and part physical and spiritual adventure. The mountains and their spirituality are central to the tale, which only fleetingly references conservation. His concluding chapter, titled "Klickitat" after the glacier on the east slope of Mount Adams, captured his constant struggle to push ahead: "The challenge is in the discovery of the outermost limits of one's own endurance."[42]

The narrative of Douglas as a person of place—mountains, rivers, prairies, and the forest floor—evolved in two later volumes that celebrate both the beauty and fragility of wilderness: *My Wilderness: The Pacific West* (1960) and *My Wilderness: East to Katahdin* (1961). In the former, Douglas took the readers to his comfort zone, the Pacific Northwest, with detours to Alaska and California. Though he celebrated the pristine beauty of these sites, he was dismayed that an alpine meadow near his beloved Mount Adams "had been desecrated by the automobile"—a place that used to be "reach[ed] only after days of hiking was now accessible to everyone without effort."[43] That sentiment captured his nostalgia for the past and his disdain for those who motored to the wilderness. In the same vein, his resentment of casual tourists substantiated the criticism that Douglas and the conservationists were elitists, wanting to save remote wilderness for themselves while effectively walling off the masses.

Douglas particularly identified with special places where he hung his hat. Over the years, he acquired or leased cabins in oases around the country, from New Hampshire to Glenwood, Washington, the Wallowa Mountains in Oregon, the Olympic peninsula, and, most important, the Cascade mountains.

In the mid-1960s Douglas built a chalet about an hour north of Yakima in Goose Prairie, Washington, which he saw as his "place in a sense that Washington, D.C. never could be."[44] He devoted an entire chapter in *My Wilderness: The Pacific West* to Goose Prairie. As a boy, he had tromped the mountains nearby. As an adult, he recalled "the country it commands. Nursery of splendid trees. Garden of brilliant flowers. . . . Home to friendly people."[45] The readers meet those friendly people, including Tom Fife, Douglas's childhood friend; Kitty Nelson and her husband Jack, the lock tender at nearby Bumping Lake; and Kay Kershaw and Isabelle Lynn, known as the "Double K girls," who ran a nearby guest ranch. These were steadfast friends who welcomed Douglas back when he was beset with illness, divorce, and public disapproval.

With its expansive meadow and wandering elk, Goose Prairie became Douglas's summer refuge, though on occasion he dispensed justice from the wilderness. During summer recesses the clerks shipped him boxes of petitions to review in his mountainside chambers. On one occasion a few persistent lawyers carrying briefcases and dressed in city-slicker suits with ties, showed up at the cabin with a petition for emergency relief, only to find no one home. They then tracked down Douglas and Cathy while they were out on a pack trip. Douglas gave them a lecture about the dangers of journeying into the mountains without proper equipment. He told them he would consider the petition and would drop off the answer the next day under a stone on a tree stump. Application denied.[46]

The terrain covered in *My Wilderness: East to Katahdin* is far more diverse, detailing trips to the Colorado Rockies; the Wind River Range in Wyoming; the Baboquivari, a granite shaft in the desert of Arizona; the Smoky Mountains along the North Carolina-Tennessee border; the Everglades in Florida; and the White Mountains of New Hampshire. Douglas's decision to title his book after Maine's Mount Katahdin reflects his continuing affection for the state, as well as his continued involvement in far-flung efforts to preserve wilderness. The many readers of Douglas's books went to these places with Douglas and left with a heightened sense of nature's majestic fragility. So primed, they were ready to be moved to action.

A Wilderness Bill of Rights

Douglas espoused a broad vision for reform in *A Wilderness Bill of Rights* (1965), which proposed "a new set of procedural rules designed to preserve wilderness against destruction by other uses."[47] The book grew out of his address, "Wilderness and Human Rights," to the 1961 Sierra Club Wilderness Conference, where he had joined Stewart Udall, Howard Zahniser, Wallace Stegner, and other conservation heroes. There he focused on the collision between "Science and its machines" and the expansion of human rights to include "the right to put one's face in clear, pure water, to discover the wonders of sphagnum moss, and to hear the song of whippoorwills at dawn in a forest where the wilderness bowl is unbroken."[48] In discussions following his speech, Douglas first surfaced a name for his proposals: "a wilderness bill of rights."[49]

The book title is pure Douglas—provocative and unorthodox. Though the writing rambles at times, in many ways the book represents the best catalog of Douglas's values and policy prescriptions. He extolled wilderness as a "therapist" and a healer, cautioning

America's Teacher

that not everything should be dollarized.[50] Connecting his judicial philosophy to his stance on conservation, he argued that in the same way that the Constitution "protects minorities, placing their rights beyond the reach of the majority," so too should "defenders of wilderness—no matter how unpopular"—be protected in their defense of "values which so far have been important in the American saga."[51] In slightly different terms, Olaus Murie had espoused the same philosophy ten years earlier: "I do think that those who take a pleasure in living trees should have equal representation with those who want to use the trees for commercial purposes."[52]

Douglas considered the automobile, population growth, technology, and (of course) unthinking bureaucracies as enemies in the wilderness war. These negative forces meant that "our power in wilderness terms is only the power to destroy, not to create." The book lays out in impressive detail the local, state, and federal management of private and public lands, along with statistics on the shrinking of protected lands.

But Douglas was not just a naysayer; he coupled his criticism with concrete policy prescriptions. At the top of his list was the refining of a standard for procedures to protect the public interest in determining multiple-use priorities. Parlaying his experience from the SEC, Douglas wrote thoughtfully about the need for public hearings and fair decisions, though he recognized that "not every decision by the agency can or should be put down for hearing."[53] That said, "in this era, when we stand to lose all, basic and important decisions concerning wilderness should be treated with high respect for administrative due process." He pointed out that conservationists were disadvantaged because the Administrative Procedure Act, the federal law governing agency hearings, had an exception for matters related "to public property," and the tax code restricted the deductibility of contributions to conservation organizations that attempted to influence legislation, unlike private companies that could expense their lobbying efforts.[54] The proposed Bill of Rights also included procedural rules and legislation for a wide swath of environmental concerns: the fencing of public lands; the restriction of mining claims in wilderness areas;

the preservation of wild rivers and wetlands; protection against dams; and "conserving natural beauties, scenic trails, trout streams, and the like" in the face of highway expansion.[55]

Percolating through many of these later Douglas writings was his plea for citizen action and education. He recalled the legacies of Wordsworth, Thoreau, Leopold, and Muir, "witnesses" in favor of nature.[56] Though the "Bill of Rights" moniker was a bold approach, Douglas's instincts were confirmed in later landmark legislation crediting the importance of the public interest in environmental decisions and the expansion of hearings and agency transparency.

Predicting Doom and Disaster

With the passage of time, Douglas became more pessimistic about the environment. In *The Three Hundred Year War: A Chronicle of Ecological Disaster* (1972), he lambasted federal agencies as public enemies and criticized industry for influencing government regulation. "The wild West is only a myth," Douglas lamented, because smog, the roar of jeeps, and small motorized vehicles ("tote goats") invade "the edges of wilderness." He quoted Ogden Nash in the same spirit, while criticizing legal loopholes over billboards that became the blight of the federal highway system:

> I think that I shall never see
> A billboard lovely as a tree
> Perhaps, unless the billboards fall,
> I'll never see a tree at all.[57]

Douglas rested his hope on fostering "more and better citizen participation in the political environment and a better method of citizen input." An "enlightened citizenry" would become "patriots without a price tag," Douglas noted, quoting environmental writer Michael Frome.[58]

Though he didn't predict global warming, Douglas wrote of an ecological holocaust that would come from threats as diverse as throwaway bottles, toxic pollutants, strip mining, and unchecked "technology and the profit motive."[59] Harkening back to how the United States had ravaged the environment since colonial times,

Douglas chastised America for putting its "priorities [in] an overseas war, not the Three Hundred Year War at home."[60]

This pessimistic view of the future was on full display in what Douglas called "a melancholy book," *Farewell to Texas: A Vanishing Wilderness* (1967).[61] Six years of field research led him to indict federal agencies, oil companies, cattle and timber barons, and the Texas establishment as "modern Ahabs"—an allusion to the biblical king cursed by God for his greed. Though Douglas had deep affection for the Lone Star State, having first gone to the Hill Country with Lyndon Johnson in the 1930s, preservationists there faced a key structural challenge. In contrast to other western states, Texas had retained control of its unappropriated lands when it joined the Union in 1845. That resulted in comparatively few federal enclaves, meaning that the usual resort for conservationists— federal protection—was not the panacea in Texas.[62]

Douglas returned to Texas in the 1960s on a whim, accepting an invitation for an outdoor adventure from Jim Bowmer, a local attorney whom he had never met. When they finished their trip to Santa Helena Canyon in Big Bend National Park, which tracks the Rio Grande River and the border with Mexico, a reporter asked Douglas if his companions were close friends. In characteristic fashion, Douglas joked, "They are now."[63]

Douglas crisscrossed Texas for several years, often with Bowmer, who offered an inside view of Texas environmental politics and drew his attention to the Big Thicket wilderness, a unique ecosystem with a name that was a harbinger of the difficulty of securing its protection. Douglas brought the full range of his talents as a writer, outdoorsman, and political and media string-puller to bear in his advocacy for the protection of this east Texas wilderness, known as "the biological crossroads of North America" for the range of habitats and species that converge within its boundaries.[64] By the 1960s Big Thicket was already a shadow of its former size and, according to Douglas, was still being rapaciously stripped by greedy "Ahabs."[65]

Douglas allied himself with Texas senator Ralph Yarborough, providing him with the media appeal that the justice characteristically attracted. Local newspapers carried headlines such as

"Gathering Book Material: Douglas Goes into Big Thicket" and "Dignitaries Tramp Texas Trails."[66] Taking his public campaign private, Douglas also tapped his extensive contacts, dealing at length with President Johnson and Secretary Udall, whose promised action never materialized.[67]

The publication of *Farewell to Texas* prompted further attention to the urgent threat. Unfortunately, Lady Bird Johnson was incensed by the book title, telling Douglas at a White House dinner that "she did not like it at all. . . . The title should have some hope in it."[68] The criticism by Texans like Lady Bird is understandable in light of the closing line of the book: "When we think of conservation, nature trails, back-packing, camping, and outdoor recreation, we must say FAREWELL TO TEXAS—unless the dedicated minority receives an overwhelming mandate from the people."[69] President Johnson may not have loved the title either, but still he provided photographs and lauded the justice's efforts in his home state.[70]

Final resolution of the fight would not come until 1974, when President Gerald Ford signed a bill to create a Big Thicket National Preserve of 84,550 acres.[71] Douglas declared it "better than nothing."[72] His efforts in Texas represented the strategy of a seasoned mover-and-shaker on conservation issues, reflecting both the lessons he had learned and his increasing confidence in his ability to effect change.

The remarkable environmental canon that Douglas generated opened America's eyes not only to the solace of open spaces, but also to the risks of impending ecological disaster. Never one to put his eggs in one basket, Douglas embraced a strategy that leveraged his relationships with America's policymakers while heightening the importance of grassroots advocacy and spreading the word through books, articles, and speeches intended to stir the public to action. He spoke to, and he hoped for, the future of wilderness.

8

Dissenting on the Court

I haven't been much of a proselytizer on the Court. I've had the
theory that the only soul I had to save was my own.

—WILLIAM O. DOUGLAS

The Constitution and the Bill of Rights were designed to get the
government off the backs of the people—all the people.

—WILLIAM O. DOUGLAS

Though Douglas had craved approbation as a child, by the
time he took his seat on the Supreme Court, he had developed confidence that turned him into a champion dissenter.
He was sure of himself—sometimes too sure. In his thirty-six years
on the court, Douglas participated in more than 4,000 opinions and
authored 524 for the majority. He dissented in 486 cases, and in a
whopping 45 percent of them, he was the sole dissenter.[1] During the
1972 term alone, Douglas dissented in 80 cases—more than the *total*
number of cases the contemporary court decides in a term.[2] No other
justice has achieved such a record, though after Douglas retired, his
successor, John Paul Stevens, took on the role of champion dissenter.

Taking on the mantle of chief dissenter was an extension of
who Douglas was—an individualist, a loner, and a nonconformist.[3] Douglas's reflection on "how lonely had been the trail [he]
walked" simply described his go-it-alone approach, which he perfected on the court.[4] The privacy and quiet of the court suited his
continuing quest for solitude.

With nine justices, there are two magic numbers: four votes to accept a case for review and five votes to garner a majority. Review by the court is never a given; the court grants only a tiny percentage of the petitions for writ of certiorari. When the court declines review, it usually issues a simple, one-line denial order. In a small number of cases, a justice issues a dissent from denial of certiorari, signaling strong views that the denial was unjust, that the case was of considerable importance, or simply that nothing substantive should be read into the denial. However, along with his other dissents, Douglas used this vehicle to make a point and publicize his views.

Notes from the now public internal files of several justices reveal that Douglas's comments during conferences with the other justices following argument were often cryptic. He simply staked out a position rather than trying to convince other justices. That approach stands in stark contrast with a justice like Sandra Day O'Connor, who "wanted to cobble together majorities however she could."[5] Douglas saw no point: "I haven't been much of a proselytizer on the Court. I've had the theory that the only soul I had to save was my own."[6] In contrast to his wilderness work, where, as a consensus builder, he fostered alliances in Congress, the executive branch, the conservation groups, and the populace, on the court he took on the role of a chief dissenter.

Douglas's dissents were not simply ego-driven pronouncements. Although much has been written about the value of consensus on the court, dissents play a crucial role in the evolution of the law. Justice Ruth Bader Ginsburg explained that she used dissenting opinions as a tool to sharpen the majority opinion, convince others on the court to change their position, spark legislative change, and "appeal[] to the intelligence of a future day."[7] Commemorating the dissents by Douglas's successor, Justice Stevens's granddaughter realized that "Grandpa dissented with hope—hope that his colleagues would be persuaded, hope that readers would be moved, hope that future generations would change the law for the better."[8] Douglas had adopted these perspectives decades earlier: "Although I appreciate the value of unanimous opinions, I

Dissenting on the Court

will continue to speak in dissent when important matters are at stake." He was "all for unity" but only if it involved "no compromise on principles."[9]

For Douglas dissenting was an extension of the democratic process and the right to free expression. In one of his early First Amendment opinions, *Terminello v. City of Chicago*, Douglas recognized that the value of a rabble-rouser "is to invite dispute."[10] He espoused this free-speech value in many of his writings, such as *An Almanac of Liberty* (1954), *The Right of the People* (1958), and *Being an American* (1971). In typical Douglas fashion, he even took the position that "the right to dissent is the only thing that makes life tolerable for a judge on an appellate court."[11] In truth, given a choice, he would have preferred to be dissenting on the road or the river than on the court.

Douglas's dissents were not futile. According to Vern Countryman, one of Douglas's former law clerks and a noted professor, Douglas succeeded in moving the law toward his views in important areas of constitutional law such as speech, privacy, and equal treatment. Countryman did not include environmental law. For Douglas the future of the environment was an important matter that demanded a full airing, and he hoped his opinions would become a marker for future generations. As Countryman optimistically noted, "In the long view, if we remain a society of decent aspirations, we may expect more of the Douglas dissents to become the law of the land."[12]

Though the legacy of dissents is not something Douglas would eschew, he also made major contributions to American jurisprudence by authoring famous majority and concurring opinions. He championed free speech, argued against censorship, warned against secrecy in government in the Pentagon Papers case, reinforced the antitrust principle prohibiting certain kinds of exclusive dealing arrangements, and established that prosecutors must turn over all evidence that might exonerate a defendant.[13] Douglas also enshrined the right to privacy in one of his landmark opinions, *Griswold v. Connecticut* (1965), in which the court overturned Connecticut's ban on contraceptives. Although the Constitution does not explicitly mention privacy, Douglas wrote that the "specific guarantees in the Bill of Rights have penumbras, formed by emanations from those guarantees that help give them life and substance."[14] Scholars derided the decision, and Justice Clarence Thomas famously has a plaque in his chambers mocking Douglas's theory: "Please don't emanate in the penumbras."[15] While his approach was controversial, Douglas's message was prescient: in the internet age, the right to privacy is a mainstay of public debate.

Douglas, the Legal Realist

Douglas came to the Supreme Court with a background in legal realism developed during his years at Yale. In concert with the famous jurist Oliver Wendell Holmes, he believed that the law encompassed not only abstract rules, but also social and policy interests. But unlike Holmes's pessimism, Douglas's brand of legal realism was pragmatism undergirded by idealism. His student and later colleague Abe Fortas noted that Douglas was "of course, an idealist; but, for him, ideals are not abstractions; they are objectives demanding present fulfillment."[16] Douglas prioritized the practical impact on citizens.

Though sometimes labeled a romantic, Douglas might better be described as a romantic realist—one who wove literary references, descriptive language, and personal experiences into his opinions.[17] His decision establishing that "freedom of movement is basic in our scheme of values" surely reflected his experience as both a traveler in the wilderness and in the world to places as distant as Mongolia.[18] Similarly, dissenting in a case about a law school minority admission program, Douglas espoused the value of diversity, writing he knew "that many of the young Indians . . . offer competitive attitudes toward life, fellow man, and nature."[19] Douglas often invoked references from his literary heroes, Henry David Thoreau, John Muir, Walt Whitman, and Carl Sandburg, who was a friend. He contrasted the life of "one who of necessity rides [buses] and street cars" with "the freedom that John Muir and Walt Whitman extolled."[20] His decisions celebrated Thoreau for his trademark "sauntering"[21] and Sandburg as a "Fellow Hobo."[22]

Douglas wrote for the public and his legacy, not for his brethren or legal scholars who could distinguish his opinions out of existence.

Douglas's jurisprudence combined what he called "feeling intellect" with broad value proclamations, interspersed with minimal legalese and precedent.[23] Douglas "saw himself as different than judges who were fact and precedent bound."[24] He would rather make precedent than follow it, and he considered it "a healthy practice (too infrequently followed) for a court to reexamine its own doctrine."[25] This approach jarred traditionalists, who called Douglas an "anti-judge."[26] What a difference a half-century makes. A majority of today's Supreme Court did not hesitate to overrule a forty-year-old precedent, claiming *stare decisis*—the legal principle that issues should be decided based on precedent—"does not compel continued adherence to [an] erroneous precedent."[27]

Douglas came to embrace the view of Chief Justice Hughes that "at the constitutional level ... ninety percent of any decision is emotional. The rational part of us supplies the reasons for supporting our predilections." Douglas went even further, believing that "no justice ... was neutral." He further explained, "The Constitution is not neutral. It was designed to take the government off the backs of people."[28] To Douglas this was not a bad thing. Indeed, according to Murphy in *Wild Bill*, he once declared at a law school gathering, "I'm ready to bend the law in favor of the environment and against the corporations."[29] Although a professor at the Law School of Syracuse University later disputed that reference, the tenor of the statement is not inconsistent with Douglas's strong views on the environment.[30] On and off the court, Douglas fought to restrain government power and campaigned to keep the government from invading his beloved wilderness.

Dissenting for Conservation—Douglas's Environmental Cases

Douglas had a knack for transforming an issue into a legal principle. In 1967 he made one of the court's first references to "ecology" in an opinion that halted construction of the High Mountain Sheep Dam in Idaho.[31] Three years later, in opposition to a proposed highway through a Texas park, Douglas employed "environmental"—

marking the first time the word appeared in Supreme Court opinions in the conservation sense.[32]

Before the golden age of environmental laws passed in the 1970s, the Supreme Court faced environmental cases primarily in the form of private property disputes. Not much can be gleaned from Douglas's participation in these early cases, with one exception: in 1946, in an opinion authored by Douglas, the court recognized noise pollution as a legitimate claim for the first time—twenty-six years before Congress moved to protect the public against its health hazards.[33] In contrast, the district court thought that "the chickens will just have to get used to the noise."

Douglas's true foray into environmental law came in 1960, a period that coincided with the increase in his active lobbying and protesting for conservation causes. That year the court declined review of *Murphy v. Butler*, a case involving the deadly pesticide DDT; the challenge was brought by a noted ornithologist and residents of Long Island who were threatened with indiscriminate spraying of their lands. The Department of Agriculture had launched a campaign to spray more than three million acres of land to eradicate the gypsy moth. Despite significant evidence of damage to dairy farms, pastures, gardens, and orchards, the case was dismissed because there was no harm to human health, the spraying had already taken place, and "another wholesale spraying operation was unlikely."[34]

When the court declined to review the case, Douglas wrote a dissent to sound the alarm about the health effects of DDT, "not only to wildlife conservationists and owners of domestic animals but to all who drink milk or eat food from sprayed gardens." Douglas knew the threat of pesticides firsthand. He and Olaus Murie despaired of the unintended consequences of the Forest Service's spraying of sagebrush in Wyoming in an effort to bring back the grasses. As expected, the sage died, but "the ecosystem received a jolt"—the process brought "vast, incredible damage."[35] Douglas warned that DDT can cause various human blood disorders and "the mounting sterility among our bald eagles," citing extensively from scientific journal research and newspaper articles, including one by Rachel Carson, describing the chemicals as "an amazing rain of death upon the surface of the earth."[36]

In her 1962 pathbreaking book, *Silent Spring*, Carson recounted the DDT case, the Douglas dissent, and the unfortunate reality that the moths had reappeared despite the spraying.[37] Douglas later wrote an effusive review, calling the book "the most important chronicle of this century for the human race." His invocation of the cycle of life, rivers of death, dying birds, and infestation of estuaries and marshes echoed his dissent. He closed with a call for "a Bill of Rights against the 20th century poisoners of the human race."[38] That call foreshadowed his 1965 book, *A Wilderness Bill of Rights*. Unfortunately, as noted scientist Edward O. Wilson observed, banning DDT did not end "the war between environmentalists and exploiters."[39] Indeed, the debate about pesticides rages on, whether related to risks to the bee population, pest control technology, or sustainable agriculture.[40]

In other environmental decisions, Douglas underscored the need to consider environmental impact to determine whether more roads and dams were truly in the public interest. For example, Douglas authored the majority opinion in *Udall v. Federal Power Commission* (1967), which brought together his antipathy toward dams, his friendship with Stewart Udall, and his views on conservation.[41] The Federal Power Commission had granted two Northwest utilities licenses to build dams at High Mountain Sheep on the Snake River in Idaho, even though eight hydroelectric dams on the Columbia-Snake Rivers had already been built and a ninth had been approved. Udall, on behalf of the Department of the Interior, intervened in the lawsuit. He suggested that Congress consider federal government oversight over the project rather than leaving it to privately funded entities. He also urged postponement in order to assess the impact on fisheries. When these views were rejected in the lower court, Udall convinced the Supreme Court to take another look.

The appeal centered on administrative issues, but Douglas reframed the case as an environmental fight. He asked why "any dam should be constructed."[42] As an avid fisherman, Douglas understood how dams threatened wildlife sanctuaries and the spawning cycle of anadromous fish (salmon and steelhead), which come up-river from the sea to spawn.

The Commission's conclusion that "we can hope for the best" was not good enough for Douglas. Quoting Justice Holmes that "a river is more than an amenity, it is a treasure," Douglas zeroed in on the congressional charge to consider the "recreational purposes" of the river. "The test is whether the project will be in the public interest. And that determination can be made only after an exploration of all issues," which included "the public interest in preserving reaches of wild rivers and wilderness areas, the preservation of anadromous fish for commercial and recreational purposes, and the protection of wildlife." Because these issues were "unexplored in this record," the case needed to be sent back to the lower court.[43] Douglas invoked his knowledge of ecology and the importance of the public interest to manufacture the grounds for a second look.

After the decision was issued, Udall sent Douglas a hand-written note on official stationery:

Dear Bill—

Your opinion in the Snake River cases (which I read last nite) is a conservation landmark.

Congratulations.[44]

Udall deserved to celebrate too. It was the first time the court had rejected a license for a dam. The continuing fight led to the creation of the Hells Canyon Wilderness in 1975 as part of the Hells Canyon National Recreation Area.

Victories often eluded Douglas in his final years on the court, which were punctuated with dissents, several involving the National Environmental Policy Act of 1969 (NEPA). A landmark procedural statute, NEPA paved the way for environmental scrutiny of federal actions by requiring advance (ex ante) environmental assessments and environmental impact statements. In theory NEPA reinforced the point that Douglas had made in his Snake River opinion—

that environmental impact must be considered *before* an agency greenlights a development project.

Prime among NEPA's intellectual visionaries was Douglas's friend Senator Henry Jackson, who sponsored the legislation and defined NEPA's legislative mission to "fulfill the responsibilities of each generation as trustee of the environment for succeeding generations."[45] Environmental plaintiffs have had victories in the lower courts under NEPA, but despite high hopes for environmental law's "Magna Carta," remarkably the Supreme Court has never found fault under NEPA with the government's action.[46]

Douglas's first NEPA dissent in 1970 brought back echoes of the impetus for the C&O Canal fight: a proposal to build a highway through a park. The San Antonio Conservation Society and its members filed suit to block federal approval and funding of an expressway through 250 acres of city parklands after the state pushed forward with the project without performing the required environmental impact study. Eager to get approval, the state proposed going ahead with building the two ends, to be somehow connected in the middle *after* the NEPA requirements were satisfied.

Douglas was determined that the court review this new NEPA case. He explained to his colleagues that this petition for review should be granted because despite "the new Act," "no effort has been made to submit the plans for scrutiny under those new requirements."[47] With support from Justices Hugo Black and William Brennan, Douglas was one vote short of the magic four justices needed to grant a writ of certiorari and hear the case.

Douglas's scathing dissent from the certiorari denial began with his trademark approach of painting pictures of bucolic retreats that would soon be overrun with roads—in this case, a super six-lane expressway. NEPA did not apply just to wilderness areas, he emphasized, but also to "parks—the breathing space of urban centers." Douglas bemoaned the court's callousness toward the "awful ... consequences" of "urban sanctuaries [being] filled with structures, paved with concrete or asphalt, and converted into thoroughfares of high speed modern traffic." To him "the ruination of a sanctuary created for urban people [was] an 'irreversible and

irretrievable' loss," and thus the court passed on the most important case of the term.[48] After more litigation, the expressway was
finally built. Douglas would have been appalled to learn that the
Federal Highway Administration named it one of the country's
three most attractive urban freeways, a designation that he would
have termed oxymoronic and abominable.

The court considered only two NEPA cases on the merits during
Douglas's last years as a justice. Both cases involved a challenge to
administrative procedures by a group of law students that called
itself SCRAP (Students Challenging Regulatory Administrative
Procedures).[49] In an important victory for future public interest
litigation, the court unanimously concluded that the students
could bring the case as users of "the forests, rivers, mountains, and
other natural resources" of the Washington DC area who alleged
"specific and perceptible harm" that they personally suffered.[50]
Although Douglas was on board with this broad endorsement
of judicial access for the public interest, he dissented from the
court's tepid view of NEPA in both cases, writing that "Congress
did not intend that [NEPA] be a paper tiger." He excoriated his colleagues for ignoring the statutory directive that "environmental
considerations are, so far as possible, to shape all agency policies
and decisions."[51] Douglas pointedly reminded his colleagues—
and the public—that NEPA was "more than a technical statute of
administrative procedure"; it represented an urgent "commitment
to the preservation of our natural environment."[52] For Douglas
NEPA was quickly becoming a paper victory for the environment,
one without teeth.

Douglas continued to beat the NEPA drum by dissenting from
denial of certiorari in a series of other cases: construction of a spill-
way dam in Texas, a scheduled detonation by the Atomic Energy
Commission, a proposed seaward runway at the Honolulu International Airport, and "the rape of Appalachia for its precious coal."[53]
His frustration in getting the court to step up on NEPA cases echoed
his early years when he noted in his diary, "Hugo & I have had
quite a struggle getting certain petitions for certiorari granted."[54]

As a former regulator himself, Douglas was skeptical of the

expanding role federal agencies took in shaping America's environmental policy. Since the early twentieth century, the arid western states had bickered over the allocation of water from the Colorado River. When the court decided in 1963 that the Department of the Interior had the power under a federal statute to allocate the water, Douglas was quick to criticize the court for making "the dream of the federal bureaucracy come true, by granting it, for the first time, the life-and-death power of dispensation of water rights."[55]

Douglas's most biting indictment of agency solicitude to private entities came in *Scenic Hudson Preservation Conference v. Federal Power Commission*, a case stemming from the Federal Power Commission's licensing of a power project on Storm King Mountain on the Hudson River. Douglas did not share the court's view that the agency's decision should be reviewed under a highly deferential standard, as the commission lacked expertise in environmental matters. Blasting the commission's attempted post-hoc effort to comply with NEPA and the agency's "industry-mindedness," Douglas reasoned that tolerating the agency's afterthought impact statement rendered "the mandate of NEPA . . . only a ritual and like the peppercorn a mere symbol that has no vital meaning."[56] Douglas's view that the court should not rubber-stamp agency actions—though controversial at the time—is gaining currency in the contemporary debate over whether courts have abdicated their duty by giving such significant deference to federal agencies.[57]

As he entered his fourth decade on the court and the stream of NEPA cases began rolling in, Douglas was a seasoned justice, but he lacked the allies that would have helped him to become a beacon, or at least a player, in the environmental arena. One study scoring the justices for their devotion to "environmental protection" gave Douglas a 100 percent rating.[58] This accolade was no surprise, but it did not command majorities and was tempered by the fact that Douglas sat on only fifteen such cases before his retirement. Instead, Douglas did what he did throughout his career: he highlighted the value of nature and conservation and spotlighted for the public the need for transparency and the folly of giving blind deference to administrative agencies.

Dissenting for Culture—Douglas's Indian Tribal Cases

Douglas was an ally of Native Americans. In an early dissent involving treaty rights to Indian land title, he complained about the Indians' claims being lost "in the fine web of legal niceties" when a tribe's grievances should have been "settled by this court in simple justice to a downtrodden people."[59] Douglas's clerks summed up his perspective: "The Justice cared deeply for the underdog" and "the person at the bottom of the heap."[60]

In broad terms Douglas endorsed the conservation of culture, just as he urged the conservation of the environment. Often illustrating the value of ancient cultures by drawing on his experience growing up near the ancestral home of the Yakama (Yakima) tribe in Washington, nonetheless he admitted, "We who were raised in Yakima did not know the Indians well."[61] So it is curious that Douglas parlayed this limited experience into claims of expertise, insisting in one of his dissents, "I do know, coming as I do from Indian country in Washington."[62] Tellingly, when he asked his friend Chief Jim of the Yakamas to find a reed pot for him, the chief brought one that was unfinished. "We kept the pot unfinished," he said, "because the work of the Yakimas is unfinished—and so is the work of the Court on Indian matters."[63]

When Douglas joined the Supreme Court, Indian law was not an organized body of law and, unlike today, was not a discipline taught in law schools. Douglas's first Indian law opinion for the majority, *United States v. Santa Fe Pacific Railroad*, came in 1941, just two years into his tenure.[64] It turned out to be "one of the most important cases ever to reach the Supreme Court in the history of our Federal Indian law," observed Felix S. Cohen, who represented the Hualapai (Walapai) tribe in the appeal and authored the key treatise in Indian law.[65] The case is often cited for the principle that Congress could not extinguish aboriginal title without making a statement of clear intent, but more important, Douglas broke new ground by accrediting cultural history as a legal fact. Noting that the Hualapai tribe had been occupying the lands in northwest Arizona "from time immemorial," Douglas confirmed that a tribe's ancestral home determined the validity of its contemporary occupancy.[66] In so doing, "the case legitimized the very notion that indigenous histories are relevant to proving [a tribe's] land claims."[67] One historian even observed that "ethnohistory ... was conceived during the Hualapai case" by initiating legal inquiry into Indian history.[68]

During Douglas's tenure, fifty-two Indian cases came before the court. Of those, Douglas wrote majority, dissenting, or concurring opinions in fourteen cases. Of particular significance is that he dissented in the majority of cases where the result disfavored Indian claims.[69] But what does a champion of the environment do when conservation goals collide with tribal rights? Although Douglas considered Indians "noble ecologist[s]" whose aims aligned with conservationist goals, he did not rubber-stamp their petitions.[70]

Fishing rights cases made for especially stark collisions of values, for in Douglas's hierarchy of priorities, fish trumped other values in the service of the public interest. When the Tlingit Indians in southeast Alaska requested a reprieve from a state ban on their powerful fish traps, the court in *Kake v. Egan* (1962) permitted the use of these traps until the end of that year's salmon-fishing season but denied a longer extension.[71] Douglas dissented because he could not abide even the short extension the majority offered. To him the Tlingit's short-term need for salmon could not justify the long-term environmental harm. Douglas dubbed the Tlingit fish traps at issue—capable of capturing up to six hundred thousand salmon in a single season—euphemistically as "efficient," "which, by conservation standards, means ... 'destructive.'" He flatly rejected a purported right to use a "lazy man's device" that caused "notorious" and "devastating" damage in just a few months.[72]

For Douglas the fish, not the Indians, again prevailed in a series of cases concerning the Puyallup tribe in his home state. A treaty gave the Puyallups the right to fish for salmon and steelhead at traditional fishing sites "in common with citizens of the Territory." In *Puyallup Tribe v. Department of Game of Washington* (Puyallup I), Douglas resolved that the treaty provided the right to fish under the "in-common clause" but that the "manner of fishing" could be regulated "in the interest of conservation" because maintaining a steady salmon population was "a question of public importance." He added a proviso: so long as "the regulation meets appropriate standards and does not discriminate against the Indians."[73] The opinion left undefined the scope of "conservation," the extent of "standards," and the meaning of the anti-discrimination language. But the result was clear: for purposes of conservation, the state could regulate the use of set nets, often referred to as gillnets, by Indians.

When the case returned to the court five years later in *Department of Game of Washington v. Puyallup Tribe* (Puyallup II), Douglas concluded that the state ban was, in fact, discriminatory. The restrictions applied only to net fishing, which Indians alone employed, but nothing was said of hook-and-line fishing, which "granted, in effect, the entire run to the sports fishermen." The issue for Douglas was "the problem of accommodating net fishing by the Puyallups with conservation needs of the river." This difficult balancing left no room for differing treatment. Douglas sent the case back to the Washington state court to adjust the formula to ensure fair apportionment, with an important caveat: "Rights can be controlled by the need to conserve a species; . . . the Treaty does not give the Indians a federal right to pursue the last living steelhead until it enters their nets."[74] Once again, conservation values rose to the top.

The denouement came in 1977, after Douglas retired. His successor, Justice Stevens, echoed Douglas's instructions to the state court: fairly apportioned Indian net fishing and sport fishing "[cannot be] effective if the Indians retained the power to take an unlimited number of anadromous fish within the reservation."[75] Indian law scholar Ralph Johnson believes that Douglas, without doubt, would have joined the decision because it "met his concern to conserve the fish while at the same time upholding the off-reservation treaty rights of the Indians."[76] Though Douglas's jurisprudence would cement his legacy as a defender of Indian rights, in the end, his environmental priorities won out.

Douglas was a lone wolf not only on the Supreme Court, but in his chambers as well. Because he was a quick writer, knew where he wanted an opinion to go, and wrote with such amazing speed, with few exceptions his law clerks were neither central to his chambers nor to his opinions.

The judge-clerk relationship is special. Clerks come to a court with sterling credentials, usually at the beginning of their legal careers. They look to the judge as a mentor, and the judge typically relies on them for research, sometimes for opinion drafting, and often as a sounding board. The relationship reflects more about the judge than the clerk. With Douglas, as with much of his life, it was more complicated.

Being a law clerk is a demanding position, and serving as a law clerk to Douglas was no picnic. To begin, because Douglas off-loaded the interview process to law professors and former clerks, his new clerks did not meet him until he returned from the summer recess, several months into the clerkship. In keeping with his sense of anti-elitism, he typically hired clerks from law schools in the West to counter the virtual monopoly that schools like Harvard, Yale, and Columbia had on clerkships.[77] For most terms Douglas had only one clerk, even when the other justices had two or three. Instead of extra clerks, Douglas had two secretaries, whom he kept busy with answering daily correspondence, mostly related to his conservation work, books, and travels. Douglas hired the first female law clerk at the court in 1944, though he didn't hire another one until 1972.

The chambers atmosphere was often tense; outbursts by Douglas were not unusual. It was a year likened to boot camp with the justice as the drill sergeant.[78] When he suspected that a clerk had written in a volume of the *United States Reports*, he threw the book out the window; luckily, no one was on the patio below. Though the clerk denied annotating the book, he got a lecture: "Books are treasures. They are temples of intellect. They must be cherished and protected."[79]

The secretaries often warned clerks that Douglas might fire them, even twice, but advised them just to show up the next day and nothing more would be said.[80] Once Douglas sent a letter to a clerk suggesting that he was not up to the clerkship and should consider leaving; the clerk stayed on anyway and later became a noted law professor. Douglas claimed he was a harsh boss because he expected clerks to be toughened up for life and the difficult practice of law. He told them, "There is nothing personal in what I say or do—this is the rough and tumble of law as it is practiced in courthouses across the nation."[81]

Douglas's independence defined the roles in his chambers. The clerks were legal researchers and citation checkers, not collaborators. His files were filled with reams of yellow, legal-sized pages of his opinion drafts. The clerks checked the drafts for accuracy and filled in details; only rarely did they get to try their hand at opinion drafting. When they branched out and rewrote paragraphs, Douglas reminded them, "If and when you are ever appointed to the Supreme Court then you can write opinions. But in the meantime, I will write the opinions."[82] And he did.

Douglas's allocation of roles also evinces his legendary work ethic, laser focus on the task, and prodigious output. He had a reputation as "one of the workhorses of the Court" and was legendary for the speed of his writing.[83] One clerk said that he "never met a mind that was faster than [Douglas's]."[84] At times Douglas may have been too fast; his writing has been criticized as slipshod, and his opinions were called "plane trip specials" that read "like rough drafts" dashed off on cross-country flights and thus were "easy to ignore."[85] The general comment among clerks was that Douglas wrote the best first drafts of anyone in the building but then never wrote a second draft. But given his work ethic and speed, one clerk said Douglas could easily have written every opinion for every justice and still have had time for his books and treks.[86] Harkening back to his view that the court work took only four days per week or less, in some years Douglas left Washington to head to Goose Prairie before the term was finished—an extraordinary slap to his colleagues, who remained for last-minute revisions and consultations.

Dissenting on the Court

Although conservation was a second, and time-consuming, career for Douglas, it is curious that his clerks knew virtually nothing about his meetings with politicians, lobbying efforts with the federal agencies, and even many of his protest activities. Interviews with the clerks revealed genuine surprise about the range of his conservation advocacy, despite the voluminous documentation in his files. Except for a few isolated occasions, like asking them to look up "the height of a Himalayan peak," Douglas typically did not ask clerks to research environmental issues, follow up on the many conservation-related requests he received, or assist in speechwriting.[87]

Douglas's sometimes abusive and formal persona contrasted with times when he was generous and personable. Many clerks respected and admired him both as a justice and a mentor.[88] More than one clerk expressed becoming "one of his most ardent admirers" by the end of the clerkship. Even though he wasn't warm, he could be "charming."[89] The clerks also were treated to his laconic humor. When a clerk asked about hiking in the Canadian Rockies, Douglas quipped: "You get on the John Muir Trail in California."[90] In a custom welcomed by the clerks, Douglas would sometimes call them into his office late on Friday afternoon, open the well-stocked liquor cabinet, pull out a silver tray and a glass of Scotch, and reminisce about his time with Roosevelt or his years on the court. Once, while he was out of town, the clerks had a few drinks from the bottle. When Douglas got back, he held up a bottle and asked: "What do you think?" Quick on his feet, one of the clerks answered, "I think you need some more booze."[91] Douglas often took them to lunch on Saturdays, and they and their families reveled in less frequent invitations to his house for dinner or a special occasion. When he was impeached, the former clerks rallied to Douglas's defense and, the night he died, they came to the hospital to be with Cathy.[92]

Despite the stern and formal work environment, many of the clerks relished their experience and have dined out for years on stories of Douglas's antics. Their experiences are so varied and their stories so rich that it is worth reading their collected recollections, including those from a 1989 celebration of the fiftieth anniversary of Douglas's appointment.[93] At a 2003 reunion in San Francisco,

Marshall Small, a clerk in 1951–52 and then a partner at the Morrison Foerster firm in San Francisco, recorded their reflections for the *Journal of Supreme Court History*.[94] In 2019, not long before he died, Small gathered the clerks again for what he said would likely be the last time. Cathy joined the group, and, as an invited guest, I observed that the feelings for the justice were warm and sincere. The assembled group of accomplished judges, lawyers, and law professors had taken his advice, which mirrored his own life: "Get out into the stream of history and swim as fast as you can."[95]

Silencing the Iconoclast and the Dissenter—The Failed Impeachment of Douglas

Douglas had the capacity, and perhaps even the need, to poke the beast. His opinions incensed many conservative politicians and academics. His private life, particularly having four wives—two of whom were under twenty-five years old when he married them in his older years—brought moral outrage from Washington's social circles. Even his conservation efforts drew pointed comment. Representative William Roth of Delaware criticized Douglas for giving a speech accusing the Army Corps of Engineers of "despoiling our natural resources ... while appeals against the government's environmental policies were pending on the Court's docket."[96]

To those who viewed Douglas as an intractable radical, it became clear that his voice had to be silenced, although they would not succeed. Douglas was threatened with impeachment more than once. The early efforts quickly fizzled, but the threat of impeachment in 1970 had to be taken seriously. It was a grave challenge to judicial independence, and for Douglas it was personal. It is exceedingly rare to impeach a judge. Of the thousands who have served as federal judges, the House of Representatives has impeached fifteen, and the Senate, which has tried only one Supreme Court justice, has convicted only eight judges.[97]

Congressman (later President) Gerald R. Ford of Michigan led the 1970 campaign against Douglas. Apart from taking aim at some of his writings, including the perceived leftist bent of the book *Points of Rebellion*, the heart of the charge was not his court or conservation work. Instead the charge was that Douglas was being paid handsomely as president of the Albert B. Parvin Foundation, a charitable organization that promoted democratic leadership in Latin America but one that opponents associated with an international gambling fraternity. What appeared to irk the politicians was that Douglas had received $96,000 over nine years for his service on the board, compared to his judicial salary of $396,000 over that period. At the time, other justices had served on foundation boards and been compensated for making speeches. Although the court had no rules on outside income, Douglas provoked a political storm that led to an investigation and a 924-page subcommittee report.[98]

Douglas took the impeachment effort seriously but never lost his sense of humor. When Attorney General John N. Mitchell made him aware of the impending impeachment inquiry, Douglas responded: "Well Mr. Attorney General, saddle your horses."[99] His former law clerks and friends rallied around him. Douglas put together a superstar legal team and hunkered down for a long fight. He wrote a note to Justice Black: "My blood pressure is 140 over 70—which indicates that the Bastards have not got me down."[100] Still, there were signs that the impeachment distressed Douglas. His first instinct was not to fight but to resign at the end of the term.[101] Even after the publication of the subcommittee report, Douglas continued to expect more attacks.

Ultimately, no impeachable wrongdoing was found or presented; instead, detractors relied on innuendo, as when Ford accused Parvin of being "a bridge between communism and organized crime on the one hand, and Douglas on the other."[102] Apart from the optics that Parvin was part owner of the Flamingo Hotel in Las Vegas, a venture supposedly backed by famous Mafia bosses, there was no evidence that Parvin was himself involved in organized crime. Douglas's alleged connection to organized crime was wholly fabricated. After a six-month-long investigation, the legislative committee voted to take no action, and the talk of impeachment quieted—although Congress later imposed limits on outside income for federal judges, including Supreme Court justices.[103]

Douglas survived the impeachment, but only a few years after the inquiry died down, he retired from the court in 1975 at the age seventy-seven. The cause was not the impeachment effort but physical impairment from a stroke. Ironically, it was President Ford who accepted Douglas's resignation with "profound personal sympathy," disingenuously gushing that Douglas's "distinguished years of service are unequalled in all the history of the Court."[104] That sardonic statement was true in more than one sense. To the clerks who were saddened by the news, Douglas told them to "keep faith in the rule of law not only for our own people, but for the people of the world."[105]

But Douglas did not leave the court easily. When his friend Charlie Reich urged him in the summer of 1975 to retire for health reasons, Douglas resisted, telling him, "Even if I am only half alive, I can still cast a liberal vote."[106] Despite official retirement just a few months later, Douglas took the unorthodox view that he could still sit on cases in which review had been granted while he was on the court. He wanted to serve up a last liberal vote. When the other justices rebuffed his effort to lodge an opinion in an important campaign finance case that was finalized after he retired, he chastised them for "political maneuvering." Eventually and reluctantly, he was forced to reckon with the reality that there could be no "tenth justice."[107]

It is fitting that Douglas's last opinion, issued just one day before he retired, arose from an environmental challenge to the site of a nuclear power plant. The justices all agreed that the Atomic Energy Commission's reasonable interpretation of its regulations was entitled to deference.[108] Douglas filed a concurrence to critique the conundrum of an agency charged with both regulating nuclear energy and protecting the public interest. He warned that the commission's ability to change the rules at any time, "even after the hearing is over," would greatly weaken "the protection afforded by the opposition of scientific and environmental groups." And "the entire federal bureaucracy," not just the agencies, had the responsibility to fight "the abuse of which the public needs protection."[109] Knowing that it would be his last, Douglas fired one final salvo for conservation.

9

The Trees Are Still Standing—The Backstory of *Sierra Club v. Morton*

The river as plaintiff speaks for the ecological
unit of life that is part of it.

—WILLIAM O. DOUGLAS

I speak for the trees, for the trees have no tongues.

—DR. SEUSS, *THE LORAX*

Though not his last opinion, just a few years before retirement, *Sierra Club v. Morton* (1972) became Douglas's most famous environmental dissent. Far from the rarified atmosphere of the Supreme Court lies Mineral King Valley, a twelve-mile glacial valley in California's southern Sierra Nevada Mountains.[1] The valley floor is an expanse of open, verdant meadows, which give way on both sides to steep, rocky slopes dotted by clusters of ancient conifers. Above the tree line, sheer granite walls form sharp, towering peaks. The valley nurtures beautiful flora along with abundant and diverse wildlife, including black bears, mule deer, yellow-bellied marmots, and an array of freshwater fish. No commercial services are available. In short, Mineral King is a true wilderness.

The battle to preserve Mineral King's pristine and unspoiled vistas began in the mid-1960s, when the U.S. Forest Service spearheaded a project to develop a year-round ski resort. Once the ambitious proposal by Walt Disney Productions was selected, the Sierra Club sued to stop the project, and the case ended up in the Supreme Court. The court rejected the Sierra Club as a plaintiff because the club did not claim that either it or its members would suffer an injury from the proposed resort. Douglas's masterpiece dissent offered a rallying cry for opening the courts to protecting nature, arguing that "the river as plaintiff speaks for the ecological unit of life that is part of it."[2] Concern about ecology, in Douglas's view, should permit "environmental objects to sue for their own preservation."[3] The query "Should trees have standing?"—one of the iconic phrases in American jurisprudence—reflected Douglas's passion for nature and cemented his reputation as the environmental justice. His dissent reinforced the proclamations he had made in *A Wilderness Bill of Rights*, in which he extolled "those whose spiritual values extend to rivers and lakes, the valley and the ridges, and who find life in a mechanized society worth living only because those splendid resources are not despoiled."[4]

How Douglas's dissenting opinion came to be is the story of a cascade of serendipity and good luck, stemming from his long-standing relationship with the Sierra Club and the happenstance of a then unpublished law review article that landed on his desk while the case was pending.[5] The case highlights the jousting among the justices and the ethical tensions surrounding judicial conflicts of interest and ex parte contacts with the court. Although a slim majority of the court ruled in favor of Walt Disney, in the end the Magic Kingdom of the mountains never materialized. But the notion that trees have standing began to take root.

Threats to Mineral King Valley

The real trouble started when Walt Disney, often viewed as a benign force for entertainment, received final approval in 1969 to develop a $35 million resort in Mineral King Valley. Construction plans included fourteen ski lifts, a chapel, an ice-skating rink, convenience shops, restaurants, a conference center, two large hotels, a heliport, a 60,000-square-foot underground facility to house resort services, and a Country Bear Jamboree. Disney estimated that the resort would attract 2.5 million visitors within its first year of operation—approximately the same as today's annual traffic at Bryce Canyon National Park in Utah.[6]

Opposition arrived quickly and forcefully. Objectors pointed out that Mineral King's official name was, after all, the Sequoia National Game *Refuge*. They insisted that development would desecrate the valley and destroy its ecosystem. In no time, bumper stickers reading "Keep Mineral King Natural" appeared across the region.[7]

Until the mid-1960s the Sierra Club had not opposed modest development in the valley, believing it would make the area more accessible.[8] The club became alarmed, however, when the scope of Disney's plans appeared to make significant commercial development inevitable. The Sierra Club refused to back down. In June 1969 the club sued in the U.S. District Court for the Northern District of California.[9] A young San Francisco lawyer, Leland R. Selna Jr., was chosen as lead counsel, and he represented the club all the way to the Supreme Court.[10] The club sued as a membership corporation with "a special interest in the conservation and sound maintenance of the national parks and forests and particularly lands on the slopes of the Sierra Nevada mountains."[11] Apart from claims that the proposed resort violated federal preservation laws and regulations, the Sierra Club wanted to stop federal officials from granting approval for Disney's development. The issue that dominated the litigation was whether the Sierra Club had the right to bring these claims—that is, whether the club had standing to sue.

In crafting its complaint, the club had to make a strategic choice. As all good lawyers know, to obtain standing to sue, some actual or imminent injury or stake in the outcome of the controversy is required. Under the standard at the time, to obtain an injunction, a plaintiff needed to demonstrate "a strong likelihood or reasonable certainty" of winning and an irreparable injury, balancing the potential damage to both parties.[12] The Sierra Club worried that if the court were to stop the project, the harm to Disney would outweigh any injury to the club or its members. In contrast, the injury to Mineral King's *environment* would likely eclipse any harm to Disney. For that reason, the Sierra Club alleged only that the environment of Mineral King Valley would suffer injury; it did not claim any injury to the club itself or its members.

Sierra Club's counsel, describing the internal debates as "tortured," recognized the peril of this approach, but "[it was] a risk the Club wanted to take." The club "was not saying the valley had standing but it was saying the irreparable harm was to the valley" if it were to become "the pathway to get to the resort."[13] At first, this bold strategy worked. The district court granted a preliminary injunction, writing that the Sierra Club was "sufficiently aggrieved to have standing as a plaintiff." The court topped off the opinion with this reminder: "The court is not concerned with the controversy between so-called progressives and so-called conservationists. Our only function is to make sure that administrative action, even when taken in the name of progress, conforms to the letter and intent of the law."[14] With environmental law just coming of age, the decision was published in the first volume of the *Environmental Law Reporter*.

The government quickly appealed—and won. In September 1970 the Ninth Circuit Court of Appeals reversed the judgment of the district court, determining that there was "no allegation in the complaint that members of the Sierra Club would be affected by the actions of [the government] other than the fact that the actions are personally displeasing or distasteful to them." The court noted: "We do not believe such club concern without a showing of more direct interest can constitute standing in the legal sense."[15]

The Sierra Club was undeterred. On November 5, 1970, the club petitioned the Supreme Court for review.[16] Douglas's relationship with two institutions—the Sierra Club and the *Southern California Law Review*—would shape both his role and his legal theory in the case. This case was made for Douglas, and Douglas was made for this case.

Justice Douglas and the Sierra Club

Douglas had been a Sierra Club life member since his resignation from the board in 1961. That was where things stood until December 2, 1970, when Douglas suddenly wrote to the president of the Sierra Club to abdicate his lifetime membership: "The problems of the environment are so numerous and so great and the Sierra Club is, or may be, in many of them. Nobody knows what the future will bring forth. I do not want to be disqualified in cases which come before the Court. *I am not thinking of any case in particular.* I have not seen one here, nor have I heard of one which is on its way."[17]

The notion that Douglas was not "thinking of any case in particular" strains credulity. According to an unsigned, undated memorandum in the Douglas case files at the Library of Congress, Douglas did check with the Clerk's Office the day before authoring this letter to see whether there were any Sierra Club cases currently on the docket and was erroneously told "No," although the Mineral King litigation had been pending for years, and the petition for certiorari had been filed a month before Douglas's letter.[18] Also, as the court's "circuit justice" assigned as liaison to the Ninth Circuit, Douglas regularly attended the circuit's judicial conferences, and he would almost certainly have been aware of key decisions coming to the Supreme Court from the Ninth Circuit Court of Appeals.[19] More likely, knowing the case was coming to the Supreme Court, Douglas wanted to participate, prompting his out-of-the-blue renunciation of the life membership eight years after resigning from the Sierra Club board.

Douglas maintained a close relationship with the Sierra Club throughout the 1960s, a period that was punctuated with continuing correspondence between Douglas and various club executives. Douglas had meticulously saved club communications and kept up with the club's docket. In particular, he kept a 1969 board report on litigation announcing that "Sierra Club standing to sue has taken a decided turn for the better with the recent decisions in *Sierra Club v. John Volpe* and in the Disney case," specifically referencing "cases such as *Sierra Club v. Hickel* in which the plaintiff has non-commercial interests and is suing to preserve a public interest."[20] And just months before oral argument in the Mineral King case, Douglas communicated with the club about wilderness status for the Cougar Lakes area in Washington State. Perhaps he saw that controversy as divorced from the Sierra Club case pending in Washington DC, thus permitting him to coordinate with the club while at the same time considering its separate appeal.

In addition, news of Disney and the Mineral King development had been percolating in the press for some time. Indeed, Douglas later acknowledged in his dissent that although he had not visited the area, he "[had] seen articles describing its proposed 'development.'"[21] Contemporary articles had also appeared in the *New York Times*, the *National Observer*, the *San Francisco Chronicle*, the *Fresno Bee*, and the *Los Angeles Times*.[22] And Douglas's long-time pal, Stewart Udall, had highlighted Mineral King in a *Newsday* article citing the Mineral King decision and commenting that "some courts have grown surprisingly receptive to ecological arguments."[23] It would have been nearly impossible for Douglas to remain oblivious to the imminent Sierra Club suit.

Douglas's extensive ties, both formal and informal, with the Sierra Club raise the kind of ethical questions that continue to command the attention of lawyers and scholars.[24] In thinking about potential conflicts, Douglas focused on his Sierra Club board membership a decade earlier, while glossing over the question of appearances and his ongoing support of and connection to the club. At the time, Supreme Court justices had a guiding ethics statute from 1948 regarding disqualification—the precursor to today's 28 U.S.C. § 455—and, of course, were always bound by their oath to "faithfully and impartially discharge and perform" the duties of judicial office.[25] The 1948 statute directly raised the question of appearance of a conflict that would "make it improper," in the opinion of a justice, to sit on the appeal. Although this version of the statute did not put in sharp relief the obligation to recuse when a justice's "impartiality might reasonably be questioned," as today's version makes explicit, the sentiment was certainly on the table.[26] Indeed, maintaining the "appearance of propriety" standard has always been important in terms of public confidence in the judiciary.[27]

Once Douglas overcame the potential actual conflict, whether he considered the *appearance* of a conflict, we will never know.

We do know that he was not insensitive to conflict issues. At the time he married Cathy some five years earlier in 1966, she said he was "getting very concerned" about conflicts and that he was "less and less active" in environmental causes because he felt "it would present an actual or apparent conflict."[28] He wrote that he had "hiked or in other ways protested certain government projects. In such cases the protester should not sit as a judge because he has at least a partial commitment on the merits."[29] The implication that it would take activism of this sort to merit disqualification reflects a somewhat cramped view of the requirements for recusal.

According to William Alsup, a clerk for the 1971–72 term and now a federal judge in San Francisco, Douglas's relationship with the Sierra Club meant that "the big question surrounding this case was whether Justice Douglas would participate—it was a source of gossip around the Court." Without consulting his clerks, Douglas decided to be on the bench during the argument, with the possibility of recusing later.[30]

The Supreme Court's Opinion in *Sierra Club v. Morton*

Morton was both historically and legally important. The Supreme Court Historical Society lists it as one of the significant arguments of the Warren Burger Court, and it has been enshrined as a "golden age classic" of environmental law.[31] Lawyers and judges nowadays are accustomed to seeing the Sierra Club in federal court, but *Morton* was the club's first appearance as a party before the Supreme Court, although it had earlier filed briefs as amicus curiae.[32] The case also forced the court to confront incongruities between traditional standing doctrine and the relatively new—and ever-evolving—field of environmental litigation.

On February 22, 1971, the court agreed to hear the Sierra Club's appeal.[33] Perhaps Douglas's concerns about conflicts informed his vote on whether to grant review: he did not take a position and simply said "pass."[34] He participated in the justices' conference without being forced to confront his ethical dilemma because Justices Hugo Black, Harry Blackmun, William Brennan, and John Marshall Harlan II voted to grant the petition. With only four votes required to accept review, the case was set for argument.

At oral argument, Justices Potter Stewart, Burger, and Blackmun dominated questioning of Selna, the Sierra Club's counsel. Blackmun pressed on whether the record showed that some of the Sierra Club members used Mineral King, a point on which Selna acknowledged there was "no direct testimony." Stewart, looking for a principle to cabin the club's claim, asked Selna how far his argument would go. Trying to save the situation, Selna pleaded: "We do not ask the Court to be wide open." Douglas, by contrast, was pretty quiet, pursuing only one point: during the government's argument, he pointed out that Michigan had "enacted a law to give standing down to [a] citizen and [the] environment" and that a pending bill in Congress "did the same thing." Solicitor General Erwin Griswold shot back: "I am not sure that even Congress has the power to create a case or controversy" necessary to confer standing.[35]

A few days following argument, the justices convened for their confidential deliberations in the court's impressive conference room. By tradition, they spoke in order of seniority. Brennan was most expansive and gave a broad explanation of his position, noting that "[the] case did not require the Sierra Club to present the issue as broadly as it did" and that the club had not pleaded any injury in fact. While the Sierra Club could have introduced evidence of members' use of Mineral King, it chose to skip that step. Brennan went on to highlight precedent that "allows aesthetic as well as economic factors to be taken into account." Brennan concluded, "I would not decide the broad question if we need not. I would reverse and remand." Justice Stewart, who would author the majority opinion, was direct and succinct: "I cannot agree with the district court; I agree with the court of appeals. I would be willing to decide the broad question and remand this, but I would prefer to affirm."[36]

We now know that by the time of the conference, Douglas had already produced a first draft of his dissent, and yet he curiously passed instead of offering his view. Blackmun's notes from the

The Trees Are Still Standing

conference are particularly revealing on the question of a potential conflict of interest: "Justice Douglas initially passed when it came his turn to vote and then later explained that he might recuse himself from the case because he had been a member of the Sierra Club for 10 years, and lately an honorary member, though he had resigned years ago."[37] Apart from veiled criticism of Douglas's role in the Sierra Club, one clerk later reported that there was a "negative feeling" among some justices that the Sierra Club had set up "a test case to try to transform standing doctrine" and recognized that its standing argument would be stretching the limits.[38]

Stewart circulated his initial draft majority opinion eight weeks after conference, and Douglas circulated his dissent the same day.[39] Chief Justice Burger and Justices Byron White and Thurgood Marshall joined the final opinion, which affirmed the Ninth Circuit in a 4–3 decision.[40] Justices William Rehnquist and Lewis Powell, who had joined the court in January 1972, after the retirements of Justices Black and Harlan, did not participate in the decision.

The court decided that the Sierra Club lacked standing to sue because it did not allege that the club *itself* was injured by Disney's planned resort.[41] Stewart explained that the club failed to "meet the prevailing constitutional requirements of standing" and instead seemed to rely on a "zone of interests" test that Douglas had announced in two recent cases.[42] Declining to clarify the meaning of the term "zone of interests," however, Stewart noted simply that broadening the categories of the necessary "injury" is fundamentally different "from abandoning the requirement" that plaintiffs be injured at all.[43] The court did not completely shatter the Sierra Club's hopes, however, and in fact offered some advice: just a week before publication, Stewart inserted a footnote indicating that the decision did not prevent the Sierra Club from amending its complaint in the district court.[44]

One commentator questioned why Marshall joined the opinion. As a civil rights advocate, he was not "sympathetic to calls to restrict standing in the federal courts."[45] Marshall's papers don't shed any light on this question, but he was not persuaded by an impassioned recommendation by his law clerk, who argued that "if conservation groups cannot sue, then *no one* can sue to protect interests clearly within the zone of interests protected by the statutes invoked."[46]

Justice Blackmun's Dissent

It is surprising that Justice Blackmun's dissent generally goes unmentioned in the legal annals, despite its being equally as passionate as Douglas's sentiment. Although Blackmun was never tagged as an "environmentalist," he was "always a lover of nature," often walking in Theodore Roosevelt Island National Park, and over time, "a reliable vote in favor of environmental interests."[47]

Blackmun's case file reflects his careful analysis before argument. Foreshadowing his dissent, Blackmun posited, as had Justice Marshall's clerk: "If petitioner has no standing, who conceivably does?"[48] His eloquent argument for nature highlighted "the Nation's and the world's deteriorating environment with its resulting ecological disturbances."[49]

Just as Justice Stewart had offered in his late-added footnote, Blackmun would have allowed the Sierra Club to amend its complaint to allege some sort of injury to the club or its members.[50] As a second option, he would have permitted "an imaginative expansion" of the traditional concepts of standing.[51] In conference, he hinted that his view was a product of emotion, acknowledging that he was "reaching for a position" resulting from desire "in the interest of Sierra Club members to sustain their standing."[52] Because an actual individual user would be unlikely to challenge the project, Blackmun queried: "Are we to be rendered helpless to consider and evaluate allegations and challenges of this land because of procedural limitations rooted in traditional concepts of standing?"[53] That stirring inquiry was largely forgotten in the face of Douglas's visionary dissent.

How Justice Douglas's Dissent Came to Be

Douglas's dissent, one of the most famous and passionate in Supreme Court history, stemmed from his heartfelt belief that the courts should open their doors to citizen challenges. He reasoned that the question of "standing" would be "simplified and also put neatly in focus if we fashioned a federal rule that allowed environmental issues to be litigated before federal agencies or federal courts in the name of the inanimate object about to be despoiled, defaced, or invaded by roads and bulldozers and where the injury is the subject of public outrage."[54] In other words, Douglas favored a rule that would recognize Mineral King Valley *itself* as the plaintiff for purposes of standing.

In piggybacking on his earlier writings, Douglas was affected in part by Aldo Leopold's view of nature as an ecological community united by "the land ethic." According to Leopold, "The land ethic simply enlarges the boundaries of the community to include soils, waters, plants, and animals, or collectively: the land." If this concept were applied to standing, Douglas believed, "then there will be assurances that all of the forms of life," including inanimate, natural objects, "will stand before the court—the pileated woodpecker as well as the coyote and bear, the lemmings as well as the trout in the streams."[55]

Douglas owed even more of the constitutional theory underlying his dissent to an article in an upcoming issue of the *Southern California Law Review*. Landing in Douglas's lap just as he put pen to paper, Professor Christopher Stone's argument that inanimate objects could have standing found its way into the dissent through a combination of strategy and serendipity.

The Genesis of Stone's Article

Douglas received Stone's article as a consequence of his agreement to write a preface for the *Southern California Law Review*'s first "Law and Technology" issue.[56] This was not an unusual commitment—Douglas often wrote for law journals, and this was a simple assignment that he could dash off quickly. In the fall of 1970 the law review's editor sent Douglas a tentative list of contributors, which did not include Stone. The editor informed Douglas that manuscripts would be sent in Spring and Summer 1971.[57]

The Law and Technology issue likely would have faded into history were it not for an off-the-cuff remark Stone made during a property class. Speaking "beyond his notes," he floated the idea that a river could have its own persona and have standing. The students' reaction was derisive, to say the least; they thought that he had "gone too far."[58]

But Stone decided to keep going. He pondered, "What would it take to give a river its own existence? What does it mean to dole out rights to non-humans?" To test this theory, he needed a case with a standing issue, an object that had its own damages. The legal reference librarian at the University of Southern California quickly came up with the Ninth Circuit's Sierra Club case, which by then was headed to the Supreme Court.[59] The match was perfect, according to Stone: "This [case], it was apparent at once, was the ready-made vehicle to bring to the Court's attention the theory that was taking shape in my mind. Perhaps the injury to the Sierra Club was tenuous, but the injury to Mineral King—the park itself—wasn't."[60]

Stone decided to write an article, so he sat down with the editor-in-chief of the *Southern California Law Review* to figure out how to get the article to the Supreme Court or, more specifically, to Douglas—who would likely lend a sympathetic ear. Ultimately, Stone and the editor elected to shoehorn the article into the upcoming technology issue. The coincidence that Douglas was writing a preface for that next volume was too good pass up, so Stone quickly drafted the piece.[61]

In Stone's view, his article, "Should Trees Have Standing?—Toward Legal Rights for Natural Objects," conceived of "other ways of looking at nature that others had not considered."[62] He observed that inanimate objects are often parties to litigation—for example, ships in matters of maritime law or corporations in most civil matters.[63] In other words, Stone believed that conferring rights on inanimate, natural objects—such as valleys, meadows, rivers, lakes, and even air—would not be extreme or unprecedented. Stone further concluded that economic and social policy favored bestowing such rights.[64]

On November 17, 1971—perhaps not coincidentally the day of the argument in *Sierra Club v. Morton*—the editor sent Doug-

The Trees Are Still Standing

las "brief synopses of the articles which will appear in the issue" and offered to send the "full text" of the articles if that "would be more helpful." The editor advised, "Professor Stone's draft has not yet been edited but because of its extraordinary nature, we are sending along a draft of the first 60 paragraphs." Alongside technology-themed articles like "Personal Liberty and Behavior Control Technology" and "Freedom, Responsibilities and Control of Science," the Stone piece on legal rights for objects in nature was decidedly out of place.[65] It was Stone's article, however, that most interested Douglas. Douglas "got a jump in looking at the article," and his dissent ultimately echoed Stone's thesis.[66]

Curiously, no one raised an ethical concern that sending a targeted legal missive to a single justice while this appeal was pending could be seen as a violation of the rule against *ex parte* (one-sided) contact. The other members of the court did not have the benefit of the draft article, which referenced the pending litigation and named the Sierra Club and other organizations as appropriate advocates for the environment.[67] To be sure, law professors and others often file briefs as friends of the court in high-profile cases, but those submissions follow the Supreme Court's rules on the filing of amicus curiae briefs.[68] The Stone article fell well outside the deadline for filing an amicus brief, but its arrival over the transom would have a monumental impact on Douglas's dissent.

Professor Stone's Article and Justice Douglas's Dissent

Douglas and Stone shared a rationale for granting standing to inanimate objects—inanimate objects, such as ships and corporations, are sometimes parties in litigation. These principles mirrored the Stone excerpt that Douglas had in hand at the time of the first draft. In language that Douglas echoed in his dissent, Stone wrote: "The river as plaintiff speaks for the ecological unit of life that is part of it," and "that is why these environment issues should be tendered by the inanimate object—itself."[69]

Douglas wrote the first draft of his dissent in about two hours on the day of the oral argument.[70] This means that the law review editor's November 17 letter to Douglas and its multiple enclosures had not arrived when Douglas wrote that first draft. But, as luck would have it, Richard Jacobson, one of Douglas's law clerks who did not work on the case, had been a protégé and friend of Stone. As Jacobson put it, "I know how WOD [William O. Douglas] knew about Chris Stone's article. I am the culprit."[71] Jacobson likely received an earlier summary directly from Stone or the law review and then passed it on to Douglas before the argument. Douglas was anxious to get the rest of the draft.

Once Douglas was privy to Stone's "trees have standing" theory, Douglas's secretary immediately wrote back to the law review editor: "Mr. Justice Douglas has your letter of November 17. The draft of Professor Christopher Stone, however, was not enclosed. Inasmuch as time is of the essence, the Justice would appreciate your getting off the copy of this to him right away."[72] The urgency was, of course, that Douglas was in the throes of drafting a dissent that relied on Stone's analysis. By February 1972 new footnotes referencing the article had been inserted into the draft, and Douglas cited the article in the final text of his dissent.[73]

The criticism that Douglas's opinions read like rough drafts did not hold true here. The opinion evolved and was polished over the course of twelve iterations, and it grew to include an assault on the Forest Service.[74] Douglas had a stack of books on his desk, which he directed his clerk, William Alsup, to "summarize into a series of footnotes to explain how the Forest Service has sold out to the logging industry."[75] As he had earlier, Douglas was keen to portray the Forest Service in a negative light. In Alsup's words, placing footnotes in the dissent was a "tough assignment." Because "there seemed to be no logical place to put the footnotes," Alsup wrote them in chronological order so they would make sense when read sequentially. Douglas offered a rare compliment: "This is great. This is just what I wanted."[76]

Alsup remembers the opinion as "the most beautiful thing [he] had ever read" and "so vintage Douglas."[77] Although the phrase "should trees have standing?" was decidedly Stone's creation, it became so closely associated with Douglas's dissent that it is often attributed to Douglas, in part because it so embodies his values, including those expressed earlier in *A Wilderness Bill of Rights*. Douglas would agree with Stone's assessment: "If you listen very, very closely, a tree will make the exact same sounds as a corporation."[78]

After Douglas's Dissent

Although hailed as a landmark standing decision, *Sierra Club v. Morton* was also a pivotal lesson in legal drafting. The Sierra Club had rolled the dice in its effort to tie standing to place, not people. In the wake of the court's ruling, the Sierra Club returned to the district court and, the second time around, claimed a sufficient injury to its members to confer standing on the club. When development of the proposed project stalled, the parties agreed to dismiss the case.[79] Disney was done. Ironically, like Douglas, Walt Disney had been a lifetime member of the Sierra Club. Although he died years before the litigation heated up, Disney might well have jettisoned the project long before the company chose to fight the fight.

An enterprising lawyer poked at the result in lyrical form:

> If Justice Douglas has his way—
>   O come not that dreadful day—
> We'll be sued by lakes and hills
>   Seeking a redress of ills.
> Great mountain peaks of name prestigious
>   Will suddenly become litigious.
> Our brooks will babble in the courts,
>   Seeking damages for torts.
> How can I rest beneath a tree
>   If it may soon be suing me?[80]

Although Douglas's views did not carry the day in *Sierra Club v. Morton*, the "rights of nature" movement has gained traction around the world. In 2008 Ecuador became the first nation to grant constitutional rights to rivers, forests, and other natural entities.[81] Several nations, especially in Latin America, followed suit with similar laws.[82] Uganda authorized nature's fundamental rights in a national act in 2019, and the Bangladeshi supreme court joined Colombia and New Zealand in recognizing the rights of rivers.[83]

In the United States conservationists have found some solace, albeit not necessarily success, by relying on Douglas's dissent in environmental litigation. The notion of standing for nature has yet to gain acceptance because of, as one commentator put it, "the attenuated, almost fictive connection between the interested or injured party and the threatened resource."[84] Not long after the *Morton* decision, lawyers in New York sued in the name of the Byram River but carefully skirted the standing issue by also naming an injured individual in their complaint. More recently, under the theory that corporations have rights, why not rivers, advocates unsuccessfully sought a judicial declaration of the legal and personhood rights of a Colorado river ecosystem.[85] While American courts have largely remained unreceptive and retained the standing hurdle, more than forty local governments have enacted ordinances that directly give nature rights. For example, Santa Monica, California, has declared that "natural communities and ecosystems possess fundamental and inalienable rights to exist and flourish." In an effort to target pollution, a town in Pennsylvania permits a civil enforcement action against a person or corporation that deprives an "ecosystem of any rights, privileges or immunities." That effort grew out of a grassroots organizing effort that Douglas would have lauded, as it mirrored his "Committees of Correspondence" to initiate local citizen action.[86]

Far more than an academic exercise, Douglas's notion of standing for inanimate objects was an expression of the themes of wilderness and sanctuary that were mainstays of his judicial philosophy. Douglas surely would have embraced the views of biologist and nature writer David George Haskell, who wrote that "because life is a network, there is no 'nature' or 'environment' separate and apart from humans. . . . The human/nature duality that lives near the heart of many philosophies is, from a biological perspective, illusory."[87] As for the Mineral King Valley itself, it remains among the most majestic examples of the values Douglas fought so hard to protect. It is now part of Sequoia National Park, where the trees remain standing.

10

Coming Home—Wilderness Bill Dissenting in His Own Backyard

Just because something is legal doesn't
necessarily mean it's right.

—WILLIAM O. DOUGLAS

The William O. Douglas Wilderness is designated in
remembrance of Justice Douglas' lifelong efforts to preserve
the Cougar Lakes area for the recreational
benefits of future generations.

—UNITED STATES CONGRESS

Douglas's independent, iconoclastic streak conjured up the nickname "Wild Bill," but his persistent work that lead to the 1964 and 1984 wilderness bills surely earned him the name "Wilderness Bill." No place symbolizes the breadth and ardor of his commitment more than his own backyard. And it was a big backyard, stretching from the Wallowa Mountains near the Oregon border to the Cascade Range running through Washington to the Canadian border. Two of the campaigns that marked Douglas's conservation career in the 1950s—fights to halt road building along the Minam River in Oregon and to achieve wilderness designation for the Cougar Lakes area in Washington state—were centered near his summer homes, a cabin on the Lostine River in Oregon and another at Goose Prairie. A third project found him protesting a copper mine atop a mountain in the North Cascades, some eighty miles north of Goose Prairie. All three campaigns brought together Douglas's unique brand of advocacy: using his position to celebrate sanctuary and solitude by chastising the Forest Service, tapping into political connections, advocating for public hearings, forming alliances with environmental groups, and stirring up publicity.

Defending the Minam River against the Forest Service—1959–1984

It is fitting that one of Douglas's early conservation fights centered on saving the Minam River, a pristine northeast Oregon waterway flowing from the glaciated Wallowa Mountains. Douglas was deeply attached to the area, which he first visited on a family vacation in 1939, months after joining the Supreme Court. He was lucky to meet Roy Schaeffer, a ranch owner who sold Douglas a parcel from his mining claim and who soon became his hiking, horseback, and nature companion. They were both rugged men of the West who teamed up to preserve the Minam. Douglas deemed Schaeffer "the man I would want with me if I were catapulted into dense woods anywhere from Maine to Oregon." Of Douglas, Schaeffer marveled, "The woods are a part of him."[1]

For the early part of his court years, Douglas's heart and soul were at home in this special corner of Oregon. He built three small log cabins. During the court's summer recesses, scores of petitions and other legal papers would arrive at the post office in the nearby town of Enterprise for the wilderness justice.[2] As he had with other unspoiled areas, Douglas called the Minam River "among the loveliest of [God's] creations."[3] The river's name came from the Nez Perce Indian word for a tall, carrot-leafed plant, apt for the almost mystical feelings that welled up in Douglas when he contemplated the wilderness.[4]

At the time, the logging industry was lagging due to decreased yield from private lands and its overdependence on streams to transport timber. When the Forest Service floated the idea of building roads to facilitate logging, it was ill-prepared to meet the wrath of Douglas and his conservation allies. Of the fifty-one miles of road that the Forest Service proposed building in Oregon, twenty-three would stretch along the Minam River.

Coming Home

For Douglas the Minam River controversy epitomized the fallacy of the Forest Service's multiple use policy: "There is no possible way to open roadless areas to cars and retain a wilderness. This is one diabolic consequence of the 'multiple use' concept as applied." Once again, Douglas saw the Forest Service regulars as "bureaucrats" whose "whims" would determine "whether the people will be left a rich wilderness area or a dust bowl of stumps."[5]

Once he got wind of the Forest Service's plans, Douglas went to Oregon senator Wayne Morse. As early as 1959 Douglas suggested that "a protest" from Morse "would be a powerful deterrent" to paving along the Minam River, but he warned that "our battle is about to be lost."[6] Morse gave the matter "emergency priority" and asked for Douglas's "help and counsel" in analyzing a Forest Service report on the region.[7] Recognizing that there were similar issues in Washington State, they looked to their northern neighbor's highly effective Senate delegation—Senators Jackson and Magnuson, known as the "twin towers of power."[8] Douglas worried that the hearings scheduled by the Forest Service would be a sham, so he suggested that Morse and Jackson join him to see Orville Freeman, the newly installed secretary of agriculture. Their mission: to get a "temporary stop-order on all these projects."[9] By then Douglas keenly understood the positive effect of high-level interventions.

Douglas also went directly to the conservation groups. The Sierra Club weighed in to stop commercial logging taking place under the Forest Service's "High Mountain" policy.[10] Through Olaus Murie, Douglas urged The Wilderness Society to use its "influence and support" against the proposed "act of desecration to log [the area] and fill it with a highway, campsites, toilets, fireplaces and everything else that goes with 'civilization.'"[11] Murie cautioned the Forest Service to consider the impact on future generations, counseling that "we are making history rapidly today, and what we do in a big way may not be approved in the time of the next generation or two."[12]

Local residents were energized. Schaeffer circulated petitions, and environmentalists formed Save the Minam, which was joined by the Federation of Outdoor Clubs, the Mazamas (a climbing club), the National Wildlife Federation, and the Idaho Wildlife

Federation.[13] Hoping to further mobilize locals, Douglas urged the Sierra Club to hire Michael McCloskey as a field organizer in the Northwest. At Douglas's suggestion, McCloskey wrote a brochure about the threatened Minam River.[14]

The early 1960s proved pivotal for the Minam effort. Two hundred people packed into the May 1961 hearings. Predictably, timber interests supported the roads, while a coalition of state officials, sportsmen, residents, and conservation groups favored wilderness preservation.[15] That summer Douglas spoke out forcefully against the Forest Service plan and couldn't resist adding, "Our forestry schools are geared primarily to serve the timber industry, and there is very little for the protection of recreation values."[16] Then the Forest Service—like many government agencies facing stiff opposition—vowed to undertake a survey, and the proposal began to stall. Even the timber companies began expressing reservations. Boise Cascade asked, "Why should we want a piddling few million boardfeet of logs in the Minam when we own 360,000 acres of timber?"[17] The Forest Service never had to answer that question.

Douglas's tactics paid off. In 1964 the Wilderness Act added 66,100 acres, including much of the Minam River watershed, to the Eagle Gap Wilderness. The fight was not quite over: the proposal was revisited in an additional round of Forest Service hearings in 1970. But public sentiment remained in favor of preserving the Minam as wilderness.[18] Finally, twenty-five years after Douglas had surfaced as a citizen advocate, the Oregon Wilderness Act of 1984 made the Minam truly safe.[19] The fight over the Minam was won, and Douglas's wish came true: "If there is to be a true wilderness in the Wallowas where trees are thick, where the canyon is filled only with the murmur of pine and fir and with the whisperings of water, roads must be kept out. The bits of wilderness left to us are only tiny islands. The Minam River is one."[20]

Saving Miners Ridge from the Kennecott Copper Company—1967

In 1967 the Sierra Club sponsored national advertisements reading, "AN OPEN PIT BIG ENOUGH TO BE SEEN FROM THE MOON." The headline was a play on the claim that the Great Wall of China

Coming Home

is "the only man-made object visible from the moon." The latter turned out to be apocryphal, as astronauts later documented, but the description of a proposed Kennecott Copper Company mine in the outback of the North Cascade Mountains made for good press, even if it too was an exaggeration.[21] Douglas's contribution to save Miners Ridge from devastation featured a variation on his celebrated protest hikes: a protest camp-in.

Miners Ridge, named for mineral exploration in the early 1900s, sits near the 10,541-foot Glacier Peak to the east of Boeing's huge airplane factory in Everett, Washington. North Cascade National Park now lies just to the north of the Glacier Peak Wilderness. The North Cascades, known as the "American Alps," feature some of the most remote and rugged mountains in the continental United States.

Douglas knew the Glacier Peak Wilderness well. Long before he took up the fight against Kennecott Copper, he saluted the region in *My Wilderness: The Pacific West*, describing how "the sun turn[s] the ice of Glacier Peak purple and then red," in a place full of "visions that halt one in his steps and produce sheer wonder and amazement." He rhapsodized on the glacial lilies, the monkey flowers, and the alpine larch, and he exchanged long, clear whistles with hoary marmots "for hours on end." He also evoked history with "[the snowberry] bush that Lewis and Clark brought back from their expedition and that Jefferson sent to Paris as a decorative plant."[22] As with *Of Men and Mountains*, one can feel Douglas's intimacy with nature and the wild in these passages.

Glacier Peak is not visible from any highway, in contrast with Mount Rainier, Mount Adams, Mount St. Helens, and Mount Hood, the other famed glaciated peaks of the Cascade Range. Offering an exaggerated but prescient prediction, Douglas worried that eventually the West Coast from Canada to Oregon "will be one continuous urban and suburban area.... The Glacier Peak area [known] for its rugged nature—its steep canyons, forbidding glaciers, and knife-edged ridges—will be a magnet to those who have daring and fortitude."[23] As usual, Douglas championed places that could be reached by foot alone.

But Douglas's most prophetic words brought him back to the region in order to protest mining. He lamented that "the Glacier Peak area is so little known it has few friends" and worried that the Forest Service would buckle under the pressure of "powerful interests to do their bidding." Always concerned about nature's "few friends," he wrote that the "aesthetic values" of places like Miners Ridge "are as much our inheritance as the veins of copper and coal in our hills and the forests in our mountains."[24]

By the early 1960s this inheritance was threatened by tensions between the Forest Service and the Park Service. Since 1906 conservation advocates had tried without success to turn part of the North Cascades into a national park. Douglas applauded efforts by Senator Magnuson to call for a study of the area, calling legislative action "just what we need."[25] Finally, in 1963, a study of the North Cascades was included in federal policy in the historic "Treaty of the Potomac" letter that Secretaries Udall and Freeman wrote to President Kennedy. The study group proposed, among many endeavors, the expansion of the existing Glacier Peak Wilderness (created in 1960) and the establishment of a North Cascades National Park.[26]

Conservationists, already concerned that little progress was being made on a national park, were distressed to learn that Kennecott was threatening to open a mine on Miners Ridge. The confluence of these events spurred the North Cascades Conservation Council, a powerful grassroots conservation group, and the Sierra Club into action.[27] The club heightened public awareness of this remote area by publishing a coffee table book, *The Wild Cascades, Forgotten Parkland*, filled with beautiful photographs and featuring a foreword by William O. Douglas. Douglas wrote that the "wilderness of the North Cascades is a national resource of the future, not merely a local commodity, and we need it all, as a nation."[28] His imprimatur—and his advocacy for a North Cascades national park—was noticed when the club circulated a copy to every member of Congress.

Critically advantageous for Kennecott, the Wilderness Act contained a significant compromise with respect to mining. Wilderness areas were protected from timbering, roads, mechanized travel, and uses incompatible with their pristine nature, but existing mining claims could be exploited without new restrictions, and there was a twenty-year grace period to prospect for new claims until 1984.[29] Kennecott planted itself squarely within this legal loophole—"like a buried bomb that hasn't been defused."[30]

The bomb went off when Kennecott started negotiations with the Forest Service in 1966. Kennecott had held claims in the area since 1954 and, to the dismay of its opponents, still had 2,650 acres of unpatented claims—that is, claims where it had a right to the minerals but not to the surface land.[31] Kennecott, the second largest copper mining company after Anaconda, justified the proposed mine on grounds of a copper shortage and military needs for the Vietnam War.[32]

Kennecott faced formidable opposition. Fred Darvill, a local doctor, gave voice to Douglas's message that an ordinary citizen can make a difference. He bought three shares of Kennecott stock and showed up at the company's annual shareholder meeting at New York's Biltmore Hotel in May 1967. Darvill displayed a painting of Image Lake, near the proposed mine site, and riled the audience further when he concluded, "Let it not be said and said to your shame, that all was beauty here, until Kennecott Copper came."[33] The next day his surprise appearance made national headlines. Darvill's commitment to the North Cascades continued, and he later wrote a Sierra Club hiking guide to the region.[34]

In addition to local zoning restrictions, Kennecott met resistance from Washington State's politicians. Senators Jackson and Magnuson, Congressman Lloyd Meeds, and Governor Daniel Evans all lined up in opposition.[35] In a show of unanimity with the other politicians, Secretary Freeman challenged Kennecott, claiming that the war effort wouldn't suffer because there were other copper deposits and citing the need to balance "a priceless, yet intangible, national treasure against ledger sheets and profits."[36] During a guest appearance at the Sierra Club's 1967 wilderness conference, Freeman sounded more like John Muir than a federal bureaucrat, describing "a timeless wilderness, a place where naturalness reigned, protected from humans' games." He warned, "We now have the power, literally, to move mountains. The next few years will determine if we have the wisdom to refrain from doing so."[37]

The Sierra Club was considering a video featuring Douglas, but when an ad hoc Statewide Committee to Stop Kennecott planned a "Camp-In, Hike-In" for August 1967, conservation groups saw an opportunity to showcase Douglas even more dramatically. Douglas would lead the hike. Heading a rag-tag group of some hundred hikers and dogs along the Suiattle River to a campground, Douglas looked the epitome of an outdoorsman, sporting a plaid shirt and well-worn hiking boots that had carried him thousands of miles. For his wife Cathy, this was a "christening," her first conservation protest.[38] In a short speech that made headlines, Douglas observed that "just because something is legal doesn't necessarily mean it's right," and he criticized "today's dollar economy in leveling our frontier."[39] He encouraged protesters to "appeal to the collective conscience of the corporate community represented by Kennecott Copper . . . so that the corporation will not become identified in the public eye with the vandalism of the kind that will result if this open-pit operation goes into effect."[40]

Despite rumors of violence, it was a peaceful hike, even when some of the loggers crashed the party. Unlike with the Minam campaign, Douglas's stalwart brigade did not necessarily reflect community sentiment as a whole. Support ran in favor of Kennecott, registered in signs reading "Hello, Birdwatchers—and GOODBY" and "WELCOME KENNECOTT." A newspaper reporter, "struck by the intensity of local support for the mining project," found the local residents "very unhappy with the out-of-towners who were there for the protest."[41] According to many locals, the preservation effort was elitist, not borne of the people and their economic needs. In the face of such antagonism, Douglas exhorted protestors to "save something for the spiritual side of man."[42]

With broader public and political support on the upswing, Congress acted in October 1968 to make the North Cascades National Park a reality.[43] Much of the park remains wilderness, where backcountry climbing and camping opportunities abound, but visitors can reach parts by car, recreational vehicle, or boat and take in views that "produce sheer wonder and amazement" and perhaps speak to "the spiritual side of man."

Leading the Cougar Lakes Wilderness Campaign—1950s–1984

The William O. Douglas Wilderness in the Cougar Lakes Basin represents the culmination of Douglas's lifelong conservation efforts. Perched almost a mile above sea level, with Mount Rainier's glaciered summit looming fifteen miles to the west, the region epitomizes the bountiful alpine lakes of the Pacific Northwest's Cascade Mountain Range. Douglas frequently felt called back to these mountains and trails of his childhood, a gateway to thousands of acres of wilderness. The Forest Service's 1930s designation of the area as "limited" meant it was only semi-protected and could be opened for logging and other development. For Douglas this uncertainty was an invitation to intervention.

Two of the most committed advocates in Douglas's wilderness army were his neighbors Kathryn "Kay" Kershaw and her partner, Isabelle "Iz" Lynn. Known as "the Double K girls" or "the Double K ladies," Kershaw and Lynn owned the Double K Mountain Ranch, 3,400 feet up the eastern slope of the Cascades, not far from Douglas's Goose Prairie cabin.[44] Kershaw, raised in Yakima, began construction on the guest ranch in 1945, after returning from service in Egypt during World War II.[45] Lynn had been the director of publications at the Red Cross's national headquarters in Washington DC, but after reading Douglas's ode to the Cascades in *Of Men and Mountains*, she decided to leave the "steaming jungle" and head west.[46] After two visits to Double K, she moved in as Kershaw's partner in 1952. With Kershaw's native knowledge of the region and Lynn's knack for whipping up "quintessential wilderness-edge cuisine," they built a successful tourist business in remote, rugged terrain.[47]

The Double K girls' second career as environmental activists kicked off in the late 1950s. When the Forest Service made a large timber sale six miles down the Bumping River from the ranch,

Kershaw and Lynn became "angry and articulate conservationists."[48] In 1958 they reached out to an Oregon wilderness group for suggestions on like-minded organizations to contact and quickly realized the need to contact "all of them."[49] Their investment in the cause was civic, not financial. Explained Kershaw, "As far as our business goes, if this fight is lost and the country is opened up by logging and roads, we will benefit financially because of more people, but we prefer less profit and an opportunity for people to enjoy it as wilderness."[50] They later curtailed large pack train trips because of the irreparable impact on campsites and lakeshores.

Before buying his first parcels at Goose Prairie in the early 1960s, Douglas made the Double K Ranch his home-away-from-home for hiking and horse pack trips. Sharing a love of the outdoors and an impatient individualism, Douglas and the Double K girls were a formidable team. When Douglas was in DC, the three corresponded frequently, planning protests and future hiking trips. When Douglas was in residence at Goose Prairie, Kershaw and Lynn could easily lure him to lunch on the ranch with "only the tinkling of the martini pitcher," along with their legendary carrot cake. The invitation went both ways. As he told them, "All you have to do is let me know the name and number of the bus that you are on. I will be down there with a cocktail shaker filled with dry martinis."[51] It is no surprise that he wrote in their guestbook, "Here's to Double K—wonderfully hospitable and not too damn respectable." In later years they invented a special drink for him—the Double K Driftpan—a concoction of vodka and gin with a whisper of vermouth that "was preserved in a special bottle that was kept more than half full at all times so it would not be apparent that anyone was drinking to the bottom of the bottle!"[52]

Together Douglas and the Double K girls embarked on a concerted and indefatigable effort against the Forest Service to stem the tide of "multiple use," which they considered thinly veiled code for logging. Kershaw and Lynn repeatedly submitted testimony to the hearings that Douglas spearheaded. "The national forests are our livelihood," they testified, "and people come from all over the United States, indeed, from all over the world, to see the wonders of the unspoiled country of the western United States. We take nothing from the forest, but we give something of the forest to all who come our way."[53]

Nothing spurred Douglas into action more than proposed logging and related road expansion because these threats would destroy the prospect of a future wilderness designation. In 1960 Douglas learned that Lawrence Barrett, supervisor of the Snoqualmie Forest, was behind an imminent timber sale out of Copper City, near an area called Blankenship Meadows, a prime stomping ground for elk. Instead of getting "corridors that surround existing wilderness areas preserved," the sale would bring the roads closer to the wilderness area and "put jeeps right on top of the Cascades."[54] Calling it "damaging and useless," Douglas implored Senator Jackson to halt the sale. In a prelude to Douglas's strategy and—not coincidentally—the Wilderness Act's crucial requirement of public hearings, Douglas requested a delay on road construction and logging "until we can get a public hearing."[55] Despite these efforts, a timber contract was signed the following summer, on a day that Douglas claimed "should be a day of mourning."[56]

Douglas tried, without success, to change Barrett's mind by going with him on a two-day hiking trip through the region. In correspondence Douglas lambasted Barrett, calling his logging plan "dangerously destructive" and "a formula which will lead ultimately to the ruin of the small bit of wilderness we have left."[57] When that didn't work, he took after Barrett personally, telling Senator Jackson that Barrett "is an intellectually dishonest person," and "unless we get rid of men like Barrett ... that whole Snoqualmie that you and I love so much is going to be completely chewed up, commercialized, civilized, motorized, and paved perhaps."[58] "In any event," Douglas grieved, "the end of the wilderness under that regime is pretty close."[59]

Lynn backed her neighbor and was equally dismissive of Barrett, calling him "a stupid, ignorant man" who took refuge in defending logging by saying, "I am the expert."[60] Neither Douglas nor the Double K girls (sometimes referred to by the Forest Service as "the blister sisters") were above harsh words, intimidation, and telling opponents what they thought. Douglas knew that candy-coated entreaties usually fell on deaf ears. A former Forest Service manager said, "They shared a unique wit, suffered fools lightly and appreciated the same quality of whiskey."[61] Just as the Forest Service ran for cover from the "blister sisters," Douglas Brinkley wrote that "dealing with Douglas on environmental protection laws had all the appeal of shaving with a blowtorch."[62]

While Congress continued its consideration of federal wilderness legislation, Douglas and his friends scrapped in defense of the Cougar Lakes area, enthusing about its "magnificent rugged country" and "the finest features of mountain wilderness."[63] Although the idea for wilderness protection had percolated for several years, in 1961 the Double K girls circulated a more formal proposal—"A Proposal to Establish a Cougar Lakes Wilderness Area"—to federal agencies and conservation supporters.[64] After Douglas tried unsuccessfully to get the usual groups fired up, he lamented, "Our dear people in conservation of course do not think in those terms of political action."[65]

Douglas served as a conduit between conservation friends in Washington State and professional connections in Washington DC. Following the concrete proposal for wilderness status, Douglas wanted to put the Cougar Lakes area on Secretary Udall's radar. During one of Udall's visits to Seattle, a wilderness supporter cornered him, suggested that Udall confer with Douglas, and "stuffed a copy of the proposal" and a map "in his coat pocket." This novel approach appealed to Douglas, who promised he would raise the matter with Udall when he next saw him.[66]

Despite these efforts, the Wilderness Act of 1964 failed to provide federal protection to the Cougar Lakes, which remained in "limited" status—a misnomer that allowed considerable commercial activity with little legal protection.[67] "Limited areas" were described as "stop, look, and listen" regions, where the Forest Service was to look first at their wild and scenic qualities before making development decisions that could lead to logging. In another hurdle for Cougar Lakes proponents, the Wilderness Act stipulated that new wilderness areas could not be added by administrative designation and instead required "a burdensome gauntlet of review and scrutiny: agency field surveys, study reports, local hearings, presidential recommendation, and congressional enactment."[68] One silver lining for Douglas was that the Forest Service lost its monopoly on wilderness designations.

Disappointed but undeterred, Douglas, the Double K girls, and other Cougar Lakes advocates redoubled their efforts. Publicly, Douglas advocated making a wilderness area out of the Cougar Lakes limited area and called to action like-minded environmentalists, even as he privately lamented he was but a "fly in the ointment" and bemoaned the "high hurdle" posed by the Wilderness Act.[69]

Douglas fell back on his old standby: a request to forestall imminent logging pending public hearings.[70] When he received no response from Freeman even as logging was set to continue, Douglas resorted to "plead[ing]" for a hearing and an opportunity to persuade Freeman and Ed Cliff, chief of the Forest Service.[71] In the end, by March 1966 Freeman's "polite rebuffs" convinced Douglas to give up on him.[72] Instead, he went back to Senator Jackson, whom Douglas believed could pressure the Forest Service into holding a hearing. He approached Jackson on two fronts: a personal meeting and a petition, drafted in part by Douglas and signed by as many Cougar Lakes devotees as possible. Attuned to Washington State politics, Douglas suggested organizers target citizens residing east of the Cascades—those closer to and more directly affected by treatment of the Cougar Lakes region.[73]

Douglas's focus on eastern Washington residents did not stop Mardy Murie, who leapt to action from Seattle, where she had moved temporarily after Olaus's death in 1963. She spoke with and wrote to activists and leaders, including Senators Jackson and Magnuson, and "wrack[ed] her brains for an inspiration on what more we can do about Cougar Lakes."[74] Douglas even volunteered to approach President Johnson directly if his meeting with Jackson did not bear fruit.[75] He initially believed it had not, writing that Jackson "is stymied on the Forest Service just like the rest of us." Nonetheless, Douglas encouraged supporters to continue the deluge of letters advocating either a hearing or a moratorium pending input from the president.[76] This was vintage Douglas, with his Committees of Correspondence idea in action.

Two weeks after his meeting with Douglas, Jackson conveyed to Mardy Murie his understanding that the Cougar Lakes area would "remain in its present status pending action" on the 1965 report commissioned by Secretaries Udall and Freeman.[77] When finally issued, the North Cascades Study Report was a disappointment, recommending four new wilderness areas, but again not Cougar Lakes. Even worse was the report's recommendation to declassify the Cougar Lakes' designation as a "limited area," a declassification that would permit the Forest Service to construct "campgrounds and other developed recreation facilities" and allow logging of "substantial acreage."[78] Cougar Lakes didn't have the same cachet as the other areas, in part because the Forest Service saw more opportunities for recreation and logging there. And at least one former Forest Service manager has suggested that the Forest Service resented Douglas's intervention and was sending a message each time Cougar Lakes was passed over.[79] Douglas's persistence and prestige may have backfired.

After a brief lull, Douglas returned to action in the 1970s, a time best described as lunches and letters. Douglas kept up his frenetic pace, dining with Freeman, Jackson, congressional aides, and Department of the Interior officials. Following the lunches, Douglas zipped off letters describing the mood of the officials and cannily trying to play them off against one another. Jackson remained unconvinced that urgent action was needed, but he was spurred on when Representative Stanley E. Saylor of Pennsylvania, one of the sponsors of the Wilderness Act of 1964, went ahead "full steam" on the Cougar Lakes wilderness project with a new wilderness bill.[80] Douglas invited Jackson to "come by Goose Prairie to shake hands with your friends" and see the region himself to understand the urgent need for protection. Declassification posed a real risk, though Freeman declared it would not happen without a hearing. Even so, a wilderness designation remained an uphill battle. "Limited areas" were not even mentioned in the Wilderness Act, and scores of truly primitive areas had jumped the queue for wilderness consideration.

By this time, the Double K girls had mastered the political process, but they still were chasing a firm victory. In reflection, Lynn wrote, "We have just completed a fourteen-year apprenticeship in the legislative process in this country. It was a frustrating, maddening, exhilarating, discouraging, and at the last, fruitful experience." Along the way, they "learned a vast amount about . . . ecology, good forestry practice, as well as the bad; and the workings of the U.S. Forest Service." Sounding a lot like Douglas, she acknowledged, "We have made many friends and a few enemies. Most important we are going to achieve our goal and we learned that the Democratic process does work—if you dragoon enough people into making it work."[81]

Despite Douglas's and the Double K girls' determination, legislative inertia was their nemesis. Though Douglas's outsized presence proved a catalyst during his lifetime, efforts to save Cougar Lakes came to a standstill and languished until after his death. More than twenty-five years after efforts began to preserve Cougar Lakes, the region had its day in the sun following public hearings in Seattle, Spokane, and Washington DC. With co-sponsorship from Senators Daniel Evans and Slade Gorton of Washington, Congress passed the Washington Wilderness Act of 1984, which— pursuant to the Wilderness Act of 1964—designated more than one million acres of wilderness in Washington State.[82] In a remarkable bipartisan effort, the Washington delegation met weekly to flyspeck the details and go over maps. By this time, wilderness designation had moved from individual designations to statewide plans. Senator Evans recalled, "We locked the staff out, not because they didn't do good work, but because we wanted to do it ourselves. We wanted our own stamp on the bill."[83] The largest wilderness designated was the 166,603 acres encompassing the "magnificent" Cougar Lakes area. As the Committee on Energy and Natural Resources acknowledged, "Douglas began hiking in this area more than 65 years ago and was active in efforts to preserve the Cougar Lakes Wilderness right up until the time of his death in 1980."[84] And that was true; Jackson's executive assistant recalls meeting with Douglas in his Supreme Court chambers and going over detailed maps and boundaries for several years after Douglas retired in 1975.[85] Douglas knew the land intimately, and he understood the political issues equally well.

Although Douglas died before the ultimate success of his tireless lobbying, four years after his death Congress formally recognized his contributions with a naming of his beloved Cougar Lakes wilderness area: "The William O. Douglas Wilderness is designated in remembrance of Justice Douglas's lifelong efforts to preserve the Cougar Lakes area for the recreational benefits of future generations. Through such designation, the Congress recognizes his persistent concern for the Cougar Lakes area, and his contribution to conservation efforts throughout the Nation."[86]

Hikers, horse riders, and bicyclists today can also enjoy the eighty-mile William O. Douglas Trail, a "story path" running from the William O. Douglas Federal Courthouse in Yakima west to Mount Rainier National Park.[87]

Of course it was not only Douglas who deserved credit: the Double K girls, Mardy Murie, and a host of supporters in Washington State and Washington DC played a vital role in protecting the Cougar Lakes area. Douglas's elevation of the democratic process—fair public hearings and open deliberation before an irretrievable altering of the landscape—allowed a cadre of dedicated advocates to play a role in the preservation of this wilderness, a living tribute to the citizen activism that Douglas inspired.

Coming Home

11

Lessons and Legacies

I would hope to be remembered as someone who made the
earth even more beautiful than it was when he came.

—WILLIAM O. DOUGLAS

Great things are done when men and mountains meet.

—WILLIAM BLAKE

Douglas blazed a trail that took him from outdoor enthusiast to conservationist to preservationist and—finally—to environmentalist. The monikers changed, yet Douglas remained constant in his passion and in his commitment to his values: preserving the wilderness, keeping the government off the backs of the people, protecting the rights of the dispossessed, using his public influence for the public good, and making America's democracy more transparent. Douglas gave his soul to nature because it brought him spiritual solace, free from judgment. This endeavor was more than the "weekend hobby" Douglas once described; it was a passion that consumed his life.[1] He gave his heart and his legacy to the American people and to the wilderness that he knew, once lost, would never be regained. Douglas was the rare visionary who decades ago understood the delicate balance necessary to sustain the planet.

East Meets West—A Tale of Two Washingtons

More comfortable at his cabin in Goose Prairie than in the marble halls of the Supreme Court, Douglas fancied himself a frontiersman. He was personally and politically loyal to FDR, to whom he owed his seat on the court, but he embodied Herbert Hoover's famous philosophy of "rugged individualism." His penchant for independence and self-reliance sometimes came at a cost, but it most often facilitated his fame and his effectiveness as a conservationist. He was a true adventurer who knew the mountains, especially those in the West, and he explored some of the world's most remote corners. He was resilient in the face of chronic financial instability, bouts of illness, and even a serious effort to impeach him. He was a dedicated New Dealer and Democrat but also a nonconformist whose focus on liberty, autonomy, and individualism reflected a libertarian bent. Whether on the road or on the court, Douglas routinely welcomed dissent, daring to take a contrary stance in order to advantage the environment.

As he chronicled in *Go East, Young Man*, Douglas's life story differed from the classic pioneer narrative of "Go West, young man" in one crucial respect: this young man went east. When he first arrived in New York City from Yakima, Washington, Douglas was an outcast, struggling to get by and get a breath of fresh air. Before long, however, his success in the East as a brilliant law professor and chairman of the sec forced him to defend the authenticity of his western roots. To earn Justice Brandeis's Supreme Court seat, Douglas had to convince President Roosevelt and the senators that he was more a cowboy than a Yale man. In truth, it wasn't a stretch.

In the decades that followed, Douglas seized opportunities to escape from Washington DC to the West. This clash between coasts shaped Douglas's career and the midcentury political landscape in which he moved. Before Douglas only four justices had come from the far West—one from Wyoming, one from Utah, and two from California.[2] Life and the culture in Washington DC remained a long way from Yakima.

Ultimately, Douglas's familiarity with both Washingtons—and the expanse of America in between—is what made him such an effective environmental champion. Admiration of nature was not enough; he was a man of action. His ability to move between the backwoods and the Beltway was a special gift. Developed over time, his political instincts, friendships, and access to decision makers, coupled with a nuanced understanding of the administrative state, made him a formidable advocate. Add to that an indefatigable drive to save the wilderness, Douglas, although once described as the "goofy bird" from the Supreme Court, became the national bandleader for the emerging conservation movement.[3] Although he didn't do it alone, embracing collective action from citizens and environmental groups, Douglas's participation in the conservation crusade was uniquely influential.

The Conservation Legacy

Transformation often begets dislocation. Just as Douglas straddled the coasts, the country shifted course with the westward expansion that began in the 1800s. With that movement came economic growth, population migration, and threats to the environment. Before Douglas was born in 1898, the explosion of railroads plowed through vast western territory at the expense of the environment. Then, at the beginning of the twentieth century, President Teddy Roosevelt, although a noted conservationist, undertook dam and reclamation projects needed to develop the West and supply water for agricultural growth and hydropower. As cars hit the road in the 1910s and 1920s, the government promoted a "See America First" campaign in the national parks. During FDR's long tenure, the focus was on overcoming economic depression and winning World War II. The era of big dams complemented these objectives. Like his cousin Teddy, FDR is credited with expanding national parks and forests and also was known for the environmental work of the Civilian Conservation Corps. After World War II phenomenal population growth and economic prosperity demanded more timber for housing and more highways for automobiles. More and more Americans began to view the environment as something beyond an economic resource, and an emerging middle class expected democratized access to nature. Wilderness was a precious commodity, though not one universally prized and prioritized. It was in this world that Douglas emerged as a national leader for conservation.

Most justices are not remembered for the opinions they authored, as the *United States Reports* are hardly beach reading for most Americans. Douglas stands out. Apart from his pathbreaking decisions on privacy, free speech, and criminal law, he authored several opinions that remain beacons for environmental law. His majority opinion in *Udall v. Federal Power Commission* helped stop a dam from destroying the Snake River. Douglas's insistence that the federal government consider the public interest in the preservation of wild rivers, wilderness areas, wildlife, and fish eventually led to the creation of the breathtaking Hells Canyon Wilderness in Idaho and Oregon. Nor should we forget Douglas's iconic dissent in *Sierra Club v. Morton*. The query whether "trees have standing" continues to bring both amusement and recognition. Douglas did not rewrite the law or move the earth, but in a single dissent, he articulated an enduring principle: nature deserves its day in court. Coupled with his earlier proclamation that aesthetic, conservation, and recreation interests should be recognized as possible sources of injuries that can be redressed by a court, Douglas brought home the importance of opening the courts to environmental disputes and arguably transformed the way environmental organizations see their mission—as standing for the trees.

Like a climate canary, Douglas sounded early warning signals about environmental hazards and "an acute ecological crisis."[4] Sometimes his alarmist rhetoric overshadowed the point he wanted to make, but his messages were trenchant. He warned of the perils of DDT and pesticides and of the health and environmental impacts of strip mining. He warned of "ghettos, poverty, and unemployment" of urban dwellers suffering from pollution and of a freeway being relocated to "roar through the Black community," foreshadowing the race-class divide in the environmental world. He warned that "if we make technology the predestined force in our lives, man will walk to the measure of its demands" and that "the voices of the mass of people [will not be] heard" by the government. And he warned that "radiation, air pollution, water pollution, [and] bulldozing the wilderness" would in the long run dilute not only the quality of life, but also life itself. Decades later,

Lessons and Legacies

many of these warnings ring true and have taken on new meaning and a sense of urgency.[5]

Long before the country first commemorated Earth Day in 1970, Douglas energized the public to think about the environment. His idea of Committees of Correspondence to petition the government for change was as old as the American Revolution. He spread the word through a monumental output of books, articles, and speeches, urging "a spiritual awakening." "Our people— young and old—must become truly activist—and aggressively so—if we and the biosphere on which we depend are to survive."[6]

Through his work on the Supreme Court, his writings, and his advocacy, Douglas galvanized the conservation conversation. Both literally and figuratively, he changed the wilderness landscape. While the West boasted many of the most famous national parks and wilderness destinations, the East, Douglas showed, also contained sacred pockets of nature worth protecting. He taught Americans that conservation was a concern that required a national crusade. For Douglas that crusade was a spiritual awakening: "When roads supplant trails, the precious, unique values of God's wilderness disappear."[7] And Douglas counseled all who would listen that something that was "legal" wasn't necessarily right.

The five million visitors who enjoy the c&o Canal each year have Douglas to thank. His outrage in 1954 toward the bearers of conventional wisdom—in this case the *Washington Post* and the National Park Service—unleashed a frenzy in Douglas that spurred two decades of environmental action. His insight that "roads, roads, roads" would be the downfall of wilderness protection prompted him to join forces with The Wilderness Society, the Sierra Club, and local conservation groups. Together they preserved remarkable pieces of America's heritage, including the last pristine coastline on Washington's Olympic Peninsula.

For Douglas preservation was not at odds with progress. When he denounced the Army Corps of Engineers and its dams, he was not opposed to innovation but rather in favor of saving wild rivers in Kentucky, Illinois, Massachusetts, and Washington. When he railed against the Forest Service for its "cut, cut, cut" attitude, he understood that timber harvesting was within the agency's legitimate province, but he wanted to make sure that "multiple use" did not eviscerate the mandate to consider wildlife and wilderness. When he chastised the Park Service, he reminded its leaders that he was among the agency's best friends. He sounded that alarm to save Florida's Everglades, Wyoming's sagebrush country, and a North Cascades mountaintop, understanding the intricate balance between nature and civilization. Recognizing that time was short and that wilderness areas were shrinking while the population was growing, Douglas put his heart into saving wild America, including the Washington backcountry that now bears his name, the William O. Douglas Wilderness. Senator Ted Kennedy summed up Douglas's remarkable career in the *Congressional Record*: "If we are to single out the one person most responsible for awakening this Nation to the hazards of inaction while our natural resources dwindled and decayed, it is to Justice Douglas that we owe our deepest gratitude."[8]

Citizen Justice Meets Judicial Ethics

Douglas lived his life outside of the Supreme Court as "a first-class citizen to the fullest extent compatible with [his] judicial duties."[9] Although the statement itself is not particularly provocative, Douglas's wide-ranging interpretation of what was "compatible" with his duties stretched—some might say eviscerated—notions of judicial propriety. He took the extreme position that being a citizen justice gave him latitude to expand his role from jurist to public environmentalist. And what he did for the environment, he "considered in the realm of public service."[10]

Judicial ethics and norms are more than feel-good declarations of adherence to a professional code. They are integral to the constitutional framework, which depends on judicial independence, the separation of powers, and confidence in the judiciary. American democracy runs on a tripartite system: Congress legislates, the executive carries out the law, and the judiciary interprets the law. Since 1789 justices and federal judges have taken an oath to "faithfully and impartially discharge" the duties of the office.[11] The guiding principles of modern judicial ethics—integrity, impartiality, and avoidance of the appearance of impropriety—serve as reminders of the public trust placed in judges, not only in their decision-making role, but also in their activities outside of the court. These principles sensitize judges to the public's expectation of the judiciary and are not only for the judges' benefit, but also for those judged and the public at large. While the specifics of judicial ethics codes have evolved, these basic principles have remained constant.

Against this backdrop Douglas lived his life not solely as a justice but as a citizen justice. Douglas's writings and speeches, which highlighted the legal and bureaucratic hurdles for conservation and extoled the beauty of wilderness, were well within the ethical canon that encourages judges to engage in civic and educational activities. Douglas was absolutely right that judges do not live in a monastery and should not be cut off from the community. Because judges provide valuable contributions to civic education, the commentary to the current Code of Conduct for Federal Judges recognizes that "complete separation of a judge from extrajudicial activities is neither possible nor wise; a judge should not become isolated from the society in which the judge lives."[12] Douglas embodied this sentiment to its fullest. There is value in judges being part of their communities rather than being separated from the public, perched on a pedestal. The challenge comes in striking a balance between isolation and immersion in advocacy to the degree represented by Douglas.

Some of Douglas's more flexible ethical views were a product of his time. For instance, in his era, aspiring to political office while sitting on the Supreme Court was unorthodox though not unprecedented. And even as Douglas pursued opportunities in the executive branch, he was aware that "partisanship . . . may at times give rise to a conflict of interest."[13] Nevertheless, his political ambitions collided with his role as a justice. Times have changed, however, and no justice since Douglas's day has tested the limits by seeking political office while on the bench. Modern ethics principles preclude political activity by judges and justices.

Some of Douglas's other views were plainly out of step even with ethical norms of his time. On one occasion he declared, "I'm ready to bend the law in favor of the environment and against corporations."[14] Impartiality has been a mainstay of the judicial system; bending the law against a particular party has not been, and it runs directly counter to the principle of fairness. Of course, dissent is always an option for a judge who disagrees with the majority or with prevailing law. But even a dissenting judge operates within a system bound by ethics. When a judge's personal views cannot be set aside in favor of a fair judgment, recusal in individual cases and ultimately retirement are the options. Douglas's provocative proclamation on bending the law remains remarkable on its own as a bold challenge to conventional propriety.

Another troubling declaration by Douglas related to his extrajudicial activities is the following: "Knowledge of a problem, prior advocacy or promotion of one side or another of a cause, long identification with a particular program for legal or constitutional reform do not disqualify a Justice."[15] Nothing is wrong with a justice having interests, or even passions, on particular subjects, whether international law, women's rights, separation of powers, the environment or even having "prior advocacy" experience. After all, every justice brings a lifetime of experience to the bench. Few questioned whether Thurgood Marshall, a strong advocate for civil rights before joining the court, could sit on race discrimination cases or if Justice Ginsburg, a prominent litigator on behalf of women's rights, could sit on sex discrimination cases. The rub comes in whether those beliefs are so fundamental and unwavering that they impair a judge's ability to be objective and affirmatively tilt the outcome of a case.

Douglas fell short in confronting whether a citizen justice could legitimately engage in public promotion of a cause and direct advocacy to the president, the Cabinet, executive agencies, and Congress. Douglas plainly diverged from accepted principles in this regard. His activity in the corridors of power presented several ethical concerns: use of prestige of the office, violation of the separation of powers, and the appearance of impropriety.

Nothing precludes justices from having friends in high places, and they often do because of their backgrounds and time in Washington. However, flexing those relationships by leveraging the prestige of the judicial office to lobby for special environmental interests crossed a line that was highly questionable then and would not be permissible today. In the same way, Douglas's identification as a national leader in the environmental movement blurred the lines between his role as a justice and his role as an advocate. Paradoxically, while pursuing a strategy of behind-the-scenes advocacy before federal decision makers, Douglas fought for public hearings before federal agencies so that important environmental decisions would be made with greater transparency, not behind closed doors. The "appearance of impropriety" should have given him pause and caused him to examine whether his relationships and his pressing for environmental actions violated his own transparency principle and undermined public confidence in the court.

Douglas chafed under ethical restrictions that he thought unnecessary. He rightly protested an effort to require the court to provide advance approval of books and articles. Such preclearance took aim at free speech rights that Douglas so cherished. When it was proposed that justices report outside income, he had the foresight to wonder why the justices did not have to report their royalties or stock holdings. Of course, his limited resources and lack of securities made this a moot question for him, though it offered him the opportunity to needle his colleagues. Although he voluntarily filed required financial declarations, he made a point to note at the bottom of his report on extrajudicial income that he "thoroughly disapproved of it."[16] After the Judicial Conference of the United States adopted a resolution precluding acceptance of "compensation of any kind" unless "in the public interest or exceptional circumstances," Douglas queried, "And whose public interest would control? Judges who had not been educated to the needs of ecology and conservation?"[17]

Much has changed with respect to judicial ethics since Douglas retired. Since 1978 justices must file detailed annual reports laying out their board memberships, gifts, debts, financial hold-ings, and stock transactions.[18] In 1991 the court adopted an inter-nal ethics resolution that focused on gifts, teaching, and outside employment. For example, justices are subject to limitations on the amount and source of gifts and generally may no longer receive honoraria. While receipt of royalties for their writing is permis-sible, other outside income is subject to a ceiling and essentially restricted to teaching.[19] In part these constraints are a result of the controversy engendered by the fact that Douglas and Fortas received considerable fees from private foundations.

Justices are increasingly under the public microscope as a result of information widely available through the internet and com-puterized case dockets. In 2004 the Sierra Club filed a motion requesting that Justice Scalia recuse himself from a case because of his duck-hunting trip with Vice President Cheney, who was a party in a case in his official capacity. In denying the motion, Sca-lia recounted historical examples of judicial friendships, from jus-tices dining at the White House with President John Adams and tossing "around a medicine ball" with Hoover's staff to Douglas's poker parties with Roosevelt. Though he cited no contemporary examples, Scalia argued that a "no-friends rule" would be "utterly disabling" and could end up disqualifying many of the justices in important cases.[20] The firestorm of publicity surrounding this con-troversy demonstrated the public concern over conflicts of inter-est and how the sheer appearance of impropriety can besmirch the court, even if an allegation is rebutted. One commentator claimed that the issue was not the connection between the court and "the other powerful elites that run the country" but the "col-lective disconnection of all of these elites, taken together, from the masses of ordinary citizens."[21] That is one charge that could not be fairly leveled at Douglas.

Although the Supreme Court is not formally subject to the fed-eral code of judicial ethics that binds lower court judges, Chief Jus-tice Roberts has responded to a push for more formal standards by emphasizing that "all Members of the Court do in fact consult the Code of Conduct in assessing their ethical obligations." Roberts has also highlighted an important ethics statute that applies to both federal judges and Supreme Court justices: 28 U.S.C. § 455 requires disqualification in "any proceeding in which his impartiality might reasonably be questioned."[22] That standard serves as a beacon for a fair and independent judiciary.

Douglas's push for transparency in government is now manifested in a continuing push for transparency in the judiciary. In some small way, Douglas may have unwittingly furthered this effort.

The Imperfect Hero

When we think of heroes, we often rhapsodize and elevate their stature, but in reality a hero need not represent perfection. Indeed, Douglas is the epitome of an imperfect hero. He was a driven, impatient man who set high standards for those around him. His work ethic was unparalleled, which made him a difficult colleague and a demanding boss, but put him on a horse or on the trail, and he was transformed. Along the way he stopped to talk with sheepherders, bartenders, postal clerks, hikers, and Boy Scouts. Those in the conservation world, including the many citizens who joined his informal conservation army, enjoyed that same personal connection. While Douglas's rough manner and disregard for social and conventional mores may have harmed his reputation and earned him detractors, his work for the wilderness also won him a wide swath of friends and admirers, not the least the Pacific Northwest William O. Douglas Society, a committed group of lawyers, hikers, academics, and foresters who continue to celebrate his memory.

Douglas's wife Cathy also remembers him as an "enormously charming and engaging" man who was "relaxed, funny, and adventuresome." To be sure, he could be difficult, but that was "not the Bill that [Cathy] knew." Because of the trials and tribulations of his childhood, he "had a sense of joy from life in his later years."[23] Cathy highlighted that "if experience was vital to Bill's understanding and interpretation of the law, humor was an essential characteristic of his experience."[24] Far too often, mention of William O. Douglas meets the retort that he is memorable as the justice with four wives. Yet even for members of the judiciary, marital status should not measure a career. That Diego Rivera had four wives hardly meant that he was not a great painter. So while the "four wives" sound bite may be a legitimate moral judgment, it should not define Douglas.

As three of his enduring friendships illustrate, Douglas's fiercely independent, and sometimes irascible, streak does not tell the whole story. He had a talent for friendships with those who understood his special connection with the outback and the lands of the West. Just as his Goose Prairie cabin became a refuge, his friendship with the nearby Double K girls, from the 1940s to the time of his death, was a leveler and a homing beacon. Like Douglas, they didn't suffer fools and were brutally honest. Together the three became "angry and articulate conservationists."[25] The Double K girls stabled Douglas's horses at their ranch, took him on extended pack trips, fixed drinks for him on the front porch of their lodge, talked politics and nature well into the night, and welcomed him home when controversy drove him out of Washington DC. They were beneficiaries of his trademark humor. And as he grew frail, it was they who miraculously convinced him to quit driving the back roads to Whistlin' Jacks, a nearby outpost with a telephone that was his lifeline to Washington.

Douglas also enjoyed a special rapport with Olaus and Mardy Murie, humble conservationists who achieved remarkable success is preserving the Arctic wilderness in Alaska. He admired them for their conservation zeal and their expertise in all things wilderness, and the feeling was mutual. Praising Douglas's literary contributions, Olaus wrote to Douglas, "I feel that mankind has important decisions to make, if he is to survive. Books like yours are a big help in having man make up his mind properly."[26] They corresponded frequently about wildlife and plant details; shared Murie's view that "the natural wilderness is a fragile thing: the material of poetry, art and music"; and spent countless hours on the trail as observers of nature and critics of the bureaucracy and its "razzle-dazzle."[27] The friendship was genuine and showed a different side of Douglas. After visiting the Murie Ranch in Moose, Wyoming, Douglas thoughtfully sent a check for three dollars for postage charges.[28] Some of the most tender moments came when they traded letters and phone calls about their illnesses. Not long before Olaus's death, Douglas proposed that the ranch be acquired by the Park Service and turned into a sanctuary "where a man or woman on a salary could go for a week or a month, or two months, to complete some writing or research on outdoor or recreational matters."[29] Years later that vision became a reality—the Murie Ranch is now a National Historic Landmark within Grand Teton National Park, where the Teton Science Schools carry on the environmental principles championed by Douglas and the Muries. Like Douglas, visitors today are treated to front porch conversations about conservation and rewarded with Mardy's famous Cry Baby Cookies. (The recipe is in the appendix; the key ingredient is a view of the Tetons.)

A third watershed relationship for Douglas was with Charles Reich, a Yale law professor and author of *The Greening of America*. Apart from their many hikes on the c&o Canal and their mutual interest in reforming regulatory oversight of federal forest land, their friendship of more than two decades was "a most mysterious and extraordinary one."[30] During their time together, Douglas was never willing to talk about the conflict between his judicial work and his environmental work, though Reich affirmatively celebrated the latter. Reich saw Douglas as loyal and nonjudgmental but was not blind to his foibles. Though Douglas was a "genius," Reich reflected that he also had a penchant for being "extraordinarily tactless."[31] Reich added, "His loneliness was ultimately similar to mine, and I was more, rather than less, his friend because I knew how isolated he really was. And so I could allow him his full greatness."[32] Reich recognized Douglas as a visionary who "had the ability to take you to the top of the mountain and show you the entire vista of future issues." Douglas was different: "You would come down from the mountain and lose sight of what you have seen. He never did."[33]

Even those with whom Douglas had difficult relationships saw the value of his legacy. His daughter Millie wrote, "William Faulkner once said to his daughter words to the effect that no one would ever remember her and they would always remember him." She found herself in the same position as she recalled that Douglas "wasn't a good father, at least by the standards of today." Yet she appreciated the values Douglas imparted to her and her brother, Bill. At the "top of the list of beliefs was honesty in all dealings" and, close behind, was the importance of the economy of words: "Never . . . use two words where one would do." Millie concluded, "Dad left us a legacy. Part of which belongs to the legal profession, part belongs to people who never knew him and part belongs to the personal side of his life, his family."[34]

Reconciling these multiple dimensions—husband, father, justice, public philosopher, icon, and conservation hero—was a lifelong challenge for Douglas.

Moving On—The Final Journey

Douglas resisted stepping down from the Supreme Court because he feared that in his absence, there would be "no one on the Court who cares for blacks, Chicanos, defendants, and the environment." When a stroke resulting in a deteriorating physical and mental condition left him no choice, he formally retired on November 12, 1975. At lunch that day, after the justices celebrated Justice Blackmun's birthday, the Douglas announcement sobered the mood.[35] True to form, Douglas's parting letter to his colleagues two days later invoked his relationship with nature: "I am reminded of many canoe trips I have taken in my lifetime. Those who start down a water course may be strangers at the beginning but almost invariably are close friends at the end." Speaking of "each happy memory of the choice parts of the journey," Douglas went on to say, "The greatest such journey I've made has been with you, my Brethren, who were strangers at the start but warm and fast friends at the end." He closed with the hope that those who follow "will leave these wilderness water courses as pure and unpolluted as we left those which we traversed."[36]

In a poignant letter to his law clerks, Douglas advised them to "keep the faith in the rule of law" and "in a system that allows a place for everyman no matter how lowly or how great." And as a

Lessons and Legacies

reminder of his enduring lessons, he counseled them to keep the faith "in a system which does not leave every issue of human rights to the ups and downs of the political campaigns."[37]

Douglas died five years later on January 19, 1980. Before his burial at Arlington National Cemetery, more than a thousand mourners came to the National Presbyterian Church in Washington DC to pay their respects. Sitting in the back pew of the church, surrounded by dignitaries like Chief Justice Burger, who gave the eulogy, and Abe Fortas, Clark Clifford, and Eric Sevareid, who offered tributes, Brock Evans, his friend who had been director of the Sierra Club's Washington DC office, scrawled this note: "My mind and heart keep coming back to those deep forests, to those wild rivers dancing in the sun, the line of great peaks rising out of the prairies in the soft first light of day. . . . These are the things of his beloved Northwest and mine. They were the touchstones of all his life . . . and of mine. These are the things he passed on."[38]

Douglas was a legal giant, a genius, a conservation hero, and a public philosopher. He always said he was "talking to the next generation."[39] Were he to look back on his remarkable journey, Douglas would despair at the environmental challenges facing the planet today, but he would delight that his relentless faith and intervention did leave "the earth more beautiful than it was when he came."[40] Many rivers are running free, choice pieces of wilderness are preserved, and the trees are still standing.

ACKNOWLEDGMENTS

The wealth of materials on William O. Douglas and those who intersected with his conservation life is overwhelming. Since I began this project on a lark in 2015 and later became more serious, I have been enriched by new friendships and the incalculable assistance of many people who were generous of time and spirit.

Olaus and Mardy Murie, naturalists, authors, adventurers, and conservationists, were the catalysts for the book. Their ranch has been a source of solitude and inspiration as I pursued the Douglas legacy and its connection with theirs. I thank the many friends—you know who you are—who have shared snowshoeing, cross-country skiing, dinners, campfires, cookies, and front porch stories at the Murie Ranch in Moose, Wyoming.

I owe a special debt to David J. Danelski, Supreme Court scholar and author of an upcoming biography of Douglas, for his guidance, thoughtful input, encouragement, and spirit of sharing. Likewise, Cathy Douglas Stone has been open and helpful throughout. The many Douglas law clerks whom I interviewed and those with whom I met kindly shared their stories. I am especially grateful for being included in their clerk reunion in 2019.

My research assistants from Stanford Law School, Magdalene Zier and Ben Higgs, have been invaluable and indefatigable.

The manuscript benefited from careful review, fact checking, and candid comments from academics, judges, lawyers, historians, and conservationists. My thanks to the following: Jonathan Aronson, Hope Babcock, John Q. Barrett, William Canby, Ross

Concillo, David Cote, Robert Deyling, Ben Hand, Mary Hartnett, Mike Hiller, Mike Hoge, Roger Kaye, Richard Lazarus, Michael McClosky, Lucas A. Powe Jr., David Martin, Judith Resnik, Adam Sowards, Scott Stern, and Joel Wacks. Special appreciation goes to William Alsup, Moon Hee Lee, Ben Shaw, and Stephen L. Wasby.

Tracking down sources and information has been a task made possible with assistance from Peter Arnold, director of the Yakima Valley Museum, and Douglas archivists Mike Hiller and Joe Miles; Michael Cary, former reporter for the *Anchorage Daily News*; Suzy Cyr, artist and resident of Bumping Lake; Steve Duerr, former director of the Murie Center; Donna Osseward, president, Olympic Park Associates; Paul Sutter, author of *Driven Wild*; and John C. Rumm, former curator of the Buffalo Bill Center of the West.

Goose Prairie, Washington, figured prominently in Douglas's life. Mike Hoge and Val Hughes, two of my former law partners, now own and are lovingly restoring the Douglas cabin. Mike has been especially helpful in making connections and offering his assistance. In 2019 Mike and Val graciously hosted a gathering of the Pacific Northwest William O. Douglas Society, where I had the opportunity to hear Douglas stories in a setting reminiscent of his many summer trips to Goose Prairie.

Although there are several Douglas biographies, along with his autobiographies, this book relies heavily on original documents and manuscripts. Research has taken me from libraries in California, Washington State, Denver, Jackson Hole, and Texas to repositories in Washington DC, New York, New Haven, and Boston. All of the librarians graciously offered assistance and put up with many questions. Special thanks to Valerie Railey and Heather Phillips of the Library of the U.S. Court of Appeals for the Ninth Circuit for their patience and resourcefulness. I spent many wonderful hours in the Manuscripts Division of the Library of Congress, which houses the Douglas collection, plus those of several of his colleagues. My thanks to the staffs at the following libraries: Supreme Court Curator's Office; the presidential libraries of John F. Kennedy and Lyndon B. Johnson; University of Washington, Manuscripts, Special Collections; Bancroft Library, University of California, Berkeley; Yakima Valley Museum, Douglas Collection; University of Southern California Special Collections; Denver Public Library, Western History Collection; University of Wyoming, American Heritage Center; Teton Science School, Murie Ranch Archives; National Museum of Forest Service History; George Washington University, Special Collections Resource Center; Yale University Library, Special Collections and Manuscripts; Peabody Museum of Natural History, Yale University; New York Zoological Society; and Washington County Free Library, Western Maryland Collection.

Gathering photos has been a challenge, especially since many of the libraries are closed due to COVID-19. But I have been blessed with photos from many sources and give special thanks to John Concillio of the William O. Douglas Film Project, Tom Hulst, Mike Hoge, Cathy Douglas Stone, David Current, and the Yakima Valley Museum.

While writing the book, I gave several public lectures sponsored by the Teton Science Schools, University of San Diego School of Law, Stanford University, and University of Wyoming. I also thank the University of Wyoming American Heritage Center and the Bill Lane Center for the American West, Stanford University, for their research support for the project.

This book would not have been possible without my agent, Jill Marsal of Marsal Literary Agency, who has patiently and expertly guided the process.

My family's unending patience cannot be overstated, from dragging them to Alaska, Wyoming, Washington State, and Washington DC to their enduring never-ending conversations about the book. They have been my sanity check, sounding board, and cheerleaders. I am blessed and cannot thank them enough—my husband, Peter Cowhey, my son Isaac Haruka McKeown Cowhey, and my sister Pat Nagel.

APPENDIX

Mardy Murie's Cry Baby Cookies

INGREDIENTS

1 cup sugar
1 cup Crisco
1 teaspoon salt
1 teaspoon ground ginger
1 teaspoon ground cinnamon
1 egg; whisk in small bowl
1 cup molasses
4 cups flour
1 cup hot water
1 teaspoon apple cider vinegar

FOR THE ICING

1 cup powdered sugar
1 tablespoon vanilla extract
Canned milk

INSTRUCTIONS

Preheat the oven to 350 degrees. Cream together sugar, shortening, salt, and spices. Add the egg. Add the molasses and mix well. Gradually add the flour. Add the water and vinegar. Bake for 10–12 minutes until golden. Cookies will be slightly soft. Place cookies on a cooling rack. While still warm, dab the tops of cookies with icing, made by mixing the powdered sugar, vanilla, and just enough canned milk to get a good consistency. Best enjoyed with a view of the Tetons.

Courtesy of Murie Ranch, Teton Science Schools, Wilson wy, from Mardy's tin recipe box.

NOTES

Abbreviations

Blackmun Papers   Harry M. Blackmun Papers, Manuscripts Division, Library of Congress, Washington DC

c&o Canal Association Records   Chesapeake & Ohio Canal Association Records, George Washington University Libraries, Special Collections Research Center, Washington DC

Double K Papers   Special Collections, University of Washington Libraries, Seattle WA

Douglas Papers   William O. Douglas Papers, Manuscripts Division, Library of Congress, Washington DC

JFK Library   William O. Douglas Correspondence, John F. Kennedy Presidential Library and Museum, Boston MA

LBJ Library   White House Central File, LBJ Presidential Library, Austin TX

Marshall Papers   Thurgood Marshall Papers, Manuscripts Collection, Library of Congress, Washington DC

Murie Ranch Papers   Papers of Olaus and Mardy Murie, Murie Ranch Archives, Teton Science Schools, Moose WY

Remembrances of William O. Douglas   "Remembrances of William O. Douglas by His Friends and Associates: In Celebration of the Fiftieth Anniversary of His Appointment as Associate Justice of the Supreme Court of the United States of America, 1939–1989," ed. William Tod Cowan and Catherine Constantinou (Washington DC: Supreme Court Historical Society)

Sierra Club Papers   Sierra Club Collection, Bancroft Library, University of California, Berkeley CA

University of Washington Collection   Special Collections, University of Washington Libraries, Seattle WA

Wilderness Society Papers   Wilderness Society Collection, Western History Collection, Denver Public Library, Denver CO

1. The Man and His Mountains

1. William O. Douglas, *Of Men and Mountains* (New York: Harper & Brothers, 1950), xiii–xiv.

2. Douglas, *Of Men and Mountains*, 327.

3. Quoted in James F. Simon, *Independent Journey: The Life of William O. Douglas* (New York: Penguin Books, 1981), 234.

4. Simon, *Independent Journey*, 20–22, 41.

5. Simon, *Independent Journey*, 20, 23; Bruce Allen Murphy, *Wild Bill: The Legend and Life of William O. Douglas* (New York: Random House, 2003), 42. Just as he was controversial in life, Douglas's biographers diverged in their accounts after his death.

6. Douglas, *Of Men and Mountains*, 7–8.

7. Murphy, *Wild Bill*, 24.

8. Douglas, *Of Men and Mountains*, 30.

9. William O. Douglas, *Go East, Young Man* (New York: Random House, 1974), 60; see also Simon, *Independent Journey*, 27.

10. William O. Douglas, *Strange Lands and Friendly People* (New York: Harper & Brothers, 1951), dedication page.

11. Murphy, *Wild Bill*, 10–11, 64–66, 273, 420–21, 481–82.

12. Douglas, *Of Men and Mountains*, 31; William Domnarski, *The Great Justices 1941–54: Black, Douglas, Frankfurter, and Jackson in Chambers* (Ann Arbor: University of Michigan Press, 2006), 130; Simon, *Independent Journey*, 21. Simon refers to the disease as infantile paralysis and polio. Murphy labeled the polio claim a myth, arguing that though Douglas was severely ill as a child, the disease could not have been polio (Murphy, *Wild Bill*, 620–22).

13. Douglas, *Of Men and Mountains*, 31.

14. Murphy, *Wild Bill*, 12, 25; Simon, *Independent Journey*, 38.

15. Douglas, *Of Men and Mountains*, 27, 30, 33, 35.

16. Douglas, *Of Men and Mountains*, 80–82.

17. Douglas, *Of Men and Mountains*, 92, 116, 126, 135, 141–43.

18. Boy Scouts of America, *Boy Scouts Handbook* (New York: Doubleday, Page, 1911).

19. Olaus Murie to Douglas, Feb. 9, 1952; Wilderness Society Papers, Olaus Murie Papers.

20. Douglas, *Of Men and Mountains*, 77, 79.

21. Douglas, *Of Men and Mountains*, 66–67, 73, 86.

22. Douglas, *Of Men and Mountains*, 109, 114–15.

23. Douglas, *Of Men and Mountains*, 109.

24. William O. Douglas, *Muir of the Mountains* (New York: Houghton Mifflin, 1961), 154.

25. Douglas, *Of Men and Mountains*, 122, 129, 155.

26. Douglas, *Of Men and Mountains*, 69.

27. Douglas, *Go East, Young Man*, 56–57.

28. Douglas, *Of Men and Mountains*, 59; Murphy, *Wild Bill*, 25.

29. Quoted in Simon, *Independent Journey*, 35.

30. Douglas, *Of Men and Mountains*, 159.

31. Quoted in City of Walla Walla, "Walla Walla's History," wallawallawa.gov.

32. Simon, *Independent Journey*, 50.

33. Murphy, *Wild Bill*, 30.

34. Douglas: *Of Men and Mountains*, 160, and *Go East, Young Man*, 92–93; Murphy, *Wild Bill*, 32.

35. Douglas's discharge papers provide his serial number, 5200182, and his rank, Private SATC (Student Army Training Corps). Despite this documentation, Murphy disputes the nature of his service (Murphy, *Wild Bill*, 509–10). For a discussion of Douglas's service and burial at Arlington National Cemetery, see Charles Lane, "Falls of Justice," *Washington Monthly*, Apr. 1, 2003, https://washingtonmonthly.com/2003/04/01/falls-of-justice/.

36. Murphy, *Wild Bill*, 33–37; Simon, *Independent Journey*, 54, 58–59.

37. Simon, *Independent Journey*, 58, 60–61.

38. Simon, *Independent Journey*, 63; Douglas, *Go East, Young Man*, 130–33.

39. Douglas, *Of Men and Mountains*, 15.

40. Douglas, *Go East, Young Man*, 128.

41. Donald W. Meyers, "It Happened Here: Yakima Billboard Compares City to Palm Springs, Calif.," *Yakima Herald*, Dec. 31, 2017.

42. Douglas, *Go East, Young Man*, 137.

43. Simon, *Independent Journey*, 64.

44. Douglas, *Go East, Young Man*, 137.

45. Douglas, *Go East, Young Man*, 135–36.

46. Murphy, *Wild Bill*, 44–45.

47. Douglas, *Go East, Young Man*, 139–40.

48. Douglas, *Go East, Young Man*, 137, 140–41.

49. Murphy, *Wild Bill*, 46–47.

50. Murphy, *Wild Bill*, 45, 49.

51. Douglas, *Go East, Young Man*, 145.

52. At the time Douglas graduated, Justice Harlan Fiske Stone had recently joined the Supreme Court and began the practice of selecting one clerk from the Columbia class. The justice chose Alfred McCormack, who was editor-in-chief of the *Columbia Law Review*. Alfred McCormack, "A Law Clerk's Recollections," *Columbia Law Review* 46, no. 5 (Sept. 1946): 710.

53. Douglas, *Go East, Young Man*, 149; "William O. Douglas: A Life on the High Court," *Showcase Yakima* (Yakima WA: KYVE 47, 1988); video on file with the Yakima Valley Museum.

54. Douglas, *Go East, Young Man*, 150; R. T. Swaine, *The Cravath Firm and Its Predecessors, 1819–1948*, vol. 1, *The Predecessor Firms, 1819–1906* (New York: Ad Press, 1946), vii.

55. Simon, *Independent Journey*, 79–80.

56. Douglas, *Go East, Young Man*, 151, 156.

57. Murphy, *Wild Bill*, 64–66.

58. Simon, *Independent Journey*, 21–22.

59. Murphy, *Wild Bill*, 46–47.

60. Douglas, *Go East, Young Man*, 157. The author was a partner in Perkins Coie before she joined the bench in 1998.

61. Murphy, *Wild Bill*, 71; emphasis in original.

62. Douglas, *Go East, Young Man*, 159.

63. Douglas, *Go East, Young Man*, 158–59; Murphy, *Wild Bill*, 73–74.

64. Douglas, *Go East, Young Man*, 163; Murphy, *Wild Bill*, 76–77.

65. Simon, *Independent Journey*, 114–15.

66. Douglas, *Go East, Young Man*, 161–62.

67. David J. Garrow, "The Tragedy of William O. Douglas," *The Nation*, Mar. 27, 2003; Simon, *Independent Journey*, 103–5.

68. Douglas, *Go East, Young Man*, 164.

69. Todd J. Zywicki, "An Economic Analysis of the Consumer Bankruptcy Crisis," *Northwestern University Law Review* 99, no. 4 (Summer 2005): 1466.

70. Douglas, *Go East, Young Man*, 174–75.

71. Kaius Tuori, "American Legal Realism and Anthropology," *Law & Social Inquiry* 42 (2017): 804.

72. Murphy, *Wild Bill*, 89.

73. Douglas, *Go East, Young Man*, 149, 175.

74. Simon, *Independent Journey*, 127–34.

75. See the articles at "William O. Douglas and the Growing Power of the SEC: From Academia to Government," *Securities and Exchange Commission Historical Society*, http://www.sechistorical.org/museum/galleries/douglas/academia.php.

76. Douglas, *Go East, Young Man*, 258–59; Simon, *Independent Journey*, 135, 139.

77. Simon, *Independent Journey*, 73, 142–43, 149–50.

78. Douglas, *Go East, Young Man*, 264.

79. Simon, *Independent Journey*, 153; "Walla Walla to Washington," *Time*, Jan. 27, 1936, 50.

80. Quoted in Douglas, *Go East, Young Man*, 265.

81. Editorial, *Yakima Daily Republic*, Aug. 10, 1937.

82. Quoted in Douglas, *Go East, Young Man*, 281.

83. Douglas, *Go East, Young Man*, 317.

84. Douglas, *Go East, Young Man*, 333.

85. Douglas, *Go East, Young Man*, 455, 334.

86. Douglas, *Go East, Young Man*, 455.

87. Murphy, *Wild Bill*, 164–65.

88. David J. Danelski, "The Appointment of William O. Douglas to the Supreme Court," *Journal of Supreme Court History* 40, no. 1 (2015): 89.

89. Simon, *Independent Journey*, 189–91.

90. Sheldon S. Cohen and Philip E. Urofsky, "The Court Diary of Justice William O. Douglas," *Journal of Supreme Court History* 20, no. 1 (1995): 80.

91. Murphy, *Wild Bill*, 166–68.

92. Danelski, "The Appointment of William O. Douglas," 83.

93. Simon, *Independent Journey*, 191–94.

94. Quoted in Douglas, *Go East, Young Man*, 463.

95. Danelski, "The Appointment of William O. Douglas," 93.

96. Simon, *Independent Journey*, 191. "Joseph Story," Oyez, https://www.oyez.org/justices/joseph_story; "Clarence Thomas," Oyez, https://www.oyez.org/justices/clarence_thomas.

97. "Douglas Sworn in as Friends Watch," *New York Times*, Apr. 18, 1939.

98. Federal Judiciary Center, *Biographical Directory of Federal Judges*, https://www.fjc.gov/history/judges/biographical-directory-article-iii-federal-judges-about-directory.

99. Clifford quoted in Murphy, *Wild Bill*, 239.

2. Political Washington

1. Quoted in Douglas, *Go East, Young Man*, 463.

2. Douglas, *Go East, Young Man*, 330, 369–70.

3. S. Cohen and Urofsky, "Court Diary of Justice William O. Douglas," 92–93.

4. William O. Douglas, *An Almanac of Liberty* (Garden City NY: Doubleday, 1954), 43.

5. Quoted in Merlo J. Pusey, *Charles Evans Hughes* (New York: Macmillan, 1951), 2:788.

6. William O. Douglas, preface to Grace Tully, *F.D.R. My Boss* (New York: Charles Scribner's Sons, 1949), vii.

7. Douglas, *Go East, Young Man*, 339.

8. O'Malley v. Woodrough (*O'Malley*), 307 U.S. 277 (1939); U.S. Const. art. III, § 1.

9. *O'Malley*, 307 U.S. at 282. Justice Pierce Butler authored a dissent that was nearly five times longer than the majority's one-page opinion.

10. Quoted in Eric Sevareid, "Mr. Justice Douglas," CBS *Reports*, Sept. 6, 1972.

11. S. Cohen and Urofsky, "Court Diary of Justice William O. Douglas," 82. Although Douglas claimed he never kept a diary, he maintained a journal of case matters from March 19, 1939, the day he learned he would be nominated, until October 9, 1940. Douglas, *Go East, Young Man*, x.

12. Douglas, *Go East, Young Man*, 467.

13. Quoted in Alpheus Thomas Mason, *William Howard Taft: Chief Justice* (New York: Simon and Schuster, 1965), 287; see also 121–56, 280–85. See also D. Danelski, *A Supreme Court Justice Is Appointed* (Chicago: University of Chicago Press, 1964), 67–70.

14. M. Margaret McKeown, "Don't Shoot the Canons: Maintaining the Appearance of Propriety Standard," *Journal of Appellate Practice and Process* 7, no. 1 (Spring 2005): 45–58. The commissioner's salary was $42,000, while federal judges made only $7,500.

15. The Canons of Judicial Ethics were adopted by the House of Delegates of the ABA on July 9, 1924. Full text of the canons is available at https://www.americanbar.org/content/dam/aba/administrative/professional_responsibility/pic_migrated/1924_canons.pdf.

16. Robert Tembeckjian, "The Supreme Court Should Adopt an Ethics Code," *Washington Post*, Feb. 6, 2019; Lincoln Caplan, "Does the Supreme Court Need a Code of Conduct?," *New Yorker*, July 27, 2015.

17. In response to an outcry for more formal standards, Chief Justice John G. Roberts emphasized in 2012 that "all Members of the Court do in fact consult the Code of Conduct in assessing their ethical obligations.... It serves the same purpose as the 1924 Canons that Chief Justice Taft helped to develop, and Justices today use the Code for precisely that purpose." U.S. Supreme Court, "2011 Year-End Report on the Federal Judiciary," Dec. 31, 2011, https://www.supremecourt.gov/publicinfo/year-end/2011year-endreport.pdf.

18. Judiciary Act of 1789, 1 Stat. 73, c. 20.

19. David J. Danelski, "The Propriety of Brandeis' Extrajudicial Conduct," in *Brandeis and America*, ed. Nelson L. Dawson (Lexington: University Press of Kentucky, 1989), 16.

20. John P. Frank, *The Marble Palace: The Supreme Court in American Life* (New York: Knopf, 1958), 275.

21. 1924 Canons, 28.

22. 1924 Canons, 23, 25, 33.

23. Although Ervin "condemned restrictions on constitutionally protected judges, he placed high value on keeping the judges in what he considered *their* place." John P. MacKenzie, *The Appearance of Justice* (New York: Scribner, 1974), 149.

24. U.S. Const. art. II, § 2.

25. Second Annual Ruth Bader Ginsburg Lecture (Georgetown University Law Center, Washington DC, October 30, 2019), https://www.c-span.org/video/?465877-1/justice-ginsburg-president-bill-clinton-secretary-state-hillary-clinton.

26. James F. Watts, Jr., "William Moody," in *The Justices of the United States Supreme Court, 1789–1969: Their Lives and Major Opinions*, ed. Leon Friedman and Fred L. Israel (New York: Chelsea House, 1995), 4:922–23; John P. Frank, "Frank Murphy," Friedman and Israel, *Justices of the United States Supreme Court*, 1255.

27. Douglas, *Go East, Young Man*, 22–23.

28. Bruce Allen Murphy, *The Brandeis/Frankfurter Connection: The Secret Political Activities of Two Supreme Court Justices* (Oxford: Oxford University Press, 1982), 9.

29. William R. Casto, "Advising Presidents: Robert Jackson and the Destroyers-For-Bases Deal," *American Journal of Legal History* 52, no. 1 (2012): 71n382.

30. Murphy, *Brandeis/Frankfurter Connection*, 204.

31. Quoted in Gordon Silverstein and John Hanley, "The Supreme Court and Public Opinion in Times of War and Crisis," *Hastings Law Journal* 61, no. 6 (2010): 1467.

32. Max Freedman, ann., *Roosevelt and Frankfurter, Their Correspondence, 1928–1945* (London: Bodley Head, 1968), 583–85.

33. Murphy, *Brandeis/Frankfurter Connection*, 303.

34. Jonathan D. Sarna, "Louis D. Brandeis: Zionist Leader," *Brandeis Review* II, no. 3 (Winter 1992): 23.

35. Murphy, *Brandeis/Frankfurter Connection*, 9.

36. Quoted in Murphy, *Brandeis/Frankfurter Connection*, 309.

37. Frank, "Frank Murphy," 1255; Frances A. Allen and Neil Walsh Allen, *A Sketch of Chief Justice Fred M. Vinson* (Washington DC: Green Bag Press, 2005), 99–100; Joshua E. Kastenberg, *The Campaign to Impeach Justice William O. Douglas: Nixon, Vietnam, and the Conservative Attack on Judicial Independence* (Lawrence: University Press of Kansas, 2019), 50; *Nominations of Abe Fortas and Homer Thornberry, Hearings before the S. Comm. on Judiciary*, 90th Cong. 103-06 (1968); Laura Kalman, *Abe Fortas, A Biography* (New Haven CT: Yale University Press, 1990) 294, 311.

38. William O. Douglas, *The Court Years: 1939 to 1975* (New York: Random House, 1980), 28–29.

39. Quoted in Philip B. Kurland, "Robert H. Jackson," *Justices of the United States Supreme Court*, 1306.

40. Paul Moke, *Earl Warren and the Struggle for Justice* (Lanham MD: Lexington Books, 2015), 249, 280; Luas A. Powe Jr., *The Warren Court and American Politics* (Cambridge MA: Belknap Press, 2000), 416-17.

41. Felix Frankfurter and Joseph P. Lash, *From the Diaries of Felix Frankfurter: With a Biographical Essay and Notes* (New York: W. W. Norton, 1975), 77.

42. Quoted in Pusey, *Charles Evans Hughes*, 1:300, 326, 332.

43. "Vinson Excelled in Federal Posts," *New York Times*, Sept. 9, 1953; Hames E. St. Clair and Linda C. Gugin, *Chief Justice Fred M. Vinson of Kentucky* (Lexington: University Press of Kentucky, 2002), 184, 195.

44. Douglas, *Go East, Young Man*, 58; "Presidential Parade Is a Feature of Senior's Class Prophecy," *Yakima Herald Tribune*; on file at Yakima Valley Museum.

45. Richard Neuberger, "Mr. Justice Douglas," in *They Never Go Back to Pocatello: The Selected Essays of Richard Neuberger*, ed. Steve Neal (Portland: Oregon Historical Society Press, 1988), 109–10; Douglas to A. Howard Meneely, Apr. 18, 1943, Douglas Papers, box 10.

46. Murphy, *Wild Bill*, 213.

47. Michael Janeway, *The Fall of the House of Roosevelt* (New York: Columbia University Press, 2004), 45.

48. Douglas, *Go East, Young Man*, 356.

49. Douglas, *Court Years*, 283; Murphy, *Wild Bill*, 229.

50. Murphy, *Wild Bill*, 218.

51. Janeway, *House of Roosevelt*, 50–57, 211; Janeway to Douglas, Aug. 4, 1944, Douglas Papers, box 537. Janeway has been called an "idea broker." "Wall St. Crumbles, Women Arise: The Janeways' Time Has Come," *People*, Jan. 20, 1975, 30–33.

52. Douglas to Francis Maloney, July 14, 1944, Douglas Papers, box 537.

53. Quoted in Simon, *Independent Journey*, 265.

54. Frankfurter and Lash, *From the Diaries of Felix Frankfurter*, 230. Frankfurter also sarcastically noted, "How many plugged nickels would you give Bill Douglas' chance of becoming president?" Quoted in Simon, *Independent Journey*, 155.

55. Douglas, *Court Years*, 285; Douglas, *Of Men and Mountains*, 230.

56. Quoted in Janeway, *House of Roosevelt*, 76–77.

57. "History of the Department of the Interior," *U.S. Department of the Interior*, https:/www.doi.gov/whoweare/history.

58. Quoted in Murphy, *Wild Bill*, 243.

59. Quoted in Janeway, *Fall of the House of Roosevelt*, 62.

60. Douglas to Harry S. Truman, Feb. 23, 1946, Douglas Papers, box 593; Douglas, *Court Years*, 218.

61. Quoted in William J. Cibes Jr., "Extra-Judicial Activities of Justices of the United States Supreme Court, 1790–1960" (PhD diss., Princeton University, 1975), 1114; Felix Belain Jr., "Douglas Refuses 2d Place on Ticket," *New York Times*, July 13, 1948.

62. Janeway, *Fall of the House of Roosevelt*, 76–77.

63. Helen Fuller, "The Funeral Is Called Off," *New Republic*, July 26, 1948.

64. Simon, *Independent Journey*, 274.

65. Arthur Krock, "Place on '52 Ticket Is Firmly Rejected by Justice Douglas," *New York Times*, Jan. 14, 1952; Douglas to Max Awner, assistant editor of the *Colorado Labor Advocate*, Feb. 5, 1952, Douglas Papers, box 621; Douglas to Olaus Murie, March 5, 1952, Murie Ranch Papers, correspondence.

66. "Recognize Peiping Justice Urges U.S.," *New York Times*, Sept. 1, 1951.

67. Quoted in "U.S. Should Recognize Red China: 'Fool Statement,' Connally Snorts," *Los Angeles Times*, Sept. 1, 1951, 2.

68. Quoted in Simon, *Independent Journey*, 274–75.

69. "Justice Douglas Is Available," *The Nation*, Jan. 1, 1952.

70. J. T. Osborne to Drew Pearson, Jan. 16, 1952, Douglas Papers, box 621. Pearson was famous for his newspaper column, "Washington Merry-Go Round."

71. Fred Rodell, "I'd Prefer Bill Douglas," *The Nation*, April 26, 1952.

72. Politicus, "Justice Douglas—Headline Hunter," *American Mercury*, Aug. 1956, 121–26.

73. Douglas to Lyndon B. Johnson, March 6, 1964, LBJ Papers, White House Famous Names File, box 1, Douglas Folder.

74. Quoted in "Commemorating the Twentieth Anniversary of Justice William O. Douglas' Appointment to the Supreme Court," Transcript of Remarks, April 17, 1959, Douglas Papers, box 1759.

75. Quoted in Murphy, *Wild Bill*, 351.

76. Douglas to Melvin D. Pedersen, Feb. 23, 1962, Douglas Papers, box 866.

3. Douglas and the Conservation Movement

1. In 1898 Webster's defined "environment" as including "surrounding conditions, influences, or forces, by which living forms are influenced and modified in their growth and development." *Webster's International Dictionary of the English Language*, 1898 ed., s.v. "Environment," https://ia800302.us.archive.org/7/items/webstersinternat00port/webstersinternat00port.pdf.

2. United States v. Students Challenging Regulatory Agency Procedures (SCRAP 1), 412 U.S. 669, 713n10 (1973) (Douglas, J., dissenting in part); Douglas quoted

from Robert Cahn, "Environmentalists Wary of Transport Trends," *Christian Science Monitor*, Feb. 28, 1973, 12.

3. Eisen v. Carlisle & Jacquelin, 417 U.S. 156, 186–87 (1974) (Douglas, J., dissenting in part).

4. "Profiles: Oh, Hawk of Mercy!" *New Yorker*, Apr. 17, 1948, 31.

5. Henry David Thoreau, "Walking," *Atlantic Monthly*, June 1862, 42; Douglas Brinkley, "Thoreau's Wilderness Legacy, beyond the Shores of Walden Pond," *New York Times*, July 7, 2017; Eliot Porter and Henry David Thoreau, *In Wildness Is the Preservation of the World* (Los Angeles: Ammo Books, 2012); first published in 1962 by Ballantine Books.

6. Roderick Frazier Nash, *The Rights of Nature: A History of Environmental Ethics* (Madison: University of Wisconsin Press, 1989), 36–37.

7. Stewart L. Udall, *The Quiet Crisis* (New York: Holt, Rinehart and Winston, 1963), 82. See also George Perkins Marsh, *Man and Nature; or, Physical Geography as Modified by Human Action* (Tacoma: Weyerhaeuser Environmental Classics, 2003); first published in 1864 by Scribner (New York).

8. Stephen Fox, *The American Conservation Movement: John Muir and His Legacy* (Boston: Little, Brown, 1981), 82; Nash, *The Rights of Nature*, 41.

9. Fox, *American Conservation Movement*, 107.

10. Quoted in Fox, *American Conservation Movement*, 115–16.

11. Michael Brune, "Pulling Down Our Monuments," July 22, 2020, Sierra Club, https://www.sierraclub.org/michael-brune/2020/07/john-muir-early-history-sierra-club; Lucy Tomkins, "Sierra Club Says It Must Confront Its Founder's Racism," July 24, 2020, *New York Times*, A14.

12. Brian G. Norton, "Conservation and Preservation: A Conceptual Rehabilitation," *Environmental Ethics* 8, no. 3 (Fall 1986): 210.

13. Fox, *American Conservation Movement*, 106.

14. Fox, *American Conservation Movement*, 107–9, 136–38.

15. Fox, *American Conservation Movement*, 136–38.

16. Fox, *American Conservation Movement*, 103–4.

17. Fox, *American Conservation Movement*, 110, 129, 139; Paul Sutter, "Putting Wilderness in Context," in *American Wilderness: A New History*, ed. Michael Lewis (New York: Oxford University Press, 2007), 181.

18. N.Y. Const. art. XIV.

19. Darrin Lunde, *The Naturalist: Theodore Roosevelt, A Lifetime of Exploration and the Triumph of American Natural History* (New York: Crown Publishers, 2016), 252.

20. Douglas Brinkley, *The Wilderness Warrior: Theodore Roosevelt and the Crusade for America* (New York: Harper, 2009), 1.

21. Fox, *American Conservation Movement*, 128–29.

22. Theodore Roosevelt, "Confession of Faith" (speech, Progressive National Convention, Chicago, Illinois, Aug. 6, 1912), Theodore Roosevelt Center, https://www.theodorerooseveltcenter.org.

23. Douglas, *Of Men and Mountains*, 129.

24. John Clayton, *Natural Rivals: John Muir, Gifford Pinchot, and the Creation of America's Public Lands* (New York: Pegasus Books, 2019), 91–94.

25. Multiple Use–Sustained Yield Act, 16 U.S.C. §§ 528–31 (1960). The statute calls for outdoor recreation, range management, wildlife and fish improvement, watershed protection, and timber production to be managed in the combination that will "best meet the needs of the American people."

26. Clayton, *Natural Rivals*, xvii.

27. Fox, *American Conservation Movement*, 108.

28. Fox, *American Conservation Movement*, 140.

29. William Colby, Sierra Club secretary, to Gifford Pinchot, 1909, in Sierra Club, Hetchy Hetchy History, www.vault.sierraclub.org; John Muir, "Let Everyone Help to Save the Famous Hetch-Hetchy Valley and Stop the Commercial Destruction Which Threatens Our National Parks" (San Francisco, 1909).

30. Sutter, "Putting Wilderness in Context," 169–72; Ken Burns, *The National Parks*, Untold Stories Project, www.pbs.org/nationalparks/pdfs/tnp-abi-untold -stories-pt-01-segregation.pdf.

31. Conservation and Protection Branch, National Park Service, *Public Use of the National Parks: A Statistical Report* (Washington DC: U.S. Department of the Interior, 1968).

32. Calvin Coolidge, "Speech to National Conference on Outdoor Recreation" (May 22, 1924), the Coolidge Foundation, https://www.coolidgefoundation.org /resources/speeches-as-president-1923-1928-4/.

33. Aldo Leopold, *Sand County Almanac* (Oxford: Oxford University Press, 1949), 243.

34. Leopold, *Sand County Almanac*, 210.

35. Douglas to Mrs. Stewart Udall, Mar. 21, 1968, Douglas Papers, box 380.

36. Julianne Lutz Warren, *Aldo Leopold's Odyssey* (Washington DC: Island Press, 2016), 299–301.

37. Aldo Leopold, "The Wilderness and Its Place in Forest Recreational Policy," *Journal of Forestry* 19, no. 7 (Nov. 1921): 718.

38. Robert Marshall, "The Problem of Wilderness," *Scientific Monthly*, Feb. 1930, 148; Harvey Broome, "Origins of The Wilderness Society," *Living Wilderness*, July 1940, Wilderness Society Papers, CONS130.

39. Paul Sutter, *Driven Wild* (Seattle: University of Washington Press, 2005), 4–6; Robert Marshall to Harold L. Ickes, Feb. 14, 1935, Wilderness Society Papers, CONS130.

40. Nash, *The Rights of Nature*, 64.

41. Fox, *American Conservation Movement*, 183.

42. Arthur M. Schlesinger, Jr., *The Coming of the New Deal* (Boston: Houghton Mifflin, 2003), 336.

43. Franklin Delano Roosevelt, "Fireside Chat 8: On Farmers and Laborers," Sept. 6, 1936, Miller Center, University of Virginia, https://millercenter.org/the -presidency/presidential-speeches/september-6-1936-fireside-chat-8-farmers-and -laborers.

44. Franklin Delano Roosevelt, "Fireside Chat 8," 3.

45. Douglas Brinkley, *Rightful Heritage: Franklin D. Roosevelt and the Land of America* (New York: Harper Perennial, 2017), appendices A-D.

46. Brinkley, *Rightful Heritage*, 238.

47. Sutter, "Putting Wilderness in Context," 173.

48. Fox, *American Conservation Movement*, 199.

49. Brinkley, *Rightful Heritage*, 416–17.

50. Sutter, "Putting Wilderness in Context," 170; Fox, *American Conservation Movement*, 201.

51. Quoted in Sutter, "Putting Wilderness in Context," 169; Fox, *American Conservation Movement*, 210.

52. Sutter, "Putting Wilderness in Context," 176, 178.

53. William O. Douglas, *A Wilderness Bill of Rights* (New York: Little, Brown, 1967), 25–26.

54. See "Franklin D. Roosevelt, Conservationist: An Early Initiative in Sustainability," *fdr4freedoms*, 11, http://fdr4freedoms.org/wp-content/themes/fdf4fdr/DownloadablePDFs/II_HopeRecoveryReform/05_FDRConservationist.pdf.

55. Brinkley, *Rightful Heritage*, 414.

56. Brinkley, *Rightful Heritage*, 414.

57. Douglas, *Go East, Young Man*, 207.

58. Fox, *American Conservation Movement*, 208.

59. Stewart Udall pegged the third wave as starting in 1963, but Michael McCloskey viewed it as starting much earlier. Compare Udall, *Quiet Crisis*, 187, with Michael McCloskey, "Wilderness Movement at the Crossroads, 1945–1970," *Pacific Historical Review* 41, no. 3 (Aug. 1972): 347.

60. McCloskey, "Wilderness Movement at the Crossroads," 347n2.

61. McCloskey, "Wilderness Movement at the Crossroads," 350, 360–61.

62. Michael McCloskey, "The Wilderness Act of 1964: Its Background and Meaning," *Oregon Law Review* 45 (1966): 288, 297–301.

63. Wilderness Act of 1964, Pub. L. No. 88-577, §§ 2(a), (c), 78 Stat. 890, 890–93 (1964).

64. Douglas, *Of Men and Mountains*, ix; Fox, *American Conservation Movement*, 239.

4. Taking on the *Washington Post*

1. William O. Douglas, *My Wilderness: East to Katahdin* (Garden City NY: Doubleday, 1961), 195.

2. Barry Mackintosh, *c&o Canal: The Making of a Park* (Washington DC: National Park Service, 1991), 1; John A. Lynch Jr., "Justice Douglas, the Chesapeake & Ohio Canal, and Maryland Legal History," *University of Baltimore Law Forum* 35 (2002): 108–9.

3. Mackintosh, *c&o Canal*, 1.

4. Lynch, "Justice Douglas," 112.

5. Lynch, "Justice Douglas," 57–70.

6. Mackintosh, *c&o Canal*, 1.

7. Mackintosh, *c&o Canal*, 2.

8. Harlan D. Unrau, *Chesapeake & Ohio Canal Historic Resource Study* (Hagerstown MD: National Park Service, 2007), 707.

9. Unrau, *Chesapeake & Ohio Canal*, 707.

10. Brinkley, *Rightful Heritage*, 246–47; Unrau, *Chesapeake & Ohio Canal*, 6–13, 19–20.

11. Unrau, *Historic Resource Study*, 49–50.

12. Unrau, *Chesapeake & Ohio Canal*, 55–56.

13. Quoted in Unrau, *Chesapeake & Ohio Canal*, 52, 55–56, 59, 66, 74.

14. "Potomac Parkway," *Washington Post*, Jan. 3, 1954, B4.

15. William O. Douglas, "Potomac Sanctuary," *Washington Post*, Jan. 19, 1954, 14. Some have speculated that Howard Zahniser of The Wilderness Society wrote the letter, but nothing in the style of the letter or in Douglas's meticulous records supports this view. See Mark Harvey, *Wilderness Forever: Howard Zahniser and the Path to the Wilderness Act* (Seattle: University of Washington Press, 2009), 272.

16. Douglas, "Potomac Sanctuary."

17. "Post Editors Accept Douglas' Challenge: We Accept," editorial, *Washington Post*, Jan. 21, 1954, 1.

18. Douglas, *My Wilderness: East to Katahdin*, 194–95.

19. Murphy, *Wild Bill*, 332.

20. Mackintosh, *C&O Canal*, 56; Jack Durham, "The C&O Canal Hike," *Living Wilderness* 19, no. 48 (Spring 1954): 1, 6.

21. Mackintosh, *C&O Canal*, 56; Durham, "The C&O Canal Hike," 3–4.

22. Murphy, *Wild Bill*, 332.

23. "Douglas Finishes His 189-Mile Hike: Justice and Eight Others Trod Chesapeake & Ohio Canal Route in Eight Days," *New York Times*, Mar. 28, 1954, 43.

24. Olaus J. Murie, Conclusions from the C&O Canal Hike, Wilderness Society Papers, Olaus Murie Papers, box 1.

25. Aubrey Graves, "AWOL Dog, Canal Hike Mascot, To Be Sent Home," *Washington Post and Times Herald*, Mar. 31, 1954, 15.

26. Aubrey Graves, "Some Kiddies Want to Know Just How to Budge a Burro," *Washington Post and Times Herald*, Nov. 14, 1954, B2.

27. Douglas, *Go East, Young Man*, 222.

28. Durham, "The C&O Canal Hike," 4, 6.

29. Mackintosh, *C&O Canal*, 70.

30. *Washington Post*, Feb. 14, 1954, B2.

31. Durham, "The C&O Canal Hike," 7.

32. Douglas notebook, C&O Canal, Mar. 1954, Douglas Papers, box 543.

33. "Douglas Hikers Make 14 Miles in Four Hours," *Chicago Daily Tribune*, Mar. 21, 1954, 24; "9 Drop Out as Douglas Hikers Chalk Up 37 Mi.," *Chicago Daily Tribune*, Mar. 22, 1954, 10.

34. Aubrey Graves, "Odds and Ends and Anecdote Add Tale to Towpath Trek," *Washington Post and Times Herald*, Apr. 4, 1954, B2.

35. Durham, "The C&O Canal Hike," 8.

36. Durham, "The C&O Canal Hike," 8.

37. "'Tow Path Lobby' Readies Douglas Party Challenge," *Washington Post and Times Herald*, Mar. 26, 1954, A1.

38. Aubrey Graves, "Canal Hikers Just 18 Miles from (Sigh!) Washington," *Washington Post and Times Herald*, Mar. 27, 1954, M1.

39. Durham, "The C&O Canal Hike," 8.

40. Murphy, *Wild Bill*, 333.

41. Graves, "Canal Hikers," M1.

42. The hike is variously referred to as 180, 185, or 189 miles, depending on the source.

43. Murphy, *Wild Bill*, 333.

44. Quoted in Durham, "The C&O Canal Hike," 8.

45. Graves, "Canal Hikers," M1.

46. "Douglas to Receive Foot Health Award," *Washington Post and Times Herald*, May 16, 1954, M3.

47. Quoted in Graves, "Canal Hikers," M1.

48. "C&O Canal: A Report," editorial, *Washington Post and Times Herald*, March 31, 1954, 12.

49. Alice Longworth to William O. Douglas, Apr. 5, 1954, Washington County Free Library Collection, Hagerstown MD, C&O Canal.

50. Murie, Conclusions from the C&O Canal Hike, Wilderness Society Papers, Olaus Murie Papers, CONS90, box 1.

51. Mackintosh, *C&O Canal*, 70.

52. Certificate of Incorporation of C&O Canal Association, May 21, 1957, C&O Association Records, MS 2027.

53. Douglas to Olaus Murie, Mar. 29, 1954, Douglas Papers, box 313; Douglas to Harvey Broome, Mar. 29, 1954, Douglas Papers, box 313; Mackintosh, *C&O Canal*, 72.

54. Mackintosh, *C&O Canal*, 72–73.

55. Durham, "The C&O Canal Hike," 24.

56. Douglas to Olaus Murie, June 11, 1954, Murie Ranch Papers, correspondence.

57. Douglas to Harvey Broome, Jan. 17, 1956, Douglas Papers, box 313; Douglas to Olaus Murie, Jan. 17, 1956, Douglas Papers, box 593.

58. Mackintosh, *C&O Canal*, 79.

59. "Potomac for the Future," editorial, *Washington Post*, May 1, 1956, 24.

60. Mackintosh, *C&O Canal*, 81–83, 85, 93; Douglas to Smith Brookhart, Apr. 12, 1957, Douglas Papers, box 362.

61. Douglas to Stewart L. Udall, Feb. 23, 1966, Douglas Papers, box 380.

62. Douglas to Stewart L. Udall, April 28, 1966, Douglas Papers, box 380.

63. Douglas to Stewart L. Udall, June 2, 1966, Douglas Papers, box 380.

64. Douglas to Stewart L. Udall, Dec. 29, 1966, Douglas Papers, box 380.

65. Colin Riter, president of the Chesapeake & Ohio Association, to President Richard Nixon, June 19, 1970, George Washington Special Collections, box 1.

66. Henry M. Jackson to Douglas, Dec. 22, 1970, Douglas Papers, box 343.

67. Mackintosh, *C&O Canal*, 101.

68. Paul Hodge, "Tribute to the Man Who Saved the Canal," *Washington Post*, May 5, 1977.

69. Douglas to Smith Brookhart, May 3, 1971, George Washington Special Collections, box 32.

70. Thomas Grubisich, "Engineer Corps Drops Support for Dams in Potomac Basin," *Washington Post*, Aug. 28, 1979.

71. Douglas to Olaus Murie, June 6, 1955, Douglas Papers, box 593.

72. Douglas to Olaus Murie, Apr. 9, 1956, Douglas Papers, box 593.

73. Murphy, *Wild Bill*, 334.

74. Charles Miller, clerk OT 1958, interview with author, March 30, 2017.

75. Charles Reich, *The Sorcerer of Bolinas Reef* (New York: Random House, 1976), 60; Charles Reich, interview with author, July 17, 2017.

76. Hodge, "Tribute to the Man Who Saved the Canal."

77. Quoted in Linda Charlton, "Officials and Nature Join to Hail Justice Douglas," *New York Times*, May 18, 1977, B1; Karen De Witt, "A Tribute to Douglas on the C&O Canal," *Washington Post*, May 18, 1977, B3.

78. C. J. S. Dunham, "In Remembrance of William O. Douglas, Associate Justice of the United States Supreme Court" (remarks, Great Falls MD, Jan. 17, 1980), C&O Association Records, box 32.

79. "About the C&O Canal," About Us, C&O Canal Trust, https://www.canaltrust.org/about-us/about-the-co-canal/.

80. DeWitt, "A Tribute to Douglas."

5. Dissenting on the Road

1. Douglas to Olaus Murie, May 5, 1954, Murie Ranch Papers, 2004.06.001.

2. Bob Swerer Productions, *Arctic Dance: The Mardy Murie Story* (1988).

3. Margaret E. Murie, *Two in the Far North* (Portland: Alaska Northwest Books, 1963), 333.

4. Douglas Brinkley, *The Quiet World: Saving Alaska's Wilderness Kingdom, 1879–1960* (New York: Harper Collins, 2011), 381.

5. "Promised Land," TIME *Magazine*, June 16, 1947, 26.

6. Roger Kaye, *The Last Great Wilderness: The Campaign to Establish the Alaska National Wildlife Refuge* (Fairbanks: University of Alaska Press, 2006), 68–70; for general background on the Muries, see Margaret and Olaus Murie, *Wapati Wilderness* (Boulder: University Press of Colorado, 1987).

7. Jequita Potts McDaniel, *Mardy Murie Did! Grandmother of Conservation* (New York: Taylor Trade Publishing, 2011).

8. Olaus Murie, "The Primitive Value of Jackson Hole," *Jackson Hole Courier*, June 11, 1936, Murie Ranch Papers, Clippings.

9. Kaye, *The Last Great Wilderness*, 2, 49.

10. National Resources Committee, Alaska: Its Resources and Development, H.R. Doc. No. 485 (1938).

11. Letter from Henry Fairfield Osborn, president of the New York Zoological Society, to Olaus Murie, Mar. 13, 1956, Murie Ranch Papers, 2004.06.001.

12. James M. Glover, "Olaus Murie's Spiritual Connection with Wilderness," *International Journal of Wilderness* 9, no. 1 (April 2003).

13. Quoted in Michael Carey (former reporter for *Anchorage Daily News*), notes from interview with Brina Kessel, May 16, 2001, Fairbanks, Alaska.

14. Margaret E. Murie, *Two in the Far North*, 273.

15. The descriptions of the expedition in the next several paragraphs are based on George Schaller, "Sheenjek, Alaska Journal, Brooks Range Expedition 1956, May 30–July 31, August 1–3" (unpublished manuscript), Peabody Museum of Natural History, Yale University; Murie Ranch Papers; Bob Krear, "Report on the Arctic National Wildlife Refuge, Murie Brooks Range Expedition—1956" (unpublished manuscript), Murie Ranch Papers; "Arctic Valley, A Report on the 1956 Murie Brooks Range, Alaska Expedition" (unpublished) (April 1957), Murie Ranch Papers; Robert Krear, letter to author, Apr. 20, 2017; Margaret E. Murie, *Two in the Far North*, part 4: Sheenjek; Douglas Diary, Brooks Range—1956, Douglas Papers, box 663; and William O. Douglas, *My Wilderness: The Pacific West* (New York: Doubleday, 1960).

16. Margaret E. Murie, *Two in the Far North*, 335.

17. Douglas notebook, Douglas Papers, box 663.

18. Margaret E. Murie, *Two in the Far North*, 335.

19. Douglas, *My Wilderness: The Pacific West*, 16.

20. Douglas, *My Wilderness: The Pacific West*, 9; William O. Douglas, "Brooks Range," in *Alaska: Reflections on Land and Spirit*, ed. Robert Hedin and Gary Holthaus (Tucson: University of Arizona Press, 1989), 124.

21. Kaye, *The Last Great Wilderness*, xiv.

22. Olaus Murie to Douglas, Dec. 15, 1958, Douglas Papers, box 358.

23. Kaye, *The Last Great Wilderness*, 140, 173–74.

24. Brinkley, *The Quiet World*, 490–91.

25. Pub. Land Order No. 2214, 25 F.R. 12598 (Dec. 6, 1960).

26. William O. Douglas, "Justice William O. Douglas Asks: 'Are We Looting Paradise?'" *West Magazine*, Mar. 5, 1967, Douglas Papers, box 881.

27. Alaska Native Claims Settlement Act, 43 U.S.C. § 1616(d)(2) (1971).

28. An act for the preservation of American antiquities (Antiquities Act of 1906), Pub. L. 59-209 (1906), 54 U.S.C. §§ 320301–320303.

29. Dermot Cole, "Thirty-Five Years Ago, Carter Drew Wrath of Many Alaskans," *Anchorage Daily News*, Nov. 30, 2013.

30. Cecil D. Andrus, interview with author, Apr. 27, 2017.

31. Cecil D. Andrus, interview with author, Apr. 27, 2017.

32. Alaska National Interest Lands Conservation Act, 16 U.S.C. §§ 1602–1784 (1980).

33. Cecil D. Andrus, interview with author, April 27, 2017.

34. Amendment of 1986 Code, Pub. L. No. 115-97, 131 Stat. 2054 (2017), § 20001.

35. Henry Fountain, "The Biden Administration Orders a New Review of Oil and Gas Development in the Arctic," *New York Times*, Aug. 3, 2021.

36. Elizabeth Harball, "Arctic National Wildlife Refuge Battle Ends, but Drilling Not a Given," NPR, Dec. 21, 2017; Henry Fountain, "Interior Dept. Takes Next Step toward Sale of Drilling Leases in Arctic Refuge," *New York Times*, Sept. 13, 2019.

37. Myrna Oliver, "Margaret 'Mardy' Murie, 101; Helped Create Arctic Refuge," *Los Angeles Times*, Oct. 22, 2003.

38. Carla Hall, "Cathy Douglas—The Woman Behind the Man," *Washington Post*, Dec. 9, 1979.

39. Alaska National Interest Lands Conservation Act of 1979: Hearings on H.R. 39, before the House Comm. on Interior and Insular Affairs, 96th Cong. 550 (1979) (statement of Cecil Andrus, secretary of the interior).

40. Roger Kaye, email to author, Dec. 9, 2019.

41. Michael Carey (former *Anchorage Daily News* columnist), "Tangled Roots: The Origins of the Arctic National Wildlife Refuge" (unpublished manuscript), 32; on file with author.

42. Brinkley, *The Quiet World*, 385; Collins quoted in Kaye, *The Last Great Wilderness*, 84.

43. Quoted in Oliver, "Margaret 'Mardy' Murie"; Inclusion of Alaska Lands in National Park, Forest, Wildlife Refuge, and Wild and Scenic Rivers Systems: Hearings on H.R. 39, 1974, 2876, 5505, 1454, 5605, 8651, et al., before the Subcomm. on General Oversight and Alaska Lands of the House Comm. on Interior and Insular Affairs, 95th Cong. 16 (1977) (statement of Margaret Murie, quoting Newton Drury, former director of the National Park Service).

44. Douglas, *My Wilderness: The Pacific West*, 32.

45. Melvin I. Urofsky, ed., *The Douglas Letters: Selections from the Private Papers of Justice William O. Douglas* (Bethesda MD: Adler and Adler, 1986), 241–42.

46. Douglas, *My Wilderness: The Pacific West*, 49.

47. Bob Spring and Ira Spring, "Coastal Controversy, Highway or Trail for Ocean Strip?" *Seattle Times*, Oct. 19, 1958, Murie Papers, Olympic Folder 1958–1975.

48. Ross Cunningham, "Sen. Jackson Urges Highway Development to Make State's Coastline More Accessible," *Seattle Times*, Apr. 21, 1957.

49. David Brower to Douglas, Apr. 1, 1957, Douglas Papers, box 559.

50. Douglas to Olaus Murie, Sept. 20, 1957, Murie Ranch Papers; Douglas Papers, box 358.

51. Urofsky, *Douglas Letters*, 241–42.

52. Quoted in Kevin Proescholdt, "Untrammeled Wilderness," *Minnesota History*, 61 (Fall 2008): 121.

53. Wilderness Act of 1964, 16 U.S.C. § 1131(c).

54. Robert Marshall, *Alaska Wilderness: Exploring the Central Brooks Range* (Berkeley: University of California Press: 1956), 2, 50.

55. Paula Becker, "Conservationists William O. Douglas, Polly Dyer and Others Begin a 22-Mile Hike along the Olympic Coastline to Protest Proposed Road Construction on August 19, 1958," *HistoryLink.org Online Encyclopedia of Washington State History*, Dec. 29, 2010, https://www.historylink.org/File/9672.

56. University of Washington Collection, Pauline Dyer Papers, Beach Hike, 1958.

57. *Beach Hike*, directed by Louis Huber (Portland: Oregon Historical Society, 1958), https://www.youtube.com/watch?v=y6oPkZsX7S4.

58. Joan H. Davidson, interview with author, May 30, 2018.

59. Quoted in Pauline Dyer to Howard Zahniser, Nov. 27, 1958, University of Washington Collection, Pauline Dyer Papers, Beach Hike, 1958.

60. Robert Serr, interview with author, June 27, 2018.

61. Mercedes H. Douglas, "The Olympic Beach Hike," *The Living Wilderness* 66 (Fall 1958): 8–9, Douglas Papers, box 862.

62. Harvey Broome, *Faces of the Wilderness* (Missoula MT: Mountain Press Publishing, 1972), 137.

63. Douglas notebook, Aug. 18–20, 1958, Douglas Papers, box 663.

64. Mercedes H. Douglas, "The Olympic Beach Hike," 10.

65. Mercedes H. Douglas, "The Olympic Beach Hike," 11.

66. Becker, "Conservationists William O. Douglas, Polly Dyer and Others Begin a 22-Mile Hike."

67. Douglas, *My Wilderness: The Pacific West*, 49.

68. Mrs. John A. Dyer to Daniel B. Beard, Jan. 15, 1958 [*sic*], University of Washington Collection, Pauline Dyer Papers.

69. Douglas to Dr. Lorin W. Roberts, Sept. 28, 1956, Douglas Papers, box 559.

70. Douglas to Pauline Dyer, Feb. 18, 1961, University of Washington Collection, Pauline Dyer Papers, Biographical Features.

71. E. M. Sterling, "Controversial 'Ocean Strip' Road Gets U.S. Backing," *Seattle Times*, Apr. 19, 1964.

72. Don Page, "Douglas Hails State Wilderness, U.S. Justice Leads 'Army' in Olympics," *Seattle Post-Intelligencer*, Aug. 18, 1964.

73. E. M. Sterling, "Tide Delays Hikers," *Seattle Times*, Aug. 18, 1964.

74. "Save Our Coast Hike Begins Today at Rialto Beach," *Peninsula Daily News* (Port Angeles WA), Aug. 19, 2018.

75. M. Margaret McKeown, "Justice Takes a Side," *Seattle Times, Pacific NW Magazine*, Aug. 19, 2018, 12–17.

6. Supreme Advocate

1. Quoted in Official Report of Proceedings before the U.S. Department of the Interior, "Commemoration of Hundredth Anniversary of Henry David Thoreau" (Dumbarton Oaks, Washington DC, May 11, 1962), Douglas Papers, box 380.

2. Douglas wrote David Brower of the Sierra Club in March 1962 that he had "very grave doubts" that the wilderness bill could pass the House. Robert Wyss, *The Man Who Built the Sierra Club: A Life of David Brower* (New York: Columbia University Press, 2016), 145.

3. David M. O'Brien, *Storm Center: The Supreme Court in American Politics*, 8th ed. (New York: W. W. Norton, 2008), 88.

4. Douglas, *Court Years*, 252; Nathaniel L. Nathanson, "The Extra-Judicial Activities of Supreme Court Justices: Where Should the Line Be Drawn?" *Northwestern University Law Review* 78 (1983–84): 521.

5. Peter Alan Bell, "Extrajudicial Activity of Supreme Court Justices," *Stanford Law Review* 22 (Feb. 1970): 587.

6. Douglas, *Court Years*, 252.

7. Douglas, *Court Years*, 253.

8. William O. Douglas, "Memorandum for the Court Re: Recommendation of the Judicial Conference," Oct. 1969, Douglas Papers, box 594.

9. Urofsky, *Douglas Letters*, 400.

10. Cathy Douglas Stone, interview with author, July 20, 2020.

11. Douglas to Charles A. Reich, Mar. 3, 1962, Douglas Papers, box 549.

12. Douglas to David R. Brower, Sept. 7, 1961, Douglas Papers, box 548.

13. Robert G. Kaiser, *So Damn Much Money* (New York: First Vintage Books, 2010), 54.

14. William O. Douglas, "The Public Be Dammed," *Playboy*, July 1969, 187.

15. See, generally, David P. Billington, Donald D. Jackson, and Martin V. Melosi, *The History of Large Federal Dams: Planning, Design, and Construction in the Era of Big Dams* (Denver: Department of the Interior, Bureau of Reclamation, 2005).

16. Douglas, "The Public Be Dammed," 187.

17. Urofsky, *Douglas Letters*, 400.

18. See, generally, Mark W. T. Harvey, *Battle for Dinosaur: Echo Park Dam and the Birth of the American Conservation Movement* (Seattle: University of Washington Press, 2000).

19. Neil Compton, *The Battle for the Buffalo River: The Story of America's First National River* (Fayetteville: University of Arkansas Press, 1992); Pat Crow, "Justice Douglas Says Keep Beauty Unspoiled," *Arkansas Gazette*, Apr. 30, 1965; William O. Douglas, "An Inquest on Our Lakes and Rivers," *Playboy*, June 1968, 96–97; Douglas to Henry M. Jackson, Apr. 18, 1967, Douglas Papers, box 343 (Buffalo River); Urofsky, *Douglas Letters*, 404.

20. Douglas, "The Public Be Dammed," 188.

21. Urofsky, *Douglas Letters*, 404.

22. United States v. Carlo Bianchi & Co., Inc., 373 U.S. 709, 719 (1963) (Douglas, J., dissenting); 2,606.84 Acres of Land in Tarrant County, Texas v. United States, 402 U.S. 917 (1971) (Douglas, J., dissenting).

23. Douglas: "The Public Be Dammed," 188; "Speech at University of Vermont," Apr. 16, 1969, Douglas Papers, box 304.

24. "Corps: No 'Mandate' for Big Hydro Project," *Seattle Times*, Nov. 3, 1981.

25. Michael C. Blumm and Andrew B. Erickson, "Dam Removal in the Pacific Northwest: Lessons for the Nation," *Environmental Law* 42, no. 4 (2012): 1043, 1072–73, 1097; Lisa W. Foderaro, "It's Fish vs. Dams, and the Dams Are Winning," *New York Times*, Jan. 20, 2020.

26. Douglas, "The Public Be Dammed," 185.

27. Quoted in Tom Eblen, "50 Years Ago, Red River Gorge Almost Became a Lake. The Story of a Hike That Saved It," *Lexington Herald Leader*, Nov. 17, 2017, https://www.kentucky.com/news/local/news-columns-blogs/tom-eblen/article185173423.html.

28. Snohomish County v. Seattle Disposal Company, 389 U.S. 1016 (1967) (Douglas, J., dissenting).

29. Quoted in Urofsky, *Douglas Letters*, 404–5.

30. *Protecting Kentucky's Red River Gorge*, produced by the Your Forest, Your Future film series, Aug. 1, 2018, https://www.outsideonline.com/2331011/kentuckys-red-river-gorge.

31. Eblen, "50 Years Ago, Red River Gorge Almost Became a Lake."

32. Douglas, "The Public Be Dammed," 185.

33. Lyndon Johnson to Douglas, Dec. 23, 1949; March 10, 1966; June 11, 1968; Douglas Papers, box 346.

34. Douglas to Lyndon B. Johnson, Nov. 20, 1967, LBJ Library, Subject File NR7, box 15.

35. Charles Maguire to Lyndon B. Johnson, Nov. 22, 1967, LBJ Library, Subject File NR7, box 15, folder 2.

36. Johnson to Douglas, Nov. 22, 1967, LBJ Library, Subject File NR7, box 15, folder 2.

37. Douglas to Stewart L. Udall, Nov. 22, 1967, and Feb. 8, 1968; Douglas Papers, box 380.

38. Stewart L. Udall to Douglas, n.d., Douglas Papers, box 380, folder 4.

39. "Daniel Boone National Forest," USDA Forest Service, updated Apr. 14, 2020, https://www.fs.usda.gov/dbnf/; Wendell Berry and Ralph Eugene Meatyard, *The Unforeseen Wilderness: Kentucky's Red River Gorge* (Berkeley: Counterpoint, 1971).

40. Douglas, *Court Years*, 312, 318.

41. Urofsky, *Douglas Letters*, 252.

42. Adrian Benepe, "How the White House Went Green: The Environmental Legacy of President Lyndon B. Johnson and Lady Bird Johnson, the Nature of Cities Summit," Nov. 1, 2015, https://www.thenatureofcities.com/2015/11/01/how-the-white-house-went-green-the-environmental-legacy-of-president-lyndon-b-johnson-and-lady-bird-johnson/.

43. Lady Bird Johnson to Douglas, Feb. 10, 1965, LBJ Library, Subject File NR7, box 15, folder 1.

44. Bureau of the Census, U.S. Dept. of Commerce, *U.S. Census of Agriculture: Special Report*, vol. 5, pt. 4 (1950), 18. In 1950 nearly 90 percent of federal and Indian lands were located in the eleven western states.

45. "History of the Department of the Interior," Who We Are, U.S. Department of the Interior, https://www.doi.gov/whoweare/history.

46. U.S. Department of the Interior, "In Case You Missed It: Interior Continues to Restore Public Access to Public Lands," press release, May 8, 2020, https://www.doi.gov/pressreleases/case-you-missed-it-interior-continues-restore-public-access-public-lands.

47. Scott Raymond Einberger, *With Distance in His Eyes: The Environmental Life and Legacy of Stewart Udall* (Reno: University of Nevada Press, 2018), 180.

48. See, for example, correspondence between Douglas and Stewart L. Udall, Nov. 3, 1967, Dec. 15, 1967, and Dec. 21, 1967 (Bumping Lake); Nov. 2, 1961, and Nov. 21, 1961 (Toppenish, Washington); and Apr. 10, 1961 (Wyoming); Douglas Papers, box 380.

49. Stewart L. Udall to Douglas, April 7, 1960, Douglas Papers, box 380.

50. See, for example, Boesche v. Udall, 373 U.S. 472 (1963); Halpert v. Udall, 379 U.S. 645 (1965); Udall v. Federal Power Commission, 387 U.S. 428 (1967).

51. Quoted in William Schwarz, ed., *Voices for the Wilderness* (New York: Ballantine Books, 1969), 278.

52. David Brower to Douglas, Jan. 13, 1961; Douglas to F. K. O'Donnell, Jan. 16, 1961; F. K. O'Donnell to Douglas, Jan. 31, 1961; JFK Library, William O. Douglas Correspondence (Jan. 1961–Dec. 1962).

53. Quoted in *Wilderness, America's Living Heritage* (San Francisco: Sierra Club, 1961), 102.

54. Murphy, *Wild Bill*, 347–49.

55. Quoted in Thomas G. Smith, *Stewart L. Udall: Steward of the Land* (Albuquerque: University of New Mexico Press, 2017), 150.

56. Douglas to John F. Kennedy, Oct. 1, 1962, JFK Library, William O. Douglas Correspondence (Jan. 1961–Dec. 1962).

57. Douglas, *The Court Years*, 303.

58. Douglas Brinkley interview with author, August 24, 2021.

59. Quoted in *Wilderness, America's Living Heritage*, 62, 100.

60. Quoted in *Wilderness, America's Living Heritage*, 98.

61. Douglas to Conrad L. Wirth, Dec. 4, 1961, Douglas Papers, box 380.

62. On Wirth's career, see Conrad L. Wirth, *Parks, Politics, and the People* (Norman: University of Oklahoma Press, 1980); Douglas, *My Wilderness: East to Katahdin*, 264.

63. Wirth to Douglas, Nov. 20, 1961, Douglas Papers, box 380.

64. Douglas to Wirth, Dec. 4, 1961, Douglas Papers, box 380; Urofsky, *Douglas Letters*, 245–46. Douglas's support for a new national park didn't end with his plea to the National Park Service. He advised the National Resources Council in Maine on how to set up a nonprofit, "Save the Allagash Committee." Douglas to Charles A. Pierce, secretary, National Resources Council, Nov. 2, 1962, Douglas Papers, box 380.

65. Quoted in Schwarz, *Voices for the Wilderness*, x.

66. Einberger, *With Distance in His Eyes*, 208.

67. Einberger, *With Distance in His Eyes*, 214. Ironically, one of Udall's greatest failures involved his support of the Bridge Canyon Dam, which would have intruded on the Grand Canyon National Monument and the Grand Canyon National Park. A change of heart saved him from environmental ignominy.

68. Douglas, *Go East, Young Man*, 215.

69. "Bridges within the National Forest System—A Historic Context," U.S. Forest Service, updated Nov. 6, 2019, https://www.fs.fed.us/eng/pubs/htmlpubs /htm00712854/page05.htm; "By the Numbers," U.S. Forest Service, updated Nov. 2013, https://www.fs.usda.gov/about-agency/newsroom/by-the-numbers.

70. Charles Wilkinson and Michael Anderson, "Land and Resource Planning in the National Forests," *Oregon Law Review* 64, no. 1 (1985): 28.

71. Wilkinson and Anderson, "Land and Resource Planning," 137.

72. Multiple-Use Sustained-Yield Act of 1960, Pub. L. 86-517, 74 Stat. 215 (1960).

73. Douglas to James Powell, Sept. 23 and 30, 1949, Douglas Papers, box 1033.

74. Douglas to Lawrence Barrett, June 12, 1954, Douglas Papers, box 548.

75. Michael McCloskey, *In the Thick of It: My Life in the Sierra Club* (Washington DC: Island Press, 2005), 44.

76. Douglas to Henry M. "Scoop" Jackson, Jan. 3, 1962, Douglas Papers, box 550.

77. Henry M. Jackson to Douglas, Feb. 6, 1962, Douglas Papers, box 343; Freeman to Douglas, Jan. 5, 1966, Douglas Papers, box 550; Douglas to P. D. Goldsworthy, May 21, 1968, Douglas Papers, box 542.

78. McCloskey, *In the Thick of It*, 29.

79. Senate Committee on Interior and Insular Affairs, North Cascades; Olympic National Park: Hearings before the Comm. on Interior and Insular Affairs, 89th Cong., 2d sess., Feb. 11–12, 1966, 9, 14.

80. Douglas to L. G. Barrett, June 22, 1961, Douglas Papers, box 550.

81. *Great Falls Tribune*, Aug. 25, 1962, photo by Harvey O. Robe, Forest Service Museum, Missoula, Montana, Robe Papers, 2016.019.019.153; Senate Committee on Interior and Insular Affairs, San Rafael Wilderness: Hearings before the Subcomm. on Public Lands, 90th Cong., 1st sess., Apr. 11, 1967, 8 (statement of Orville Freeman, secretary of the interior).

82. Douglas Papers, box 1775.

83. See, for example, Holmes v. United States, 391 U.S. 936 (1968) (Douglas, J., dissenting). Douglas wrote eight dissents on this subject.

84. Sharon Boswell and Lorraine McConaghy, "Twin Towers of Power," *Seattle Times*, Sept. 29, 1996.

85. See, for example, Urofsky, *Douglas Letters*, 242–43; Douglas to Warren Grant Magnuson, Apr. 6, 1960 (contacting Magnuson about his bill to establish the North Cascades Park); Henry M. Jackson to Douglas, Sept. 7, 1961; Douglas Papers, box 548 (follow-up regarding the Boise Cascade mill).

86. See, generally, correspondence with Henry M. Jackson, Douglas Papers, box 343.

87. Douglas to Robert Strange McNamara, July 3, 1967, and July 28, 1967; Douglas to Lyndon Baines Johnson, Aug. 12, 1967; Douglas to Henry M. Jackson, Feb. 1, 1968; Douglas Papers, box 343.

88. Douglas to Charles McCurdy Mathias, June 17, 1961; Clair Engle to Douglas, Aug. 1, 1961; Douglas Papers, box 548.

89. Douglas to Wirth, Dec. 4, 1961, Douglas Papers, box 380.

7. America's Teacher

1. Douglas, *An Almanac of Liberty*, 42.

2. United States v. Rumely, 345 U.S. 41, 56 (1953) (Douglas, J., concurring).

3. See example of tagline in Olaus Murie to Howard Zahniser, May 5, 1956, Wilderness Society Papers, CONS130; Porter and Thoreau, *In Wildness Is the Preservation of the World*. Thoreau first uttered this famous refrain in an April 23, 1851, oration at the Concord Lyceum. See Brinkley, "Thoreau's Wilderness Legacy."

4. Howard Zahniser to Douglas, Feb. 11, 1954, Wilderness Society Papers, CONS130, box 7.

5. Douglas to Olaus Murie, June 20, 1959, Douglas Papers, box 352 (Brooks Range); Douglas to Olaus Murie and Carrol Noble, Feb. 17, 1960 (seeking review "with a fine tooth comb" of a draft chapter in *My Wilderness: East to Katahdin*); Douglas to Olaus Murie, Feb. 23, 1960, Douglas Papers, box 358 (Yellowstone elk); Douglas to Olaus Murie, Apr. 17, 1961, Douglas Papers, box 351 (antelope and fencing).

6. Zahniser to Douglas, n.d., Douglas Papers, box 383.

7. Douglas to Zahniser, Feb. 26, 1960, Douglas Papers, box 383.

8. Michael McCloskey, email to author, Apr. 17, 2020; McCloskey, *In the Thick of It*, 20.

9. Tom Turner, *David Brower, The Making of the Environmental Movement* (Berkeley: University of California Press, 2015), 106–7.

10. Douglas to Dr. Edgar Wayburn, president of the Sierra Club, Oct. 1, 1962, Douglas Papers, box 1763. See also Urofsky, *Douglas Letters*, 62.

11. Douglas to Charles Reich, Sept. 11, 1962, Douglas Papers, box 365.

12. Douglas to Dr. Philip Berry, president of the Sierra Club, Dec. 2, 1970, Douglas Papers, box 1764.

13. Douglas to David Brower, Feb. 21, 1962, Bancroft Library, Brower Correspondence, box 2.

14. Dr. Edgar Wayburn to Douglas, Oct. 23, 1962, and Nov. 6, 1962, Douglas Papers, box 1763.

15. Michael McCloskey, interview with author, Apr. 19, 2019; Michael McCloskey, "Taking Over as Environmentalism Takes Off," *Forest History Today*, Spring 2008, 29.

16. Quoted in Official Report of Proceedings before the U.S. Department of the Interior, "Commemoration of Hundredth Anniversary of Henry David Thoreau." Douglas Papers, box. 380.

17. Telephone message from Sigurd Olson and David Brower to Douglas, Apr. 11, 1961, Douglas Papers, box 548; Douglas to Red Higgins of Red's Wallowa Horse Ranch, Apr. 1, 1961, Douglas Papers, box 548.

18. Ann Gilliam, ed., *Voices for the Earth: A Treasury of the Sierra Club Bulletin, 1893–1977* (San Francisco: Sierra Club Books, 1979), 538–39. These laudatory remarks were made in connection with a speech by Douglas, "Nature and Value of Diversity."

19. William O. Douglas, "America's Vanishing Wilderness," *Ladies' Home Journal*, July 1964, 37, 77.

20. Edward D. Collins, "Committees of Correspondence of the American Revolution," *American Historical Association Annual Report* 1 (1901): 245–46.

21. Douglas, "America's Vanishing Wilderness," 77.

22. Ernest Gruening to Douglas, July 7, 1964, Douglas Papers, 877.

23. Ernest Gruening to Douglas, July 7, 1964, Douglas Papers, 877.

24. Douglas to Marian G. Laurie, Mar. 11, 1965, Douglas Papers, box 550; Douglas to David M. Seymour, Jan. 11, 1960, Douglas Papers, box 548.

25. Douglas to United Conservation Fund, Mar. 17, 1955, Douglas Papers, box 548.

26. Douglas to Meyer Lefkowitz, Dec. 15, 1961, Douglas Papers, box 548.

27. Douglas to Hon. Jean-Paul Harroy, vice-governor general, Ruanda-Urundi, Africa, May 5, 1960, Douglas Papers, box 548.

28. Mike Wallace interview with William O. Douglas, ABC, New York, May 11, 1958; "Mr. Justice Douglas," hosted by Eric Sevareid, *CBS Reports*, Sept. 6, 1972; *Good Morning America*, featuring Justice Douglas and Cathy Douglas, ABC, New York, Nov. 14, 1975.

29. *What's My Line*, CBS, New York, May 5, 1956.

30. Richard Davis, "The Symbiotic Relationship between the U. S. Supreme Court and the Press," in *Covering the United States Supreme Court in the Digital Age*, ed. Richard Davis (Cambridge: Cambridge University Press, 2014), 14; Harvard Law School, John Roberts, "Supreme Court and Appellate Advocacy," YouTube, Nov. 21, 2017; National Portrait Gallery, Elena Kagan, "The Four Justices," YouTube, Mar. 16, 2015; Ruth Bader Ginsburg, "Stephen Works Out with Ruth Bader Ginsburg," *The Late Show with Stephen Colbert*, CBS, New York Mar. 21, 2018; Stephen Breyer, "Justice Stephen Breyer Interview," *The Late Show with Stephen Colbert*, CBS, New York Sept. 15, 2015; Sonia Sotomayor, "Justice Sonia Sotomayor Allows Stephen to Approach the Bench," *The Late Show with Stephen Colbert*, CBS, New York Nov. 16, 2018; Conversations with Bill Kristol, "Samuel Alito: Justice Alito Reflects on the Supreme Court, Recent Controversial Cases, and His Education," July 20, 2015, https://conversationswithbillkristol.org/video/samuel-alito/; Conversations with Bill Kristol, "Clarence Thomas: Personal Reflections on Twenty-Five Years on the Court, His Jurisprudence, and His Education," Oct. 22, 2016, https://conversationswithbillkristol.org/video/clarence-thomas/; Stephen Breyer, "Justice Stephen Breyer: His View from the Bench," CBS *Sunday Morning*, New York Sept. 13, 2015; "Created Equal: Clarence Thomas in His Own Words," PBS, May 18, 2020.

31. For an overview of Supreme Court justices' autobiographies published in the nineteenth and twentieth centuries, see Laura Krugman Ray, "Lives of the Justices: Supreme Court Autobiographies," *Connecticut Law Review* 37 (2004): 233–320.

32. Ray, "Lives of the Justices," 315–16.

33. Douglas, *Court Years*, 172.

34. Warth v. Seldin, 422 U.S. 490, 519 (1975) (Douglas, J., dissenting).

35. Douglas, *Court Years*, 4.

36. Murphy, *Wild Bill*, 285; "Salaries: Supreme Court Justices," Federal Judicial Center, https://www.fjc.gov/history/judges/judicial-salaries-supreme-court-justices.

37. William O. Douglas, *We the Judges: Studies in American and Indian Constitutional Law from Marshall to Mukherjea* (Garden City NY: Doubleday, 1956), 334.

38. See Douglas Papers, boxes 852–91.

39. CBS *Reports*, "Mr. Justice Douglas," hosted by Eric Sevareid, Sept. 6, 1972.

40. Mrs. Olaus J. Murie to the editors, *Ladies' Home Journal*, June 22, 1964, Douglas Papers, box 877.

41. William O. Douglas, *Beyond the High Himalayas* (New York: Doubleday, 1952), 40.

42. Douglas, *Of Men and Mountains*, 313.

43. Douglas, *My Wilderness: The Pacific West*, 94–95.

44. Douglas, *Go East, Young Man*, 237.

45. Douglas, *My Wilderness: The Pacific West*, 125–26.

46. Cathy Douglas Stone, interview with author, July 20, 2020; "Remembrances of William O. Douglas by His Friends and Associates, In Celebration of the Fiftieth Anniversary of His Appointment as Associate Justice of the Supreme Court

of the United States of America 1939–1989" (remarks by Jerome B. Falk Jr., former law clerk), *Supreme Court Historical Society*, 1990 Yearbook, 22.

47. Douglas, *Wilderness Bill of Rights*, 109.

48. William O. Douglas, "Wilderness and Human Rights," in Schwarz, *Voices for the Wilderness*, 109, 121.

49. Adam M. Sowards, *The Environmental Justice: William O. Douglas and American Conservation* (Corvallis: Oregon State University Press, 2009), 75.

50. Douglas, *Wilderness Bill of Rights*, 33.

51. Douglas, *Wilderness Bill of Rights*, 25.

52. Olaus Murie to Richard E. McArdle, chief forester, Dec. 7, 1955, Wilderness Society Papers, CONS130.

53. Douglas, *Wilderness Bill of Rights*, 108.

54. Douglas, *Wilderness Bill of Rights*, 101, 110.

55. Douglas, *Wilderness Bill of Rights*, 150.

56. Douglas, *Wilderness Bill of Rights*, 34.

57. William O. Douglas, *The Three Hundred Year War: A Chronicle of Ecological Disaster* (New York: Random House, 1972), 152.

58. Douglas, *Three Hundred Year War*, 188.

59. Douglas, *Three Hundred Year War*, 168.

60. Douglas, *Three Hundred Year War*, 199.

61. William O. Douglas, *Farewell to Texas: A Vanishing Wilderness* (New York: McGraw-Hill, 1967), 231.

62. Adam M. Sowards, "Modern Ahabs in Texas: William O. Douglas and Lone Star Conservation," *Journal of the West* 44, no. 4 (Fall 2005): 39–40.

63. Quoted in Simon, *Independent Journey*, 327.

64. "Nature & Science," National Park Service, updated Sept. 13, 2017, https://www.nps.gov/bith/learn/nature/index.htm.

65. James Cozine, "Defining the Big Thicket: Prelude to Preservation," *East Texas Historical Journal* 31, no. 2 (1993): 57–58; Douglas, *Farewell to Texas*, 37, 230.

66. 112 Cong. Rec. s8621–22 (daily ed. Apr. 20, 1966) (statement of Senator Yarborough).

67. Stewart Udall to Douglas, June 17, 1969, Douglas Papers, box 380; Sowards, "Modern Ahabs in Texas," 41.

68. Douglas to Jim D. Bowmer, May 26, 1966, Douglas Papers, box 310.

69. Douglas, *Farewell to Texas*, 231.

70. Douglas to Lyndon Johnson, July 21, 1965, LBJ Library, folder 1.

71. 16 U.S.C. § 698 (1974), Big Thicket National Preserve Act.

72. Douglas to Jim D. Bowmer, Nov. 1, 1974, Douglas Papers, box 312; Sowards, "Modern Ahabs in Texas, 46."

8. Dissenting on the Court

1. Lee Epstein et al., *The Supreme Court Compendium: Data, Decisions, and Developments*, 6th ed. (Washington DC: CQ Press, 2015), 636, tables 6–9; Lone Dissent: An Exercise in Supreme Court Obstinacy, lonedissent.org. The statistics vary slightly across sources. Schultz, for example, has Douglas authoring 500 major-

ity opinions and 583 dissents. David Schultz, *Encyclopedia of the Supreme Court* (New York: Facts on File, 2005), 131.

2. Adam Feldman, "King of Dissents," *Empirical scotus*, June 22, 2016, https://empiricalscotus.com/2016/06/22/king-of-dissents/.

3. Melvin I. Urofsky, "William O. Douglas as a Common Law Judge," *Duke Law Journal* 41, no. 1 (1991): 137.

4. Douglas, *Go East, Young Man*, 334.

5. Evan Thomas, *First: Sandra Day O'Connor* (New York: Random House, 2019), 297.

6. Quoted in Simon, *Independent Journey*, 250.

7. Ruth Bader Ginsburg, "Lecture: The Role of Dissenting Opinions," *Minnesota Law Review* 95 (2011): 1–8. Justice Ginsburg was quoting Chief Justice Hughes in the phrase "appealing to the intelligence of a future day."

8. Hannah Mullen, "In Memoriam," *Northwestern University Law Review* 114 (2020): 1777.

9. S. Cohen and Urofsky, "Court Diary of Justice William O. Douglas," 91.

10. Terminiello v. City of Chicago, 337 U.S. 1, 4 (1949).

11. Melvin I. Urofsky, *Dissent and the Supreme Court: Its Role in the Court's History and the Nation's Constitutional Dialogue* (New York: Pantheon, 2015), 4.

12. Vern Countryman, "The Contribution of the Douglas Dissents," *Georgia Law Review* 10 (1976): 331–52.

13. See Terminiello v. City of Chicago, 337 U.S. 1 (1949); New York Times Co. v. United States, 403 U.S. 713 (1971) (Douglas, J., concurring); United States v. Paramount Pictures, Inc., 334 U.S. 131 (1949); Brady v. Maryland, 373 U.S. 83 (1963).

14. Griswold v. Connecticut, 381 U.S. 479, 484 (1965).

15. David J. Garrow, "The Tragedy of William O. Douglas," *Nation*, Mar. 27, 2003, https://www.thenation.com/article/tragedy-william-o-douglas/.

16. Abe Fortas, "William O. Douglas: An Appreciation," *Indiana Law Journal* 51 (1975): 3.

17. Laura Krugman Ray, "Autobiography and Opinion: The Romantic Jurisprudence of Justice William O. Douglas," *University of Pittsburgh Law Review* 60 (1999): 707.

18. Kent v. Dulles, 357 U.S. 116, 126 (1958).

19. DeFunis v. Odegaard, 416 U.S. 312, 335 (1974) (Douglas, J., dissenting).

20. International Association of Machinists v. Street, 367 U.S. 740, 775 (1961) (Douglas, J., concurring).

21. Papachristou v. City of Jacksonville, 405 U.S. 156, 165 and n. 7 (1972).

22. William O. Douglas, "Vagrancy and Arrest on Suspicion," *Yale Law Journal* 70 (1960): 3.

23. Douglas, *Go East, Young Man*, xi.

24. Charles Miller, clerk OT 1958, interview with author, March 30, 2017.

25. Urofsky, "William O. Douglas as a Common Law Judge," 140; Simon, *Independent Journey*, 251.

26. G. Edward White, "The Anti-Judge: William O. Douglas and the Ambiguities of Individuality," *Virginia Law Review* 74 (1988): 17.

27. Franchise Tax Board of California v. Hyatt, 139 S. Ct. 1485, 1492 (2019) (over-ruling Nevada v. Hall, 440 U.S. 410 [1979] and holding that states are immune from suit in courts of another state).

28. Douglas, *Court Years*, 8.

29. Quoted in Murphy, *Wild Bill*, 455 (Murphy interview with Richard "Red" Schwartz, College of Law of Syracuse University, Syracuse NY, Jan. 27, 1993).

30. Ten years later Professor Schwartz, referencing a dinner with Douglas, wrote that Douglas "certainly said nothing about bending the law." At a break-fast the next morning, Schwartz said he did not recall "[Douglas's] saying that he was 'ready to bend the law' to deal with pollution or any of our other prob-lems." (Schwartz email to David Cote, June 10, 2003; email on file with David Danelski and copy of text on file with author.) Unfortunately, Schwartz died in 2017, so this dispute cannot be clarified.

31. Udall v. Federal Power Commission, 387 U.S. 428, 440 (1967). Justice Frank-furter first used the word "ecology" in a 1952 reference to "sciences as young as human ecology and cultural anthropology." Beauharnais v. Illinois, 343 U.S. 250, 262 (1952).

32. San Antonio Conservation Society v. Texas Highway Department, 400 U.S. 968, 975 (1970) (Douglas, J., dissenting). Strictly speaking, the earliest appearance of the word "environmental" was in Power Reactor Development Co. v. Interna-tional Union of Electrical, Radio and Machine Workers, AFL-CIO, 367 U.S. 396, 419 n. 10 (1961), but only by way of a congressional hearing title cited in a footnote.

33. United States v. Causby, 328 U.S. 256 (1946); Noise Control Act of 1972, 42 U.S.C. § 4901.

34. Murphy v. Benson, 362 U.S. 929, 931 (1960) (Douglas, J., dissenting).

35. Douglas, *My Wilderness: East to Katahdin*, 49–55.

36. Murphy v. Benson, 362 U.S. 932–33, 933 n. 8 (1960) (Douglas, J., dissenting) (quoting Rachel Carson, "Vanishing Americans," *Washington Post*, Apr. 10, 1959).

37. Rachel Carson, *Silent Spring* (New York: Houghton Mifflin, 1962), 158–61.

38. William O. Douglas, "Report," *Book-of-the-Month-Club News*, Sept. 1962, 2–4.

39. Edward O. Wilson, afterword to Carson, *Silent Spring*.

40. Liza Gross, "Pesticides Are Harming Bees in Literally Every Possible Way," *Wired*, Jan. 24, 2019, https://www.wired.com/story/pesticides-are-harming-bees-in-literally-every-possible-way/.

41. Udall v. Federal Power Commission, 387 U.S. 428 (1967).

42. Udall v. Federal Power Commission, 387 U.S. 428, 436 (1967).

43. Udall v. Federal Power Commission, 387 U.S. 428, 439, 443, 449–50 (1967).

44. Stewart Udall to Douglas, undated correspondence, Douglas Papers, box 380.

45. Noise Control Act of 1972, 42 U.S.C. § 4331(b)(1).

46. Richard Lazarus, "The National Environmental Policy Act in the U.S. Supreme Court: A Reappraisal and a Peek behind the Curtain," *Georgetown Law Journal* 11 (2012): 1507. Although the Lazarus study covered data only through 2012, the plaintiffs' losing record did not change through 2019.

47. Memorandum by William O. Douglas to the conference, Dec. 7, 1970, Douglas Papers, box 1520.

48. San Antonio Conservation Society v. Texas Highway Department, 400 U.S. 968, 972, 974, 977 (1970) (Douglas, J., dissenting).

49. United States v. Students Challenging Regulatory Agency Procedures, 412 U.S. 669 (1973) (SCRAP I); Aberdeen & Rockfish R. Co. v. Students Challenging Regulatory Agency Procedures, 422 U.S. 289 (1975) (SCRAP II).

50. SCRAP I, 412 U.S. at 670, 689.

51. SCRAP I, 412 U.S. at 710, 714.

52. SCRAP I, 422 U.S. at 331 (Douglas, J., dissenting).

53. 2,606.84 Acres of Land in Tarrant County, Texas, v. United States, 402 U.S. 916 (1971) (Douglas, J., dissenting); Committee for Nuclear Responsibility, Inc. v. Schlesinger, 404 U.S. 917 (1971) (Douglas, J., dissenting); Life of the Land v. Claude S. Brinegar, Secretary of Transportation, 414 U.S. 1052 (1973) (Douglas, J., dissenting); Watson v. Kenlick Coal Co., Inc., 422 U.S. 1012, 1013 (1975) (Douglas, J., dissenting).

54. Douglas handwritten diary, Oct. 12, 1940, Douglas Papers, box 1781.

55. Arizona v. California, 373 U.S. 546, 630 (1963) (Douglas, J., dissenting).

56. Scenic Hudson Preservation Conference v. Federal Power Commission, 407 U.S. 926, 932–33 (1972) (Douglas, J., dissenting).

57. See, for example, Kisor v. Wilkie, 139 S. Ct. 2400 (2019); Baldwin v. United States, 140 S. Ct. 690, 691–92 (2020) (Thomas, J., dissenting from denial of certiorari).

58. Richard Lazarus, "Restoring What's Environmental about Environmental Law in the Supreme Court," UCLA Law Review 47 (1999–2000): 727.

59. Northwest Band of Shoshone Indians v. United States, 324 U.S. 335, 361–62 (1945) (Douglas J., dissenting) (quoting brief of amicus curiae with respect to "simple justice").

60. Kastenberg, Campaign to Impeach, xiv.

61. Douglas, Of Men and Mountains, 25–27.

62. DeFunis v. Odegaard, 416 U.S. 312, 335 (1974) (Douglas, J., dissenting).

63. Quoted in Douglas, Go East, Young Man, 75.

64. United States v. Santa Fe Pacific Railroad, 314 U.S. 339 (1941).

65. Quoted in Christian W. McMillen, "The Birth of an Activist: Fred Mahone and the Politicization of the Hualapai, 1918 to 1923," American Indian Culture and Research Journal 27 (2003): 35.

66. Santa Fe Pacific Railroad, 314 U.S., at 359.

67. Sarah Krakoff, "Not Yet America's Best Idea: Law, Inequality, and Grand Canyon National Park," University of Colorado Law Review 91 (2020): 594.

68. Christian W. McMillen, Making Indian Law: The Hualapai Case and the Birth of Ethnohistory (New Haven CT: Yale University Press, 2007), xv.

69. Ralph W. Johnson, "Douglas and the American Indian Cases," in "He Shall Not Pass This Way Again": The Legacy of Justice William O. Douglas, ed. Stephen L. Wasby (Pittsburgh: University of Pittsburgh Press, 1990), 206; Robert Keller, Jr., "William O. Douglas, the Supreme Court, and American Indians," American Indian Law Review 3 (1975): 339.

70. Keller, "William O. Douglas, the Supreme Court, and American Indians," 349 (citing Douglas, The Three Hundred Year War).

71. Organized v. Egan "Village of Kake," 369 U.S., 60, 76 (1962).

72. *Village of Kake*, 369 U.S. at 77, 79, 80–81, 83 (Douglas, J., dissenting).

73. Puyallup Tribe v. Department of Game of Washington, 391 U.S. 392, 393, 398 (1968) (Puyallup I).

74. Department of Game of Washington v. Puyallup Tribe, 414 U.S. 44, 46–49 (1973) (Puyallup II).

75. Puyallup Tribe v. Department of Game of Washington, 433 U.S. 165, 175 (1977).

76. Johnson, "Douglas and the American Indian Cases," 202. Johnson also notes that by this time, the court had resolved its "equal protection analysis as applied to Indians" (p, 201).

77. Douglas, *Court Years*, 171.

78. Melvin I. Urofsky, "Getting the Job Done: William O. Douglas and Collegiality in the Supreme Court," in Wasby, *"He Shall Not Pass This Way Again,"* 37–41.

79. "Remembrances of William O. Douglas by His Friends and Associates," 21; Jerome B. Falk Jr., clerk OT 1965, interview with author, Mar. 23, 2017.

80. Evan Schwab, clerk OT 1963, interview with author, Jan. 11, 2017.

81. Quoted in Marshall L. Small, "William O. Douglas Remembered: A Collective Memory by WOD's Law Clerks," *Journal of Supreme Court History* 32, no. 3 (2007): 307 (Carol Bruch, clerk OT 1972); Cathy Douglas Stone, interview with author, July 20, 2020.

82. Quoted in Small, "William O. Douglas Remembered," 306 (Alan Austin, clerk OT 1974).

83. Kastenberg, *Campaign to Impeach*, 245.

84. Charles Ares, clerk OT 1952, interview with author, April 5, 2017.

85. Bob Woodward and Scott Armstrong, *The Brethren: Inside the Supreme Court* (New York: Simon and Schuster, 2011), 63. L. A. Powe Jr., clerk OT 1970 and now a professor of the University of Texas Law School, has been a pointed critic. See Garrow, "The Tragedy of William O. Douglas."

86. William Canby, clerk to Justice Whittaker, now a judge on the U.S. Court of Appeals for the Ninth Circuit, email to author, June 20, 2020.

87. William Cohen, "Justice Douglas: A Law Clerk's View," *University of Chicago Law Review* 26 (1958): 6, 8.

88. William Alsup, "Accurately Remembering Justice Douglas: A Reply to *Wild Bill* and Recent Critics," *Federal Lawyer*, Nov.–Dec. 2003, 28 (clerk OT 1971); Todd C. Peppers and Artemus Ward, *In Chambers: Stories of Supreme Court Law Clerks and Their Justices* (Charlottesville: University of Virginia Press, 2013), 192–93.

89. For example, Steven Duke, clerk OT 1959, email to author, April 24, 2017.

90. George Rutherglen, clerk OT 1975, email to author, June 5, 2019.

91. Tom Klitgaard, OT 1961, interview with author, Mar. 8, 2019.

92. Kastenberg, *Campaign to Impeach*, 139; Richard Jacobsen, clerk OT 1971, interview with author, March 20, 2018.

93. "Remembrances of William O. Douglas by His Friends and Associates."

94. Small, "William O. Douglas Remembered."

95. Small, "William O. Douglas Remembered," 308 (Warren Christopher, clerk OT 1949).

96. Kastenberg, *Campaign to Impeach*, 22.

97. Kastenberg, *Campaign to Impeach*, 2, 201–2.

98. Kastenberg, *Campaign to Impeach*, 5, 41, 53.

99. Quoted in Kastenberg, *Campaign to Impeach*, 110.

100. Douglas, *Court Years*, 371.

101. Kastenberg, *Campaign to Impeach*, 108.

102. Quoted in Kastenberg, *Campaign to Impeach*, 9–10.

103. Ethics Reform Act of 1989, Pub. L. 101-94, 13 Stat. 1716 (1989).

104. Quoted in Lesley Oelsner, "Douglas Quits Supreme Court; Ford Hails 36½-Year Service," *New York Times*, Nov. 13, 1975.

105. Douglas to clerks, Nov. 14, 1975, Douglas Papers, box 374.

106. Quoted in Simon, *Independent Journey*, 451.

107. Simon, *Independent Journey*, 453.

108. Northern Indiana Public Service Company v. Porter County Chapter of the Izak Walton League of America, Inc. (*Northern Indiana Public Service*), 423 U.S. 12, 15 (1975).

109. *Northern Indiana Public Service*, 423 U.S. at 15–18 (Douglas, J., concurring).

9. The Trees Are Still Standing

1. Adapted from M. Margaret McKeown, "The Trees Are Still Standing," *Journal of Supreme Court History* 44, no. 2 (2019): 189. For a general description of Mineral King, see Roger Rapoport, "Disney's War against the Wilderness," *Ramparts*, Nov. 1971; see also Sierra Club Advocacy Flyer, Sierra Club Papers, container 6:11.

2. Sierra Club v. Morton (*Morton*), 405 U.S., 727, 743 (1972) (Douglas, J., dissenting).

3. *Morton*, 405 U.S. at 742.

4. Douglas, *Wilderness Bill of Rights*, 86.

5. Christopher D. Stone, "Should Trees Have Standing?—Toward Legal Rights for Natural Objects," *Southern California Law Review* 45 (1972): 450.

6. "Stats Report Viewer," National Park Service, https://irma.nps.gov/STATS/SSRSReports/Park%20Specific%20Reports/Annual%20Park%20Recreation%20Visitation%20(1904%20-%20Last%20Calendar%20Year)?Park=BRCA.

7. Flyers from University of Southern California Libraries, Special Collections, Mineral King Development Records, box 1.

8. Peter Browning, "Mickey Mouse in the Mountains," *Harper's Magazine*, Mar. 1972, 65; see also United States Forest Service, "Draft Forest Service-Michigan State Study re Litigation Related to Management of Forest Service Lands," July 6, 1970, 21, 46–50, Sierra Club Papers, container 6:11.

9. Sierra Club v. Hickel, 1 Environmental Law Reporter 20010 (N.D. Cal. 1969). The case began as Sierra Club v. Hickel—not *Morton*—because Walter J. Hickel was the secretary of the interior when the club filed suit.

10. Leland R. Selna Jr., interview with author, Dec. 4, 2018.

11. Sierra Club v. Hickel, 433 F.2d 24, 26, 29 (9th Cir. 1970).

12. *Hickel*, 433 F.2d at 33; Charles Alan Wright, Arthur Raphael Miller, and Mary Kay Kane, *Federal Practice and Procedure* (St. Paul: West Publishing, 1955), § 2948.1.

13. Leland R. Selna, Jr., interview with author, Dec. 4, 2018.

14. See *Hickel*, 1 Environmental Law Reporter at 20014.

15. *Hickel*, 433 F.2d at 30, 33.

16. Petition for Writ of Certiorari, Sierra Club v. Morton, 405 U.S. 727 (No. 70-34).

17. Douglas to Edgar Wayburn, Oct. 23, 1962, Douglas Papers, box 1763 (emphasis added); see also Wayburn to Douglas, Nov. 6, 1962, Douglas Papers, box 1763.

18. Memorandum, "WOD and the Sierra Club," n.d., Douglas Papers, box 1545. This note lists key dates concerning Douglas's involvement with the Sierra Club.

19. Allotment of Supreme Court Justices to Circuits, 28 U.S.C. § 42 (1948).

20. Minutes of Sierra Club board meeting, July 25, 1969, Douglas Papers, box 1764.

21. *Morton*, 405 U.S. at 743–44 (Douglas, J., dissenting) (footnote omitted).

22. "Sierra Club Role Disputed by U.S.," *New York Times*, Feb. 10, 1970; "'American Alpine' in Style," *National Observer*, Dec. 27, 1965; "Government's View on Mineral King Case," *San Francisco Chronicle*, Jan. 10, 1970; "Wilderness Backers' Leaders Oppose Disney's Mineral King," *Fresno Bee*, Dec. 11, 1968; "Disney Profits Sharply, Higher for 1st Quarter," *Los Angeles Times*, Feb. 4, 1970.

23. Quoted in "When Government Turns Its Back on Pollution," *Newsday*, Aug. 25, 1970.

24. See, for example, Caplan, "Does the Supreme Court Need a Code of Conduct?"

25. 28 U.S.C. § 24 (1948) provided that any "justice or judge of the United States shall disqualify himself in any case in which he has a substantial interest ... or is so related to or connected with any party or his attorney as to render it improper, in his opinion, for him to sit on the trial, appeal or other proceeding." The Judiciary Act of 1789, ch. 20, 1 Stat. 73, set out the oath of office.

26. The current version of 28 U.S.C. § 455 requires disqualification of any justice, judge, or magistrate judge "in which his impartiality might reasonably be questioned."

27. McKeown, "Don't Shoot the Canons," 45.

28. Cathy Douglas Stone, interview with author, Nov. 27, 2018.

29. Douglas, *The Court Years*, 370.

30. William Alsup, interview with author, Jan. 18, 2017.

31. "Significant Oral Arguments 1955–1993: The Burger Court," Supreme Court Historical Society, http://supremecourthistory.org/history_oral_decisions_burger .html; James Salzman and J. B. Ruhl, "New Kids on the Block—A Survey of Practitioner Views on Important Cases in Environmental and Natural Resources Law," *Natural Resources and Environment* 25 (2010): 45.

32. See, for example, Association of Data Processing Service Organizations, Inc. v. Camp, 396 U.S. 808 (1969) (order granting motion to appear as amicus).

33. Order Granting Petition for Certiorari, 401 U.S. 907 (1971).

34. Untitled note in *Morton* case file, Douglas Papers, box 1545.

35. The oral argument in *Morton* (heard Nov. 17, 1971) is available through the Oyez Project, https://www.oyez.org/cases/1971/70-34. See also Brian S. Tomaso-

vic, "Soundscape History and Environmental Law in the Supreme Court," *Lewis & Clark Law Review* 45 (Fall 2015): 929.

36. Quoted in Del Dickson, ed., *The Supreme Court in Conference (1940–1985): The Private Discussions behind Nearly 300 Supreme Court Decisions* (New York: Oxford University Press, 2001), 133–34.

37. Quoted in Robert V. Percival, "Environmental Law in the Supreme Court: Highlights from the Blackmun Papers," *Environmental Law Reporter* 35 (2005): 10657.

38. Paul Gewirtz (law clerk to Justice Thurgood Marshall and now a professor at Yale Law School), interview with the author, Nov. 26, 2018. Gewirtz emphasized that it was definitely not Marshall who spread this view and speculates it may have been Stewart.

39. First Draft Stewart Opinion for the Court, Marshall Papers, box 81.

40. *Morton*, 405 U.S. at 741.

41. *Morton*, 405 U.S. at 740–41.

42. *Morton*, 405 U.S. at 733 (citing Data Processing Services Organizations v. Camp, 397 U.S. 150 [1970] and Barlow v. Collins, 397 U.S. 159 [1970]).

43. *Morton*, 405 U.S. at 738.

44. Percival, "Environmental Law in the Supreme Court," 10657; *Morton*, 405 U.S. at 736 n. 8.

45. Jonathan Zasloff, "The Mystery of Sierra Club v. Morton," *Legal Planet*, Apr. 24, 2011, http://legal-planet.org/2011/04/24/the-mystery-of-sierra-club-v-morton/.

46. Memorandum by Paul Gewirtz, Marshall Papers, box 81; emphasis in original.

47. Tinsley Yarborough, *Harry A. Blackmun: The Outsider Justice* (New York: Oxford University Press, 2008), 271; Percival, "Environmental Law in the Supreme Court," 10663. During law school in the early 1970s, I often went to Theodore Roosevelt Island, where I saw Justice Blackmun taking a solitary stroll.

48. Typewritten questions by H.A.B., Nov. 15, 1971, Blackmun Papers, box 137.

49. *Morton*, 405 U.S. at 755 (Blackmun, J., dissenting).

50. *Morton*, 405 U.S. at 756–57 (Blackmun, J., dissenting).

51. *Morton*, 405 U.S. at 757 (Blackmun, J., dissenting).

52. Quoted in Dickson, *The Supreme Court in Conference*, 72.

53. *Morton*, 405 U.S. 759 (Blackmun, J., dissenting).

54. *Morton*, 405 U.S. 741 (Douglas, J., dissenting).

55. *Morton*, 405 U.S. at 752 (quoting Leopold, *A Sand County Almanac*, 204).

56. Douglas to M. D. Talbot, articles editor of the *Southern California Law Review*, Oct. 10, 1970, Douglas Papers, box 889; M. D. Talbot to Douglas, Nov. 17, 1971, Douglas Papers, box 889 (enclosing a preview paragraph of Professor Christopher D. Stone's article, then titled "Legal Rights for the Environment Too?").

57. M. D. Talbot to Douglas, Nov. 10, 1971, Douglas Papers, box 889.

58. Christopher D. Stone, interview with author, Apr. 4, 2018.

59. Christopher D. Stone, interview with author, Apr. 4, 2018.

60. Christopher D. Stone, *Should Trees Have Standing? Law, Morality, and the Environment* (New York: Oxford University Press, 2010), iii.

61. The link between Stone and the law review remains somewhat of a mystery. He wrote: "I can't recall how I learned that the law review had lined up Douglas; I am sure it was widely circulated. I was not the faculty advisor. I seem to remember that the editor in chief was behind the idea of adding the piece in the Tech Symposium. He was encouraging. It was written in short order." Stone, email to author, Apr. 18, 2018.

62. Christopher D. Stone, interview with author, Apr. 4, 2018.

63. Stone, "Should Trees Have Standing?," 450, 452–53.

64. Stone, "Should Trees Have Standing?," 450, 473–80.

65. M. D. Talbot to Douglas, Nov. 17, 1971, Douglas Papers, box 889.

66. Christopher D. Stone, interview with author, Apr. 4, 2018.

67. Stone, "Should Trees Have Standing?," 466.

68. *Rules of the Supreme Court*, 1970 ed. (Washington DC: Thiel Press, 1970), Rule 42, Briefs of an *Amicus Curiae*, 40.

69. Quoted in M. D. Talbot to Douglas, Nov. 17, 1971, Douglas Papers, box 889; *Rules of the Supreme Court*, 1970 ed., Rule 42, Briefs of an *Amicus Curiae*, 40.

70. William Alsup, interview with author, Jan. 18, 2017.

71. Richard Jacobson, email to author, Mar. 19, 2018.

72. Nan Burgess, secretary to Justice William O. Douglas, to M. D. Talbot, Nov. 21, 1971, Douglas Papers, box 809.

73. Case file for Sierra Club v. Morton, Douglas Papers, box 1545. Douglas asked Alsup to look at the tentative draft of Stone's article, and the final version of the dissent was adjusted to reflect the new title of the article. Alsup to Douglas, Feb. 18, 1972, Douglas Papers, box 1545; Alsup to Douglas, Mar. 14, 1972, Douglas Papers, box 1545.

74. The twelve opinion drafts are contained in the case file, Douglas Papers, box 1545.

75. William Alsup, interviews with author, Jan. 18, 2017, and Oct. 3, 2018.

76. William Alsup, interview with author, Oct. 3, 2018.

77. William Alsup, interview with author, Jan. 18, 2017.

78. Quoted in Stanley Mosk, "William O. Douglas," 5 *Ecology Law Quarterly*, 229, 230 (1976).

79. Sierra Club v. Morton, 348 F. Supp. 219, 219–20 (N.D. Cal. 1972); Order Dismissing Action Pursuant to Stipulation, Sierra Club Papers, container 5:3.

80. John M. Naff Jr., "Reflections on the Dissent of Douglas, J., in *Sierra Club v. Morton*," *American Bar Association Journal* 58 (Aug. 1972): 819.

81. Andrew Revkin, "Ecuador Constitution Grants Rights to Nature," *Dot Earth* (blog), *New York Times*, Sept. 29, 2008, https://dotearth.blogs.nytimes.com /2008/09/29/ecuador-constitution-grants-nature-rights/.

82. Oliver A. Houck, "Noah's Second Voyage: The Rights of Nature As Law," *Tulane Environmental Law Journal* 31 (Winter 2017): 5.

83. Hannibal Rhoades, "Reviving Nature and Culture in Uganda," *Ecologist*, Apr. 2, 2020, https://theecologist.org/2020/apr/02/reviving-nature-and-culture-uganda; Sigal Samuel, "This Country Gave All Its Rivers Their Own Legal Rights," *Vox*,

Aug. 18, 2019, https://www.vox.com/future-perfect/2019/8/18/20803956/bangladesh-rivers-legal-personhood-rights-nature.

84. Hope M. Babcock, "A Brook with Legal Rights: The Rights of Nature in Court," *Ecology Law Quarterly* 43, no. 1 (2016): 1–51.

85. Byram River v. Village of Port Chester, N.Y., 394 F. Supp. 618, 620 (S.D.N.Y. 1975); Colorado River Ecosystem v. Colorado, No. 1:17-cv-02316 (D. Colo. 2017); Julie Turkewitz, "Corporations Have Rights. Why Shouldn't Rivers?," *New York Times*, Sept. 26, 2017.

86. Stephen J. Turner et al., eds., *Environmental Rights: The Development of Standards* (New York: Cambridge University Press, 2019), 346; Santa Monica, Cal., Municipal Code, Ordinance No. 2421, ch. 4.75 (Apr. 9, 2013); Tamaqua Borough, Schuylkill County, Pa., Ordinance No. 612 § 12.1 (Sept. 19, 2006).

87. David George Haskell, *The Songs of Trees* (New York: Viking Press, 2017), x.

10. Coming Home

1. Douglas, *Of Men and Mountains*, 232.

2. For a description of Schaeffer and the property transaction, see Simon, *Independent Journey*, 276–77. When Douglas and Mildred faced financial problems upon their divorce, Mildred apparently spited Douglas by taking the cabins, knowing his attachment to the property. Murphy, *Wild Bill*, 299.

3. Douglas, *My Wilderness: The Pacific West*, 201.

4. Jon M. and Donna McDaniel Skovlin, *Into the Minam: The History of a River and Its People* (Cove OR: Reflections Publishing, 2011).

5. Douglas, *My Wilderness: The Pacific West*, 201.

6. Douglas to Wayne L. Morse, Aug. 2, 1959, and Oct. 15, 1959, Douglas Papers, box 548. Douglas also sought similar support from Representative Al Ullman of the Oregon congressional delegation. Al Ullman to Douglas, Aug. 9, 1961, Douglas Papers, box 548.

7. Wayne L. Morse to William Berg, assistant to Morse, Oct. 19, 1959, Douglas Papers, box 548; Morse to Douglas, Nov. 20, 1959, Douglas Papers, box 548.

8. Boswell and McConaghy, "Twin Towers of Power."

9. Douglas to Wayne L. Morse, Apr. 1, 1961, Douglas Papers, box 548.

10. Michael McCloskey, email to author, Apr. 9, 2020.

11. Douglas to Olaus Murie, Apr. 5, 1960, Murie Ranch Papers.

12. Olaus Murie to Richard E. McArdle, chief, Forest Service, Oct. 23, 1960, Wilderness Society Papers, Olaus Murie Papers.

13. Skovlin and Skovlin, *Into the Minam*, 149.

14. Michael McCloskey, interview with author, Apr. 19, 2019.

15. "Out of the Past," *The Chieftan*, Feb. 18, 2010, https://www.wallowa.com/opinion/columnists/out-of-the-past/article_17f9bd62-8e2c-51c6-82f6-9c39cc7bf051.html.

16. Quoted in Skovlin and Skovlin, *Into the Minam*, 147–48.

17. Transcribed notes of telephone conversation between Douglas and George Zahl of Save the Minam, Jan. 27, 1962, Douglas Papers, box 549.

18. "Save the Minam!," *High Country News*, Sept. 29, 1972, 10.

19. Oregon Wilderness Act, Pub. L. 98-328, 98 Stat. 272 (June 26, 1984).

20. Douglas, *My Wilderness: The Pacific West*, 200.

21. Kennecott, named after a glacier in Alaska, was formed in the early 1900s through a venture of the Guggenheim family and J. P. Morgan. Kennecott Corporation History, http:/www.fundinguniverse.com/company-histories/kennecott -corporation-history/. For an extensive treatment of the controversy, see Adam M. Sowards, *An Open Pit Visible from the Moon: The Wilderness Act and the Fight to Protect Miners Ridge and the Public Interest* (Norman: University of Oklahoma Press, 2020).

22. Douglas, *My Wilderness: The Pacific West*, 157, 159, 162–63.

23. Douglas, *My Wilderness: The Pacific West*, 155.

24. Douglas, *My Wilderness: The Pacific West*, 159–60.

25. Urofsky, *Douglas Letters*, 242.

26. North Cascades Study Team, *The North Cascades Study Report* (Washington DC, 1965), https://www.nps.gov/parkhistory/online_books/noca/study_report /contents.htm.

27. John McPhee chronicled the story of the protest and the Sierra Club's executive director, David Brower, in his well-known book, *Encounters with the Archdruid: Narratives about a Conservationist and Three of His Natural Enemies* (New York: Farrar, Straus and Giroux, 1971).

28. William O. Douglas, foreword to Harvey Manning, *The Wild Cascades, Forgotten Parkland* (San Francisco: Sierra Club, 1965), 18.

29. 16 U.S.C. § 1133(d)(3).

30. Paul Brooks, "A Copper Company vs. the North Cascades," *Harper's Magazine*, Sept. 1967, 48. See also Paul Brooks, *Roadless Area* (New York: Knopf, 1964).

31. John McPhee, "Encounters with the Archdruid, I-a Mountain," *New Yorker*, Mar. 20, 1971, 42.

32. Kathleen Sperry, "North Cascades National Park: Copper Mining vs. Conservation," *Science* 157 (Sept. 1, 1967): 1021–22.

33. Quoted in "Crisis at Miner's Ridge," *Washington Post*, May 3, 1967.

34. Fred T. Darvill Jr., *Hiking the North Cascades* (Berkeley: Sierra Club, 1982).

35. *The Wild Cascades* (Issaquah WA: Northwest Conservation Council, June–July 1967), http://npshistory.com/newsletters/the-wild-cascades/june-july-1967 .pdf; "Evans Urges Greater Area for New Park," *Skagit Valley Herald*, May 26, 1967.

36. Quoted in Sperry, "North Cascades National Park," 1022.

37. Quoted in Maxine E. McCloskey and James P. Gilligan, eds., *Wilderness and the Quality of Life* (San Francisco: Sierra Club, 1969), 109–10.

38. Cathleen Douglas Stone, interview with author, July 20, 2020.

39. Quoted in Maribeth Morris, "Protestors Crash Douglas Camp-In," *Post-Intelligencer*, Aug. 7, 1967.

40. "Remarks of Justice William O. Douglas Regarding Kennecott Copper Corp. Proposed Open-Pit Mine on Miners Ridge, July 21, 1968," Kennecott (Mine) Film 1967–68, North Cascades Conservation Council, Special Collections, University of Washington; Sowards, *An Open Pit Visible from the Moon*, 118.

41. Stephen Ponder (former reporter for the Associated Press), email to author, Apr. 15, 2019.

42. Quoted in Marjorie Jones, "Douglas Leads Glacier Peak Protest," *Seattle Times*, Aug. 6, 1967, 24; Douglas, *My Wilderness: The Pacific West*, 164.

43. Pub. L. No. 90-544, 82 Stat. 926 (1968).

44. Isabelle Lynn, "Year 'Round in the Mountains," *The Mountaineer*, 1962, 33.

45. Lynn, "Year 'Round in the Mountains," 34; "In Memoriam: Isabelle Lynn and Kathryn Kershaw," *The Wild Cascades*, Summer/Fall 1996, 15.

46. Lynn, "Year 'Round in the Mountains," 36–37.

47. "In Memoriam: Isabelle Lynn and Kathryn Kershaw," 15.

48. Lynn, "Year 'Round in the Mountains," 38.

49. Kathryn Kershaw and Isabelle Lynn to Karl Onthank, president of Friends of the Three Sisters Wilderness, July 30, 1958, Double K Papers, box 2-2. See also Onthank to Lynn and Kershaw, July 15, 1958, Double K Papers, box 2-2.

50. Kathryn Kershaw to Dr. A. W. Stevenson, Feb. 25, 1966, Double K Papers, box 1-41.

51. "In Memoriam: Isabelle Lynn and Kathryn Kershaw," 15; Douglas to Isabelle Lynn, Feb. 25, 1971, 2, Double K Papers, box 1-1.

52. Suzy Cyr (artist and author), interview with Tim Franklin (former wrangler at the Double K Ranch), Aug. 2019 (notes on file with author).

53. Kathryn Kershaw and Isabelle Lynn, "Statement on the 'National Wilderness Preservation Act,'" submitted to Nov. 7, 1958, hearings (authored Oct. 31, 1958), Double K Papers, box 2-2.

54. Douglas to Henry M. Jackson, Nov. 15, 1960, and Oct. 17, 1960, Douglas Papers, box 343.

55. Douglas to Henry M. Jackson, Oct. 17, 1960, Douglas Papers, box 343. See also Adam P. Sowards, "William O. Douglas's Wilderness Politics: Public Protest and Committees of Correspondence in the Pacific Northwest," *Western History Quarterly* 37, no. 1 (Spring 2006): 37.

56. Douglas to L. O. Barrett, Oct. 12, 1961, Douglas Papers, box 343.

57. Douglas to L. O. Barrett, Oct. 12, 1961, Douglas Papers, box 343.

58. Douglas to Henry M. Jackson, Dec. 1, 1961, and Jan. 3, 1962, Douglas Papers, box 343.

59. Douglas to Henry M. Jackson, Dec. 1, 1961, Douglas Papers, box 343.

60. Isabelle Lynn to Stewart Brandborg, The Wilderness Society, Mar. 31, 1961, Double K Papers, box 2-4.

61. Mike Hiler, former Forest Service manager in Naches, Washington, to Tom Hulst, Aug. 12, 2001 (copy on file with the author).

62. Brinkley, *Quiet World*, 378.

63. Kathryn Kershaw, Feb. 24, 1961, Double K Papers, box 2-2.

64. Kathryn Kershaw and Isabelle Lynn, "A Proposal to Establish a Cougar Lakes Wilderness Area," Feb. 12, 1961, Double K Papers, box 2-12.

65. Douglas to Kathryn Kershaw, Apr. 12, 1962, Double K Papers, box 1-1.

66. Eileen Ryan to Douglas, June 11, 1961; Douglas to Ryan, June 15, 1961, Douglas Papers, box 553.

67. Sowards, "William O. Douglas's Wilderness Politics," 37.

68. Michael McCloskey, email to author, Apr. 9, 2020.

69. William O. Douglas, "Cougar Lakes Wilderness Recommendations," *The Mountaineer* 58 (Mar. 15, 1965): 66–67; Douglas to Isabelle Lynn, Oct. 14, 1964, Douglas Papers, box 553.

70. Douglas to Freeman, Jan. 25, 1966, Douglas Papers, box 553.

71. Douglas to Freeman, Mar. 2, 1966, Douglas Papers, box 553.

72. Douglas to Cragg Gilbert, Yakima orchardist, Mar. 29, 1966, and Douglas to John Larsen, Mar. 31, 1966, Douglas Papers, box 553.

73. Douglas to Cragg Gilbert, Mar. 29, 1966, Douglas Papers, box 553.

74. Mardy Murie to Douglas, Mar. 29, 1966, Douglas Papers, box 553.

75. Douglas to Mardy Murie, Mar. 31, 1966, Douglas Papers, box 553.

76. Douglas to Cragg Gilbert, Apr. 1, 1966, Douglas Papers, box 553.

77. Douglas to Mardy Murie, Mar. 31, 1966, Douglas Papers, box 553; Jackson to Mardy Murie, Apr. 15, 1966, Douglas Papers, box 553; North Cascades Study Team, *North Cascades Study Report* § I, https://www.nps.gov/parkhistory/online_books/noca/study_report/contents.htm.

78. North Cascades Study Team, *North Cascades Study Report* § III, "Wilderness Areas."

79. Mike Hiler, former Forest Service manager, email to author, April 4, 2020.

80. Douglas to J. Alex "Lex" Maxwell, president of Yakima Savings and Loan Association, Feb. 16, 1971, Douglas Papers, box 553. See also Sowards, "William O. Douglas's Wilderness Politics," 40.

81. Undated typewritten document, Double K Papers, box 2-12.

82. Washington Wilderness Act of 1984, Pub. L. No. 98-339, § 3(21), 98 Stat. 299, 302 (1984); S. Rep. No. 98-461, at 6–7 (1984).

83. Daniel Evans (former governor of Washington and U.S. senator), interview with author, Oct. 31, 2019.

84. S. Rep. No. 98-461, at 14.

85. Denny Miller, interview with author, Aug. 20, 2019.

86. Pub. L. No. 98-339, § 3(21), 302.

87. Harris Meyer, "A Historic New Trail for Washington Hikers," *Crosscut*, Sept. 17, 2012, https:crosscut.com/2012/harris-william-o-douglas-trail.

11. Lessons and Legacies

1. "Wood, Field and Stream; A Stirring Plea for U.S. Conservation Is Made by Justice Douglas," *New York Times*, May 3, 1964.

2. Stephen Field (1863–97) and Joseph McKenna (1898–1925) were appointed from California; Willis Van Devanter (1911–37), from Wyoming; and George Sutherland, from Utah (1922–38). "Justices 1789 to Present," Supreme Court of the United States, https://www.supremecourt.gov/about/members_text.aspx.

3. George Collins quoted in Kaye, *The Last Great Wilderness*, 84.

4. Speech to Associated Students of the University of Hawaii, Honolulu ʜɪ, Jan. 5, 1970, Douglas Papers, box 816.

5. William O. Douglas, *Points of Rebellion* (New York: First Vintage Books, 1969), 50, 52, 80; Douglas, *Three Hundred Year War*, 198.

6. Douglas, *Three Hundred Year War*, 199–200.

7. Douglas, *My Wilderness: The Pacific West*, 199.

8. Senator Edward Kennedy, *Congressional Record—Senate*, Feb. 6, 1976.

9. Douglas, *Go East, Young Man*, 467.

10. Douglas to Howard Zahniser, Feb. 26, 1960, Douglas Papers, box 383.

11. Judiciary Act of 1789, ch. 20, § 8, 1 Stat 73.

12. Code of Conduct for United States Judges, Commentary to Canon 4, last revised Mar. 12, 2019, https://www.uscourts.gov/judges-judgeships/code-conduct -united-states-judges.

13. Urofsky, *Douglas Letters*, 400.

14. Quoted in Murphy, *Wild Bill*, 455.

15. Urofsky, *Douglas Letters*, 400.

16. Douglas Memorandum to the Judicial Conference of the United States, Aug. 8, 1970, Douglas Papers, box 1736; Public Report of Extra-Judicial Income, June 30, 1972, Douglas Papers, box 1736.

17. Chandler v. Judicial Council, 398 U.S. 74, 139 (1970) (Douglas, J., dissenting).

18. Ethics in Government Act of 1978, Pub. L. 95-521, 92 Stat. 1824, 1851–61 (1978).

19. U.S. Supreme Court, "Resolution," Jan. 18, 1991, https://www.washingtonpost .com/r/2010-2019/WashingtonPost/2012/02/21/National-Politics/Graphics/1991 _Resolution.pdf; https://www.uscourts.gov/rules-policies/judiciary-policies/code -conduct/outside-earned-income-honoraria-and-employment. The resolution states that subject to certain clarifications, the officers and employees of the court will comply with the substance of the Judicial Conference Regulations under Titles III and IV of the Ethics Reform Act of 1989.

20. Cheney v. United States District Court for the District of Columbia, 541 U.S. 913, 916–17 (2004) (Scalia, J., mem.).

21. Michael C. Dorf, "Justice Scalia's Persuasive but Elitist Response to the Duck Hunting Controversy," Mar. 24, 2004, https://supreme.findlaw.com/legal -commentary/justice-scalias-persuasive-but-elitist-response-to-the-duck-hunting -controversy.html.

22. U.S. Supreme Court, "2011 Year-End Report on the Federal Judiciary," Dec. 31, 2011, https://www.supremecourt.gov/publicinfo/year-end/2011year-endreport.pdf.

23. Cathleen Douglas Stone, interview with author, July 20, 2020.

24. Cathleen H. Douglas, "William O. Douglas: The Man," *1981 Yearbook, Supreme Court Historical Society*, 7–8.

25. Lynn, "Year 'Round in the Mountains," 38.

26. Olaus Murie to Douglas, Nov. 5, 1962, Douglas Papers, box 358; Murie Ranch Papers, correspondence.

27. "The Joys and Solitude of Nature," *LIFE*, Dec. 28, 1959; Douglas to Olaus Murie, April 26, 1961, Murie Ranch Papers.

28. Fay Aull to Olaus Murie, June 29, 1959, Douglas Papers, box 358.

29. Douglas to Mardy Murie, Oct. 20, 1963, Douglas Papers, box 358.

30. Reich, *Sorcerer of Bolinas Reef*, 59.

31. Charles Reich, interview with author, July 17, 2017.

32. Reich, *Sorcerer of Bolinas Reef*, 61.

33. Quoted in Murphy, *Wild Bill*, 329.

34. Undated statement of Mildred Douglas Read, copy on file with David Danelski and author.

35. Simon, *Independent Journey*, 451–52; Artemus Ward, *Deciding to Leave: The Politics of Retirement from the United States Supreme Court* (Albany: State University of New York Press, 1971), 190.

36. Retirement of Mr. Justice Douglas, 423 U.S. vii, ix–x (1975) (quoting Douglas's November 14 letter to the chief justice and associate justices).

37. Douglas letter to clerks, Nov. 14, 1975, Douglas Papers, box 374.

38. Brock Evans, email to author, July 24, 2019 (sharing notes from the funeral).

39. Cathleen Douglas Stone, interview with author, July 20, 2020.

40. *Good Morning America*, featuring Justice Douglas and Cathy Douglas, aired Nov. 14, 1975, on ABC, https://www.youtube.com/watch?v=CjLJ0bmMqtI&feature=youtu.be&t=322.

FURTHER READING

Selected Books by William O. Douglas

An Almanac of Liberty. Garden City NY: Doubleday, 1954.

The Anatomy of Liberty: The Rights of Man without Force. New York: Simon and Schuster, 1963.

Beyond the High Himalayas. Garden City NY: Doubleday, 1952.

The Court Years, 1939–1975: The Autobiography of William O. Douglas. New York: Random House, 1980.

Farewell to Texas: A Vanishing Wilderness. New York: McGraw-Hill, 1967.

Go East, Young Man: The Early Years: The Autobiography of William O. Douglas. New York: Random House, 1974.

My Wilderness: East to Katahdin. New York: Doubleday, 1961.

My Wilderness: The Pacific West. New York: Doubleday, 1960.

Of Men and Mountains. New York: Harper and Brothers, 1950.

The Three Hundred Year War: A Chronicle of Ecological Disaster. New York: Random House, 1972.

A Wilderness Bill of Rights. Boston: Little, Brown, 1965.

Selected Books

Ball, Howard, and Philip Cooper. *Of Power and Right: Hugo Black, William O. Douglas, and America's Constitutional Revolution*. New York: Oxford University Press, 1992.

Berry, Wendall, and Gene Meatyard. *The Unforseen Wilderness: An Essay on Kentucky's Red River Gorge*. Lexington: University Press of Kentucky, 1971.

Brinkley, Douglas. *The Quiet World: Saving Alaska's Wilderness Kingdom, 1879–1960*. New York: Harper Collins, 2011.

———. *Rightful Heritage: Franklin D. Roosevelt and the Land of America*. New York: Harper Collins, 2016.

———. *The Wilderness Warrior: Theodore Roosevelt and the Crusade for America*. New York: Harper Collins, 2009.

Broome, Harvey. *Faces of the Wilderness*. Missoula MT: Mountain Press Publishing, 1972 (with foreword by William O. Douglas).

Brower, David, ed. *Wilderness, America's Living Heritage*. San Francisco: Sierra Club, 1961.

Clayton, John. *Natural Rivals: John Muir, Gifford Pinchot, and the Creation of America's Public Lands*. New York: Pegasus Books, 2019.

Countryman, Vern. *The Judicial Record of Justice William O. Douglas*. Cambridge MA: Harvard University Press, 1974.

Danelski, David J. *A Supreme Court Justice Is Appointed*. Westport CT: Praeger, 1980.

Dickson, Del. *The Supreme Court in Conference (1940–1985)*. New York: Oxford University Press, 2001.

Domnarski, William. *The Great Justices 1941–54: Black, Douglas, Frankfurter, and Jackson in Chambers*. Ann Arbor: University of Michigan Press, 2006.

Duram, James C. *Justice William O. Douglas*. Boston: Twayne Publishers, 1981.

Fox, Stephen. *The American Conservation Movement: John Muir and His Legacy*. Boston: Little, Brown, 1981.

Frank, John P. *Marble Palace: The Supreme Court in American Life*. New York: Alfred A. Knopf, 1958.

Harvey, Mark. *Wilderness Forever: Howard Zahniser and the Path to the Wilderness Act*. Seattle: University of Washington Press, 2007.

Hulst, Tom R. *The Footpaths of Justice William O. Douglas: A Legacy of Place*. New York: iUniverse, 2004.

Hume, Robert. *Ethics and Accountability on the US Supreme Court: An Analysis of Recusal Practices*. Albany: SUNY Press, 2017.

Ickes, Harold L. *The Secret Diary of Harold L. Ickes*, vol. 3: *The Lowering Cloud 1939–1941*. New York: Simon and Shuster, 1954.

Janeway, Michael. *The Fall of the House of Roosevelt*. New York: Columbia University Press, 2004.

Kalman, Laura. *Abe Fortas: A Biography*. New Haven CT: Yale University Press, 1990.

Kastenberg, Joshua E. *The Campaign to Impeach Justice William O. Douglas: Nixon, Vietnam and the Conservative Attack on Judicial Independence*. Lawrence: University Press of Kansas, 2019.

Lash, Joseph P., ed. *From the Diaries of Felix Frankfurter*. New York: W. W. Norton, 1975.

Leopold, Aldo. *A Sand County Almanac*. Oxford: Oxford University Press, 1949.

Lerner, Max. *Nine Scorpions in a Bottle: Great Judges and Cases of the Supreme Court*. New York: Arcade Publishing, 1994.

Lewis, Michael, ed., *American Wilderness: A New History*. New York: Oxford University Press, 2007.

Lubet, Steven. *Beyond Reproach: Ethical Restrictions on the Extrajudicial Activities of State and Federal Judges*. Chicago: American Judicature Society, 1984.

Lunde, Darrin. *The Naturalist: Theodore Roosevelt, a Lifetime of Exploration, and the Triumph of American Natural History*. New York: Broadway Books, 2016.

MacKenzie, John P. *The Appearance of Justice*. New York: Charles Scribner's Sons, 1974.

Further Reading

Manning, Harvey. *The Wild Cascades, Forgotten Parkland*. San Francisco: Sierra Club, 1965 (with foreword by William O. Douglas).

Marshall, Robert. *Arctic Wilderness*. Berkeley: University of California Press, 1956.

McCloskey, Michael. *In the Thick of It: My Life in the Sierra Club*. Washington DC: Island Press, 2005.

Murie, Margaret E. *Two in the Far North*. Portland OR: Alaska Northwest Books, 1977.

Murphy, Bruce Allen. *The Brandeis/Frankfurter Connection: The Secret Political Activities of Two Supreme Court Justices*. Oxford: Oxford University Press, 1982.

———. *Wild Bill: The Legend and Life of William O. Douglas*. New York: Random House, 2003.

Murphy, Walter F. *Elements of Judicial Strategy*. Chicago: University of Chicago Press, 1964.

Nash, Roderick Frazier. *The Rights of Nature: A History of Environmental Ethics*. Madison: University of Wisconsin Press, 1989.

O'Brien, David M. *Storm Center: The Supreme Court in American Politics*. New York: W. W. Norton, 2017.

O'Fallon, James M. *Nature's Justice: Writings of William O. Douglas*. Corvalis: Oregon State University Press, 2000.

Petulla, Joseph M. *American Environmental History*. San Francisco: Boyd and Fraser, 1977.

Porter, Eliot, and Henry David Thoreau. *In Wildness Is the Preservation of the World*. Los Angeles: Ammo Books, 2012 (first published in 1962 by Ballantine Books).

Reich, Charles A. *The Greening of America*. New York: Random House, 1970.

———. *The Sorcerer of Bolinas Reef*. New York: Random House, 1976.

"Remembrances of William O. Douglas by His Friends and Associates, in Celebration of the Fiftieth Anniversary of his Appointment as Associate Justice of the Supreme Court of the United States of America 1939–1989." *Supreme Court Historical Society*, 1990 yearbook.

Rodell, Fred. *Nine Men: A Political History of the Supreme Court 1790–1955*. New York: Random House, 1955.

Rosen, Jeffrey. *The Supreme Court: The Personalities and Rivalries That Defined America*. New York: Henry Holt, 2007.

Scigliano, Robert. *The Supreme Court and the President*. New York: Free Press, 1971.

Simon, James F. *Independent Journey: The Life of William O. Douglas*. New York: Harper and Row, 1980.

Skovlin, Jon M., and Donna McDaniel Skovlin. *Into the Minam: The History of a River and Its People*. Cove OR: Reflections Publishing, 2001.

Sowards, Adam M. *The Environmental Justice: William O. Douglas and American Conservation*. Corvallis: Oregon State University Press, 2009.

———. *An Open Pit Visible from the Moon: The Wilderness Act and the Fight to Protect Miners Ridge and the Public Interest*. Norman: University of Oklahoma Press, 2020.

Stone, Christopher D. *Should Trees Have Standing? Law, Morality and the Environment*, 3rd ed. Oxford: Oxford University Press, 2010.

Sutter, Paul. *Driven Wild*. Seattle: University of Washington Press, 2005.

Turner, Tom. *David Brower: The Making of the Environmental Movement*. Berkeley: University of California Press, 2015.

Udall, Stewart. *The Quiet Crisis*. New York: Holt, Rinehart and Winston, 1963.

Urofsky, Melvin I. *Dissent and the Supreme Court: Its Role in the Court's History and the Nation's Constitutional Dialogue*. New York: Pantheon Books, 2015.

———, ed. *The Douglas Letters: Selections from the Private Papers of Justice William O. Douglas*. Bethesda MD: Adler and Adler, 1987.

Warren, Julianne Lutz. *Aldo Leopold's Odyssey*. Washington DC: Island Press, 2016.

Wasby, Stephen L., ed. *He Shall Not Pass This Way Again: The Legacy of Justice William O. Douglas*. Pittsburgh: University of Pittsburgh Press, 1990.

Woodward, Bob, and Scott Armstrong. *The Brethren: Inside the Supreme Court*. New York: Simon and Shuster, 1979.

Wuethner, George, Eileen Crist, and Tom Butler, eds. *Protecting the Wild: Parks and Wilderness, the Foundation for Conservation*. Washington DC: Island Press, 2015.

INDEX

Red River Gorge, 93–96

Rehnquist, William, 151

Reich, Charles, 67, 90, 109, 142, 187

relationships: Arthur (brother), 3, 5, 17;
Bill Jr. (son), 12; Cathy Heffernan (fourth
wife), 79, 89, 94, 149, 166, 185; Charles
Evans Hughes, 22; Charles Reich, 187–
88; Department of the Interior, 100, 172;
Double K girls, 117, 167–71, 173–74, 186; as
father, 187–88; FDR, 17, 22, 27, 32; frontier
justice, 34; Isabelle "Iz" Lynn, 117, 167–71,
173–74; JFK, 91, 99–100, 103; Joan (step-
daughter), 82; Joan Martin (third wife),
94; Joe Kennedy, 31–33; judge-clerk, 137–
40, 188–89; Julia (mother), 3, 4; Kathryn
"Kay" Kershaw, 117, 167–71, 173–74; Kendall (horse), 1; LBJ, 91, 95–97, 105, 121–
22; Margaret "Mardy" Murie, 69–70, 186;
Martha (sister), 3, 4; Mercedes "Merci"
Hester Davidson (second wife), 37, 70,
79, 82, 83; Mildred Riddle (first wife),
8, 10, 11, 37, 70; Millie (daughter), 2, 12,
187–88; and "no-friends rule," 184; Olaus
J. Murie, 69–70, 186; Sandy (dog), 82;
Sierra Club, 147; Stewart Udall, 91, 98–
101, 122; Tom Fife (childhood friend), 117;
William (father), 2–3

reputation/personality, 137–38; "anti-
judge," 127; for bending the law, 127, 182,
222n30; in chambers, 137–42; as citizen justice, 22–24, 38, 90, 112, 180–85; as
civil libertarian, 18; as confident, 7–8, 35,
122, 123, 148, 180, 183; and enemies, 27–
28, 91–94, 101–4, 119–20, 122, 140, 179; as
environmental justice, 144; as frontier
justice, 34; as generous/personable, 139–
40; as "goofy bird," 79–80, 176; as "go-to"
contact, 110; and impeachment threats,
140–42; as imperfect hero, 185–88; as
independent judiciary, 138; and many
wives, 140, 185; as prominent conservationist, 52; as resilient, 176; as serious, 7;
as storyteller, 113; as teacher, 12; as tem-
peramental, 137–38; as visionary, 175, 187;
as "wild" liberal, 15. See also dissents

Revolutionary War, 111

Riddle, Mildred (first wife), 8, 10, 11, 37, 70.
See also relationships

The Right of the People (Douglas), 125

rights: Bill of, 113, 118–20, 123, 126, 129, 144,
157; civil, 42, 46, 49, 151, 178, 182; elitism and, 49; First Amendment, 49, 90;
nature's, 157–58; wilderness, 118–20

River Bend Dam, 66

Roberts, John G., 184–85, 202n17

Roberts, Owen, 31

Rockefellers, 43

Rodell, Fred, 37

"Roll on Columbia," 50

Roosevelt, Franklin Delano: appointment of Douglas, 16–18; and Civilian
Conservation Corps, 177; and dams,
49–50; death, 33; and environmental
protection, 47; and foreign affairs, 29;
friendship with Douglas, 14–15; and
New Deal, 13–14; and poker parties, 15,
22, 32, 184; and Potomac River parkway,
55; values of, 40

Roosevelt, Theodore, 39–40, 43, 44, 77,
78, 177

Roth, William, 140

Russian Journey (Douglas), 115

Salmon River, 92

Sandburg, Carl, 126

A Sand County Almanac (Leopold), 46

Sandy (dog), 82

Sangamon River, 92

Sawyer, Diane, 95

Saylor, Stanley E., 171

Scalia, Antonin, 113, 184

*Scenic Hudson Preservation Conference v.
Federal Power Commission*, 133

Schaeffer, Roy, 160

Schaller, George, 72–73

SCRAP (Students Challenging Regulatory
Administrative Procedures), 132

Seaton, Fred, 76

Securities and Exchange Commission
(SEC), 7, 13–14, 16

Selna, Leland R., Jr., 145

Sequoia National Game Refuge, 145

Sequoia National Park, 110, 158

Serr, Robert, 82

Sevareid, Eric, 23, 112, 189

Sheenjek expedition, 70–80, 211n15

"Should Trees Have Standing?—Toward